EXPLORING GREEN LANES

and the stories they tell

SOUTH & SOUTH-EAST DEVON

FIFTY WALKS

Valerie Belsey

green books

First published in 2009
by Green Books Ltd
Foxhole, Dartington, Totnes, Devon TQ9 6EB
edit@greenbooks.co.uk www.greenbooks.co.uk

Text printed by TJ International, Padstow, Cornwall
on 100% recycled paper

To the best of our knowledge all details in
this book are correct at the time of going to print, but the publishers
accept no liability for inadvertent errors beyond their control.
We welcome any feedback from users:
please email valeriebelsey@lycos.co.uk

ISBN 978 1 900322 29 4

ACKNOWLEDGEMENTS

My thanks to the following for invaluable help in preparing this book:

Stowford Paper Mill, Tiverton Tourist Office,
Porlock Tourist Office, Totnes Tourist Office, Uffculme Local History
Society, especially Mr John Bell, The National Gallery of Ireland, Dublin,
Steve C. Taylor for wild flower sketches, Totnes Image Bank for many
photos, including the stonebreakers on page 223, the Staff of Harberton Art
Workshop, Totnes, David Archer Maps.

A big thank-you to the staff of Green Books for their friendly encouragement, and in particular to Stephen Prior for his good humour and expertise.

CONTENTS

There is no set way in which to explore these lanes, which range over 5,000 square miles. The list below begins in Exeter and works its way towards Tiverton and out to the far north-east to Shute, down to the south-east at Sidmouth, up the Otter valley and back to the south coast at Teignmouth. Certain lanes in the South Hams are covered, but many have already been explored in my book *Exploring Green Lanes in the South Hams*. The listing finishes with some in the Plymouth area on the Cornish border. But whichever order you to choose to explore the lanes, you will always find yourself wondering what lies just beyond the end of the lane you are in. Happy exploring!

Contents

WHAT IS A GREEN LANE?

An unmetalled road bounded on either side which may or may not be a right of way and which once was used for a variety of purposes, but now is mainly used for recreation.

– The Dartington Institute Study on Green Lanes, 1985

INTRODUCTION

If you have ever wandered away from the centre of a busy holiday resort or bustling train station and found yourself walking further and further away from the hub with no desire to return for a while, then this is the book for you.

For when you step into the green lanes of south and south-east Devon you enter a network of ways which once thronged not just with holidaymakers, as is sometimes now the case, but with travellers and traders of all kinds, both by day and by night.

Most of the lanes were formed when the majority of the population lived and worked in the countryside. Travellers came from the towns into the villages, not as is the reverse today. To find out why a given lane follows the particular route that it does, we need to look for clues to solve the mystery that it offers.

You can start by considering its name. Is the lane named after the place to which it leads or where it is situated, such as 'Mill Lane', 'Quarry Lane' or 'Well Lane'? Or did its physical appearance lead to its naming, such as 'Clay', 'Lime' or 'Long'? Or is it about what happened there, such as 'Strawberry', 'Thatchers' or 'College'?

How this selection was made

As long as people have used these lanes there have been stories, and the people who told them were those who worked and walked the lanes and the land. They may have been talking about the sumptuous meal they had seen brought into the Bishop's Palace and whose scraps they had tasted; the runaway rebel whom they had helped; the beautiful flower girl they had seen; or the mighty stag which their master Raleigh had not caught. Until the second half of the twentieth century they were probably just walking between work and home, church and home, the local market or seaside town and home, with plenty of time for tales to be told.

Everyone walked everywhere, and journey times were not to be measured – just endured and tramped. These stories have been taken from all the centuries that the lanes have known and from the people who have trodden, driven or ridden along them. This was my main criterion in making this selection of walks.

Alongside their dramatic potential – and in reality preceding it – comes the landscape itself. This selection of lanes covers all the different habitats of the area. The south and south-east Devonshire coastline is longer and more accessible than its wilder northern shores, so it is not surprising that in this volume a third of those routes are within sight of the sea. There are hidden beaches, wide-rolling sands, chalk and red sandstone cliffs to discover.

The ways inland for early traders, farmers and fishermen threaded up and down steep, narrow lanes, few of which were widened by the Enclosure Acts. Riverside lanes are many here, as it is an area catching waters wrung out from Dartmoor's sponge along the Tamar, the Plym, the Yealm, the Dart, the Exe, the Otter and the Axe. There are fertile plains here which provided Exeter with its food.

There are rolling hills still clad with sizeable forests, such as those at Haldon, Ashclyst and along the River Tamar. Within the folds of the hills lie hidden valleys once home to dairies, some on a large scale; there are orchards both great and small here. There are villages linked to each other by winding lanes leading through folds of rolling hills. There is the watery Culm Valley, and the low-lying watery area known as the South Hams.

There are heathlands bordering Dartmoor, as well as individual commons such as those near Newton Abbot and Newton Poppleford. Dartmoor is visible nearly everywhere throughout the area. Defoe's description written in the early 1700s on descending Honiton Hill is still true today:

I beheld the most beautiful landscape in the world, I do not remember the like in any one place in England.

This was the area which first inspired the Romantic poets Wordsworth and in particular Coleridge, a Devonian. Their writings led to a change in the way people saw the countryside. We must not forget the underlying nature of the landscape, with its rich deposits of minerals, which also formed the way that people worked in the countryside; there are many industrial archaeological sites here apart from Morwellham which have been abandoned for nature – especially many species of bat – to recolonise.

The lanes themselves are busy wildlife corridors where you may see gannets and seals on the coast below, but where lizards scuttle across your path. Elms struggle for survival, and there are many clumps of stately Scots and Monterey pines on your way.

There are muddy and wetland crossings to be made, from which will fly up many varieties of dragonflies and butterflies; at night you can catch the twinkling of glow-worms in the hedges.

This is an area well-known for its holiday attractions, yet these attractions are more like distractions – for if you want to discover this area's true beauty, lushness and tranquillity, just step into any minor road or green lane. Stop, look and listen.

When writing about Dorset holloways, which run close to some of the routes here, Robert McFarlane in his book *The Wild Places* observes:

Unseen by maps, untenanted by the human, undeveloped because of their steepness, these vertical worlds add thousands of square miles to the area of Britain and Ireland – and many of them are its wildest miles.

Once you discover them, you will agree.

The chronological approach for the armchair reader

There are many ways of exploring highway history. The history of individuals and the nature of the topography through which they pass are just two. For the armchair walker in particular, there is the chronological approach. If you wish to follow the course of history through these lanes, then the following is one way to do so.

A glance through the modern-day OS maps for this area shows that there are many prehistoric hillforts and castles, from the shore to the moor. The walks which cover some of these include the one which takes you to Cadbury hillfort, Hembury, Membury and Stockland, and many more along the border areas of Somerset and Dorset. When the Romans arrived, cutting up through the estuaries, they built some of their major roads along the coast, particularly round Kilmington and Axminster and Exeter. They also reinforced the

Anglo-Saxon and earlier ridgeway patterns between settlements and villages, especially in east Devon, around Kentisbeare for example.

There are references to Anglo-Saxon charters, which give detailed records of roads as boundaries and can be found along the Moreleigh route; other distinctive Anglo-Saxon field patterns can be found around Ashill near Uffculme. We are in an area where some of the most powerful monasteries in the west in medieval times once maintained the roads between Sherborne, Dunkeswell, Buckfastleigh and Tavistock. They brought sheep and the woollen industry into these areas, which led to the setting up of many local markets by the end of the first Elizabethan Age. Some battles and routes to and from them can be found in this area: fighting the Danes at Whipton, the Dumnonii at Denbury, as part of the Prayer Book Rebellion at Feniton, rallying to support Monmouth at Colyton, and fleeing down Runaway Lane in the Civil War at Modbury. Then there are those lanes which saw agricultural workers seeking to better their working and living conditions, to be found at Stockland, Axmouth, Culmstock, Ilsington and Payhembury. The variety of agricultural practices, combined with fishing and mining, began as far back as the fourteenth century, and can be seen at Bere Ferrers, Beesands and Starcross. Mineral extraction took place throughout the region: at Bridford, at Blackborough where the whetstone mines were, as well as at the famous Morwellham copper bonanza. Evidence of smuggling and wreckers is to be found close to any of the coastal routes – at Branscombe for example, where they rose and fell along with the fear of invaders from France and the rise and fall of the lace-making industry. Dairies such as those found in the Culm Valley at Hemyock proved to be big employers, helped by the coming of the railways, when flowers and fruit were sent from Devon up to London from many centres such as those at Dawlish and Newton Poppleford. There are the turbaries, providing peat (mainly as fuel) for areas along the Culm Valley and Dunkeswell. There are the ways walked by the Quakers around Kilmington, Uffculme and Kentisbeare.

You will meet many colourful local characters, from Thomas Wakeley, founder of *The Lancet* at Membury, The Beggar King at Butterleigh, to the vicar who planted roses round his parishioners' doors at Hawkchurch, and the masons who made their mark at Tiverton.

Because there are so many mines and quarries throughout this area, you are walking through a post-industrial landscape, following in the steps of those workers who kept the green lanes open in order to get to work. The idea of them being used for recreation would amaze them, just as we in turn are amazed how the desire to make short-term profits hewed out these ways for quick returns, but not for everyone. The story of Devon's miners and quarry workers still remains largely unexplored.

There are many green lanes which form entire networks behind the main road patterns, and as Sheldon points out, they are powerful reminders of the past:

> *Therefore roads, generally speaking, have great vitality, and their vitality is strongest at those spots where two tracks cross one another. The points of intersection serve as pegs, holding the framework of the highways together, and giving it stability.*

The maps

In 1983 a government scheme called the Green Lanes Project set out to survey, research and restore green lanes in the county of Devon. It was a scheme which wanted to see the results of its survey available to the public in the form of maps, written walks and educational material. At the time of its closure, when I was no longer participating in the project, I heard that over forty Ordnance Survey maps to the scale of 1:2500 covering the whole of the county and covering the walls of the project's headquarters had been put in a waste bin. I recovered the binful, and spent two days prising them apart and labelling them up. Most, but not all, showed where green lanes were to be found. The South Hams have used information from these maps to produce maintenance programmes, guided walks and cycle routes. In the South Hams there is also the 'On the Right Tracks' scheme, and my book *Exploring Green Lanes in the South Hams* – but what about the rest of the county?

Not until the making of the Definitive Map, and the publication of the new OS Explorer series of maps in 2005, did I begin to find out what had been happening over the years.

When writing this book and using the old maps I had rescued, I did not look at the new ones until the final stages. It then became obvious that the Green Lanes Project information had been used to expand the Rights of Way system throughout the county. This collection includes many of those lanes which once appeared as white roads on the old maps; they are shown in this book overlaid with a line of broken green dots or green crosses, sometimes complete with local names. I have tried to incorporate and refer to as many of them as possible. I have also tried to include in the walks some of the new areas of moor and woodland that can be explored as a result of the new Right to Roam Act. Many walks link to established trails such as the Tarka Trail or the Two Moors Way.

The base maps here use the 1890 one-inch-to-a-mile OS series of maps, and also the Popular and the New Popular editions. Many features such as smithies, corn mills, railway lines, rifle ranges, orchards, woodlands, chapels etc., have gone, but most of the basic road patterns remain unchanged, and this includes, above all, green lanes. By using these older maps you will feel more in touch with the landscape through which you pass, and be given one more piece of the highway history jigsaw to fit in.

This is not a gazetteer of all the green lanes in the area, or an in-depth consideration of their status and uses. Many of the circuits include long sections of made-up roads, with surfaces upon which walkers have as much of a right to tread as tyres. These minor roads thread through the countryside and settlements which parcel up the Devon landscape into many different habitats.

I have indicated when there is more than one green lane which seems to cover the same route, and have marked these with crosses, along with footpaths or minor roads, to add variety to the route.

How to walk your way through this selection

Preferably using the public transport links from Exeter, Seaton, Tavistock and Plymouth, you can work your way around the routes as and when you pass through an area. The routes are arranged here starting in the Exeter area, going up to the Blackdown Hills then along to the Dorset and Somerset borders.

The routes then drop down to the coast at Sidmouth and along to the South Hams, ending up on the Cornish borders. All routes appear on the following OS Explorer and Outdoor Leisure (OL) series of maps:

OS 108 Lower Tamar Valley and Plymouth / Tavistock and Callington
OS 110 Torquay and Dawlish / Newton Abbot
OS 114 Exeter and the Exe Valley / Crediton, Tiverton and Dulverton
OS 115 Exmouth and Sidmouth / Honiton
OS 116 Lyme Regis and Bridport / Chard
OS 128 Taunton and Blackdown Hills / Wellington and Ilminster
OS Explorer OL20 South Devon Brixham to Newton Ferrers
OS Explorer OL28 Dartmoor

Questions

These are placed at the end of each walk and relate to something you see or read about whilst walking. Some are very straightforward, and others require a little detective work. Answers can be found on page 272.

Links to public transport

Some of the walks here cross over into Cornwall, Dorset and Somerset. But, if you are a bus-pass owner, since 2008 you have been able to cross county borders quite freely. The daily passes issued by the bus companies are great value, as are train tickets bought after 9.30 a.m. and at the weekends. The main Paddington to Penzance and Waterloo to Paignton railway lines and the Plymouth to Gunnislake branch line can be used when exploring these routes. The routes have been researched and written using public transport only, as this is the best way to get into the heart of the countryside.

You will not have to worry about parking up against hedgerows in narrow lanes, hoping that tractors can squeeze past and lorries will not smash in your wing mirrors. You don't have to return to the place from where you started, but are free to catch the bus or train further along its route or on its return. Some routes link up with both buses and trains. Some areas towards the Dorset and Cornwall borders may best be approached from outside the county, and you have to pick your days – mainly Fridays – to get to far-flung

Hawkchurch or Sydenham Damerel. Some of these routes set off from towns such as Sidmouth or Tavistock but drop you off in the middle of nowhere. As the bus trundles away and the silence of the countryside surrounds you, your exploration begins.

Numbered routes across south & south-east Devon

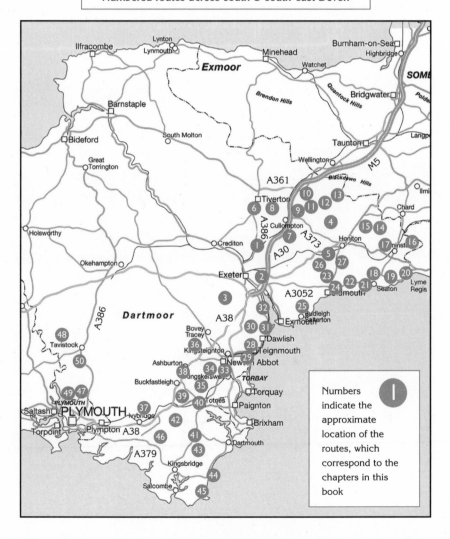

Numbers indicate the approximate location of the routes, which correspond to the chapters in this book

THORVERTON to CADBURY

The sweet waters and rolling hills of W.G. Hoskins' homeland

OS Explorer 114

This walk begins and ends in the beautifully tranquil village of Thorverton, which once had many shops and rural trades. It still has three pubs, and a post office which is housed in a portakabin, full of hidden delights. There is some minor road walking on this route, but traffic is always light. This walk is dedicated to the historian, W.G. Hoskins, a Devonian and father of all local history studies who, as you will see, passed many a summer here in his youth with his cousins who had lived here since the time of Alfred the Great. Whilst writing his standard work on Devon he visited all 407 parishes on foot or by using public transport. I have been proud to follow in quite a number of his footsteps.

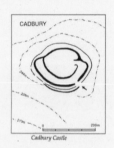

Cadbury Castle

Conditions: Some overgrown and steep lanes.

Distance: 5-6 miles.

Starting point: SY 924031. Take a look around the village and, as at the beginning of any green lanes route, do not ignore the parish church – it will always give you a good historical background, and will have details of the former residents of the area you are about to explore. Here at SY 924023 stands the church of St Thomas of Canterbury, which is dominated by angelic clerks on roof bosses in the porch and elsewhere. Its pew ends are carved with poppy heads and have a well-worn sheen to them. The village itself is rich in blossoming gardens watered by the stream which begins at Windmill Plantation which we ascend on this circuit.

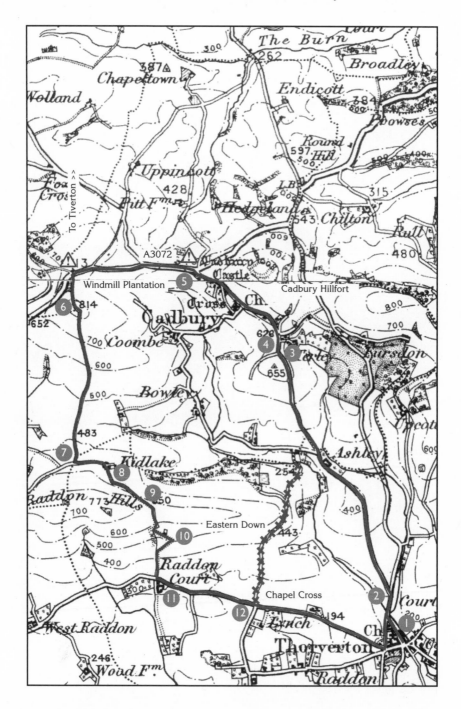

One of the essential things for any settlement, especially a big village, is a constant water supply, and here at Thorverton there seems to be an absolutely endless spring. In all my life I have never seen it fail. – W. G. Hoskins

(1) The spring is to your left on the Cadbury road after you leave the church. Follow the road where it forks and take the left to Cadbury passing the well. Pause just before Dinneford Bridge to admire the little seating area at what looks like another tumbling weir such as the one found at Ottery St Mary. Thanks to J.T. (look for the plaque with his initials) for this lovely area backing onto a very productive allotment.

(2) Keep left at Thatcher's Lane End, but as you ascend watch out on the right for a view of Fursdon Manor House, occupied by the family of that name for over 750 years (see *By the way* on next page). Cadbury Castle, an early Iron Age hillfort, also becomes visible to your right. You pass a group of lanes on your right.

(3) This is Terley, with a fine exposed cob wall; you are on the foothills of this camp, once occupied by the Romans, who placed votive offerings here. Climb the next signed footpath to your right, which has a cobbled surface, and over which Fairfax's troops clattered when they camped here in the Civil War. Spend time here exploring this large area and retrace your steps to the lane, turning right towards Cadbury.

(4) Before reaching the church, look out for the Furzeland Deer Park and Rescue Centre on your left, where roe, red and some very white reindeer can be seen. The church of St Michael was built in this dark hollow in the thirteenth century, but it is light and welcoming inside – especially bright are the colours of the window dedicated to the Fursdons.

(5) On reaching Cadbury Cross, turn left into the Crediton to Tiverton road for a brief, busy section of the A3072.

(6) Turn left at Windmill Plantation into a very long green lane. This lane is one used by Hoskins to demonstrate how Devon's hedges often started life as ancient manorial boundaries. Today this lane is a parish boundary, and it once formed part of the way for traffic coming directly from Exeter to the north towards Witheridge. The views which open up before you as you descend are wide and rolling with, in the distance, the twin peaks of west Dartmoor. There is some tarmac here; the surface of the lane is even, and in parts is the full width of a carriage. The hedges contain oaks and ashes, and merit a dating based on Hooper's hedge-dating theory. Count the number of different hardwood species on one side for thirty yards: each species represents a hundred years (see page 86).

(7) Take the footpath, keeping to the right round the field, then over a stile and left along the field edge again until you are in a green lane once more.

(8) This is a narrow lane running along the ridge at the top of a field and, given the documentary evidence, another ideal place for hedge-dating, which provides the field evidence too. There are at least ten species here, including spindle and honeysuckle. Spindle is considered to date from late-Medieval and Elizabethan times.

(9) Cross over the field edge, where there is a line of big pollarded ashes to your left, and on the edge of the further field to your right a line of furze, as you enter another green lane.

(10) By Raddon Hill Farm keep to the left, passing Raddon Hall's front lawn on the edge of a ridge looking right down over the Exe Valley. Follow the lane down to the road at the bottom which runs from Bradninch along a ridge road into Crediton.

(11) Turn left with Raddon Court on your right-hand side, towards Thorverton.

(12) On the corner on the left by Chapple Farm is a lane signed to Eastern and Eastern Down. Unfortunately it no longer links up to give access to Cadbury Hill Fort, but is worth walking along for the field maple and elm in the hedges and, by turning right at the top through the metal farm gate, you reach a line of ancient oaks and beeches on the ridge, Surely they were planted to mark the importance of this way to the fort? On descending go back into Thorverton to your left, noticing the Monterey pine which mark the way down to Old Lynch Farm on the right by a typical short green lane access way. On the left there is a fine monkey puzzle tree at Lynch. You return into Thorverton, passing the Exeter and Thorverton Arms and a plaque to three generations of Cummings, all postmen in the area from 1870-1994.

By the way

The village of Thorverton, with its proximity to Cadbury Hillfort, is an appropriate place to start this exploration of green lanes in south and south-east Devon. Firstly, it stands on the east-west axis of roads going down to the ports on the river Exe as far apart as Exmouth and Starcross. For the sea and rivers were the first choice of the traveller from prehistoric times until the development of wheeled transport transferred these movements to the land.

Secondly, it was where W.G. Hoskins, professor and pioneer in the study of local history at a university level, spent his childhood. He writes of Fursdon, where his cousins lived who told him tales which he was later to discover through his own researches were indeed true:

> *What still fascinates me is that when I was a youngster, my country cousins who lived round here used to stuff me with the yarn – so I thought then – that it had all belonged to Alfred the Great. Now they could not have known this historical fact, it was not written down anywhere.*

> *Devon is a mixture of more or less isolated single farmsteads, and of hamlets, which are usually three or four farmsteads grouped together.*

Hoskins spent his life investigating the relationship between these farmsteads and villages, and the lanes which link them. I quote once more:

> *Every lane has its own history; it is not there by accident: and every twist it makes once had some historical meaning, which we can sometimes decipher today, but not often.*

In the twenties he spent his childhood summers amongst his cousins in this area, and he gives us a clear picture of how Thorverton developed. It was a collection of farmsteads taken over by the Anglo-Saxons in the seventh century; the Dumnonii were pushed out up into the hills, and the village developed as a stockaded shape which you can see as you walk around here today. These patterns which he identified will appear again and again on our green lane explorations throughout this part of the county.

Other green lanes in the area

There are those on the other side of the A 396 at Silverton and Butterleigh.

Links

Buses run through Thorverton from Exeter and Tiverton.
The Exe Valley Way.

Question

What is the name of the house by which the well stands?

A sketch of the Cadbury Tree, after the symbol which is based on trees in nearby Kentisbeare (see Route 9). It was used from 1906 until just after the Second World War, and lives on as the logo for Cadbury World.

Hoskins' Demonstration Lane – see (6) in the text.

WHIPTON to BROADCLYST

A battleground and a lot of Bampfyldes

OS Explorer 114

This walk takes in a great deal, but is really quite short. It can begin from Exeter or Broadclyst, using the B3181 as your base line. It takes you through stretches of old parkland, and gives views right out over the Exe Estuary and over to Haytor on Dartmoor.

Conditions: Steep and mucky from motor-bike activity in places.

Distance: 2-3 miles.

Starting point: SX948943, on the B3212 at Whipton.

(1) At Summer Lane, opposite the church, go under the railway bridge and up passing the school on your left; or you can begin at Pinhoe Station.

(2) Turn right into a road which runs past the impressive small red-bricked Pinhoe House on your left.

(3) At the junction with Church Lane to your right, notice on the left a metalwork kissing gate and footpath with views up to Pinhoe Church of St Michael and All Angels. Follow this winding footpath, bordered by hawthorn and hazel, which looks down into the crater of a sandstone quarry.

(4) You emerge with the church on your left. It is a dramatic position for the church, which has a swinging lychgate. Like Butterleigh, it still has a Poor Box. Go through the churchyard and take the footpath, which is by Beacon House and runs up through Church Lawn – you could meet some alpacas on the way. You climb up over the meadow, from where you can see across to Haytor and get a glimpse of the Exe estuary at Topsham and beyond.

(5) Turn left into Beacon Hill Lane, another green lane running towards the Roman Signal Station at Stoke.

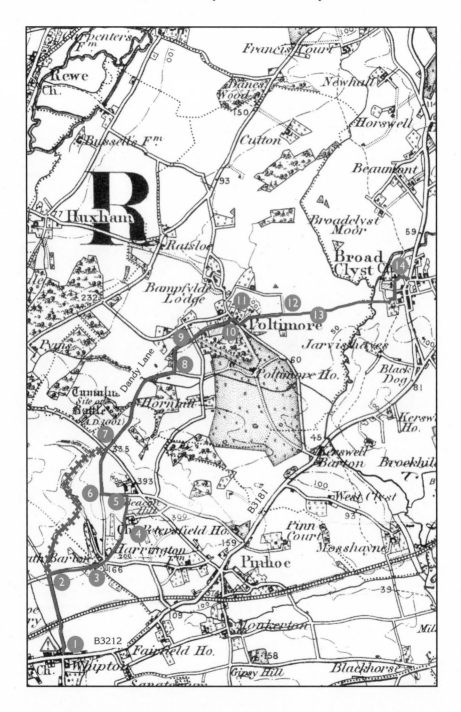

(**6**) Turn right, climbing up to Cheynegate House at the crossroads at the top. As shown by the 'Battle' sign on the map, this is where the Battle of Pinhoe was fought in a field directly to the left of the entrance to Dandy Lane. In A.D. 1001 an army of about 2,000 Englishmen faced a Viking army which outnumbered them by two to one. Although the Vikings were victorious, they fled back to Exmouth without taking any English commanders as hostages, which was unusual for these invaders.

(**7**) Cross straight over here and down into Dandy Lane, where memories of bloody battles will soon fade as we enter Bampfylde country. The lane begins narrowly and widens out at the bottom. It is used by motor trial bikes and mountain bikes, so is muddy but firm in the centre. There are patches of pedunculate grass growing towards its end, where it has fine-clipped, almost box-like hedges. Perhaps it is named Dandy Lane after the Bampfyldes: Arthur Mee records that on Sundays the last of the Bampfyldes

marched to church with his servants, the men in top hats, the women in poke bonnets, one of the sights of this countryside last century. – Arthur Mee, *Devon* (1938)

There have been Bampfyldes at Poltimore since the fourteenth century. One was a Speaker in the House of Commons in the days of the Commonwealth, another a preacher reformer. One was a poet who got into trouble with Joshua Reynolds, the Plympton-born painter, for unsuccessfully courting his niece. If you are following this route in winter, his lines on the robin are very apt:

But when pale Winter lights the social fire,
And meads with slime are sprent, and ways with mire,
Thou charm'st us with thy soft and solemn hymn
From battlement, or barn, or haystack trim . . .

(**8**) The lane meets the road by Appleby Stables. Further on there is a notice claiming that the lane is 'Unsuitable for Motor Vehicles'. Follow the road round to the left.

(**9**) Go straight across at this crossroads. You will soon have the wall of Poltimore Gardens on your right.

(**10**) You come out into the hamlet of Poltimore by a house with a beautiful square-bay leaded-light window. Turn right to visit the church of St Mary's, whose Poltimore Pew lowers over the congregation. (From here you may want to go on to the left route to see Poltimore House itself.) At the crossroads opposite the church stand the Alms Houses, to the right of Hatchland Road, set up by a Bampfylde in 1631 to commemorate his wife and son. But his other children live on, as you can see from the cameo portraits which appear on the wall.

(11) Go down into Hatchland Road here, passing a row of Cornish Unit Council Houses. You can contrast these later with the Acland Estate houses at Broadclyst. The lane is full of rabbit holes in the banks and drops straight down by some stables.

(12) Take the footbridge over the M5 here. This section of the road was built between 1975 and 1977.

(13) There is a piggery here which you soon leave behind as you take the footpath out over the fields, making for Broadclyst Church Tower ahead. You pass an entrance to Clyston Mill (now owned by the National Trust and open in the summer months) where corn is ground twice a week. There were 600 working watermills in Devon up until the middle of the twentieth century.

(14) Take the lane into Wilthier Close, where there are some fine almshouses to the right. You are now in Broadclyst, where there is much to explore and from where you can take a bus to Exeter.

By the way

It is not unusual in old postcards or archive photographic collections to come across as well as scenes by the old mill, scenes of dog carts and waggons, and sometimes just ponies with one man or a lady out on their milk round. There must have been rivalry amongst the deliverers, and overlapping territories along the lanes throughout east Devon. In Broadclyst Church I met a lady who remembers how a member of her family from one delivery round married into a rival one

Other green lanes in the area

There are quite a few out towards Stoke in the west.

Links

On bus and train routes to Pinhoe from Exeter.
By bus to Broadclyst from Exeter.
The National Trust

Question

How many children survived the Bampfylde who built the almshouses?

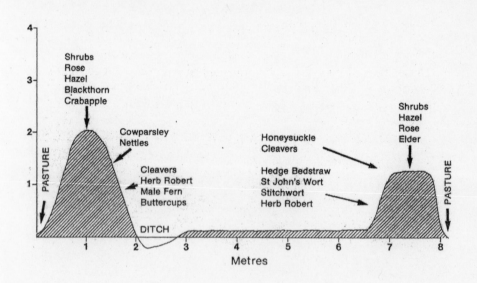

Profile of a lane. *Courtesy of Stephen Westcott.*

BRIDFORD

"Forty men are sad but have no complaints."
– the end of a toxic trade

OS Explorer 110

So read the headline in Exeter's *Express and Echo* of August 1958, referring to the closure of the Bridford Barytes Mine (Wheal Augusta) near Exeter, which had been working from 1838. This certainly echoes all the tales which emerge in the many now 'disused' mining districts of south and east Devon, where so many green lanes are to be found and where the fortunes of a few rose and fell but for many remained constant. A vein of manganese crosses beneath Haldon from Christow and Doddiscombsleigh, and appears again at Newton St Cyres and Upton Pyne. The mines and quarries here and around Christow are set amongst an almost Swiss-like scenery of rising and falling hills, with Dartmoor looming behind and the lakes of the reservoirs close at hand – ideal for wandering around, but they must have been hard going for those walking to work up and down the heights every day.

Conditions: Muddy in places, with some minor road walking.

Distance: 2-3 miles.

Starting point: SY 817865. The crossroads by the chapel. Take a walk to the right from here and then left for the older part of the village.

(1) There is a green lane of sorts which runs from the back of the church of St Thomas à Becket for those coming from the west. It takes you out to the main entrance.

(2) Turn left out of the lychgate. Granite is all around now as you descend into the green lane by a dead end sign, passing the Bridford Inn to your right with its religious motto *Laus Deo*. You pass the Old Rectory, and

the lane becomes wide and cobbled with granite walls. There is a sign where the bridleway meets the swiftly running (and sounding) Rookery Brook. Cross over and climb to the left, soon passing Middle Hole. There are views back over the village and the overlapping valleys from here. The lane becomes tarmacked for a while and then up to 5 metres wide where it runs down into Lower Hole Farmyard.

(3) Keep to the left here, and pass through a gate marked "Paths" and over someone's front lawn into a steep, granite-flanked green lane again.

(4) At the top, turn down left and down over a field at the back of Middle Hole Farm, where there is a fine granite trough.

(5) Once in the minor road, turn left towards Bridford again. There is now a footpath to your right which will take you up onto the edge of Christow Common, or you can carry on down passing Poole House to the left, with red bricks and Candy tiles shining forth.

(6) Turn left and down by a stream to the face of Scatter Rock Quarry. No doubt some workers didn't scatter quickly enough.

(7) Take the footpath to the left up here, where there are signs to Paynes and Searle's. Follow the signs carefully, keeping to the left round the back of the houses and back to the Bridford road on Pound Lane above Welcombe.

(8) If you turn right here you are very close to the site of the Barytes mine. On the map close by is Windhill Gate (SX 819871). This is 800 feet (235 metres) above sea level, and is thought to be on the route from Exeter to Dartmoor's Great Central Trackway. You pass this point on the alternate northerly route crossed in on the map. To return to Bridford, turn left.

By the way

The white mineral known as barytes has been used in the manufacture of hydrogen peroxide, paint and cosmetics, and is also used in the oil drilling process. There were also silver lead mines in the area. It is not surprising that the folklorist C.H. Laycock saw an *ignis fatuus* here. Birch Aller Mine went down 50 fathoms, and had a waterwheel 30 feet in diameter. But prior to the digging of the mines, there is a record of how the Quakers were involved in the serge woollen trade here.

The founder of Exeter's General Bank, a Quaker, employed home spinners and weavers here. He set off once a month with his foreman to bring new supplies, collect pieces of cloth and pay the workers. If a collection was particularly heavy, they took a sumpter horse with them – this was a pack-

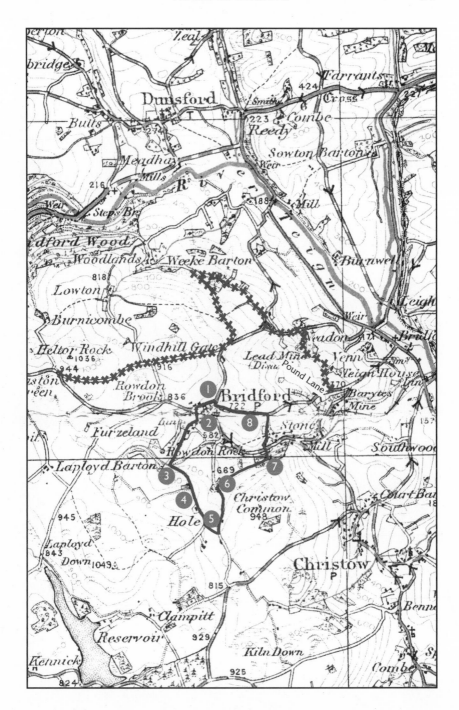

horse of larger proportions.

In W. Harding Thompson's *Devon*, Sir John Fortescue wrote in 1932:

The Packhorse and the Devon road. For it was no joke in the old days to meet a train of packhorses. They occupied the whole of the road, leaving no room for a mounted man to pass, and they plodded on steadily, nose to tail, without a thought of stopping before any living obstruction. . . . We hardly know what manner of beast it was. When I was a boy I remember a mare of my father's which was said by very old men to 'throw back' certainly to the old packhorse. I can see her now, a long, low, not very comely creature of about fifteen hands, dark muddy chestnut in colour, with a crupper mark and horizontal dark stripes on her forelegs. She had a queer temper, but a strong constitution, and was a willing slave in harness.

By 1958, when the mines were closed, local people were well treated – but it had not always been so. This village was one where the ancient lords still had the power to inflict capital punishment independently. It seems that miners in the past were always considered a difficult and dangerous group to deal with, and the local historian Reverend Carrington expressed his fears in the 1830s:

Contraband spirit was plenty in the district but little illicit trade remains, except around the mines to the west. The miners are a wild people and the district would be unsafe for a revenue officer.

Don't worry – all is quite peaceful in this Swiss-like enclave now.

Other green lanes in the area

Many to the north and east.

Links

There is a bus service from Newton Abbot and Exeter.
Waperwell to Bishopsteignton route (no. 30).

Question

The luminous escaping gas which was sometimes seen close to mines was called *ignis fatuus*. What does this mean?

DUNKESWELL

Weaving through the medieval ways, where monks behaved badly

OS Explorer 115

This walk goes through the beautiful rural valleys behind Honiton. Although more famous now for its American (and now privately run) aerodrome and the Canadian Chapel at Wolford, this parish contains the remains of a Cistercian Abbey founded by King John in the thirteenth century. If you visit the Church of St Nicholas, you can see how the essential rural and non-military nature of this area is prized, when you read the altar window inscription:

While the Earth remaineth Seed Time and Harvest Shall not Cease.

This is not a circular route, but can be made by studying the buses which run from Honiton to Taunton through the village. The first tucking mill in Devon was first recorded at Dunkeswell in 1238.

Conditions: Very muddy and wet in places.

Distance: 2-3 miles.

Starting point: ST138058, Wolford Cross at the junction with Long Lane and Limer's Lane.

(1) Turn right, leaving the conifer-lined avenue behind you, which is replaced by indigenous oaks and beeches. The line of the rhododendrons becomes visible to the right.

(2) Take the footpath sign on the left, and follow it through by taking the footpath to the left. This lane is at least thirty feet wide, with the rather straggly rhododendrons at its centre and two moulded boundary banks with coppiced and layered beeches – these must be part of the medieval monastic lands. There are some flintstone rocks on the path, and some muddy patches which have been bridged over by fallen branches layered horizontally. This is how 'corduroy' roads were made through mud and watery ways for centuries: they were supplemented with 'bavines', bundles of furze, or heather layed across them.

(3) The rhododendrons disappear here, and there is a footpath sign taking you over a stile into and over a rolling hill pasture and out onto another long section of green lane.

(4) The pines to your left here form a dark canopy, but the path takes you along by open fields, giving good views towards Luppitt Common and initially towards the long red brick milking parlour of Old Highwoods Farm. There is a group of well-pollarded large elders along here. Skylarks sing by the Highwoods, and you may catch a glimpse of a private plane from the nearby aerodrome cruising by here.

(5) More holly appears towards the end of this lane. Once at its end, turn left and down through the woods with more beech boundary banks. There is a fine bridge with interesting drainage channels. You climb up past Fishponds House. The Cistercian Abbey further up the valley was in operation from 1201-1539. Continue passing Windwhistle and Southlands Farms with a view of Dunkeswell village below.

(6) Before Cox's Hill Farm drop down right at a lane with lots of holly and beech, which feels as though it must once have been one of the ways through to the Abbey up the valley. It is roughly tarmacked in places now, and passing Mansells on the left you go through a landscape of alders and scrubby birches in the valley, which in spring is home to swathes of bluebells.

(7) Keep to the left, and go down to the footbridge. Cross over and take the snakey path up towards Knapp Farm which is lined by gnarled, layered-down beeches.

(8) Go through the gate, and keep to the left by Knapp Farm. You follow an increasingly red-brick-surfaced road up to the groups of farm buildings at Bowerhayes Farm.

(9) There is an alternative footpath to the left here which leads back down to the village, but keep on and go through to where the green lane joins

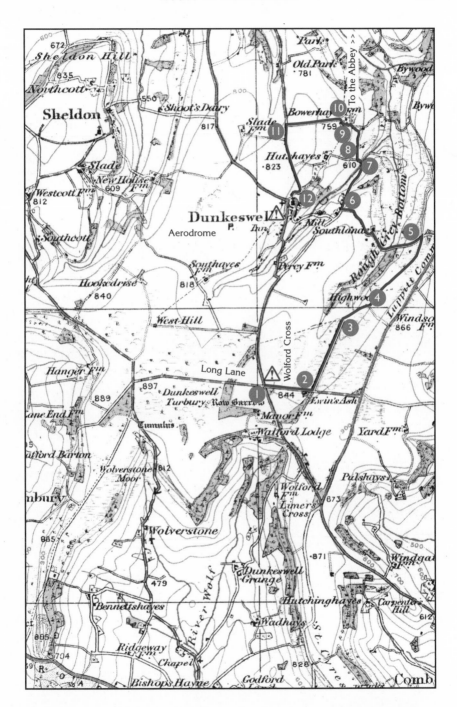

a minor road.

(10) Turn left into this minor road, which becomes increasingly green at its centre and carries a dead end sign – far from the truth!

(11) Turn left along a minor road which runs along the back of houses which seem to have their own personal hangars attached. This will bring you down into the village, with the Methodist Church up above and the road running down to the Tercery area.

(12) The church of St Nicholas is to your right, with its solid square tower. The font has some strange carvings around its base: it is possible to make out a bishop, a doctor and elephant. Elephants were found on tiles amongst the remains of the Abbey too. The elephants are what Pevsner saw, whereas Mee saw Sagittarius drawing his bow at a double-headed monster! What do they look like to you? The Beer stone pillars show the figureheads of the six daughters of General Simcoe, the first Governor of Canada, together with a grand-daughter who fell with Wolfe at Quebec.

By the way

The ruins of Dunkeswell Abbey close by are worth visiting. Whenever a Cistercian monastery was founded, it had to be beyond the sound of another church bell tolling, which shows how close religious communities were throughout the landscape then.

If you wish to pay a visit to the Abbey and walk in the footsteps of rebels, then maybe you should set out from Hackpen on the Ashill Route (No. 11). It was from here that a lay person called Cogan set out in 1299 to get even with the monks for a wrong they had done him. He and his allies drove out all the monks, wounded the servants, took the gallows to Uffculme and burnt them along with 60 oxen and 20 cows. This was a lot of wrongdoing, and he was fined £80. Had he committed these crimes in later years, surely he would not have got off so lightly? (See Route 15, Stockland.)

Other green lanes in the area

Route 5, Feniton; Route 9, Blackborough; and Route 11, Ashill.

Links

There is a bus service through the village stopping at The Royal Oak from Taunton to Honiton.
The ruined Abbey buildings to the north, the Wolford Chapel and the Aerodrome Museum are all close by.

Question

The three colours which predominate in the church are to be found in the American flag. What are they?

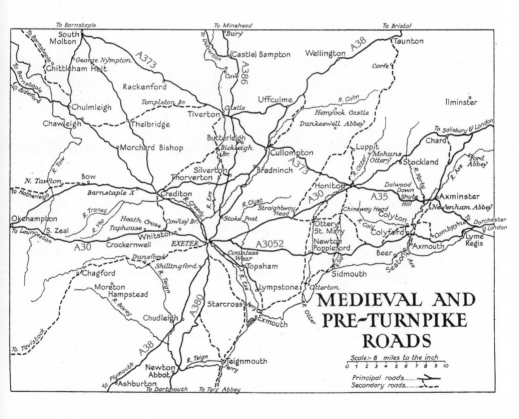

FENITON

An unquiet land between Neolithic hillfort and Roman highway

OS Explorer 115

This walk follows the footsteps of those early Neolithic settlers who built Hembury hillfort to overlook the Otter Valley in the south, and also to guard against invaders approaching from the north. There are views all around over a green and red patchwork of fertile lands, and one of the longest green lanes in Devon to enjoy. This is a railway-based route. You are close to Whimple here, which also has many green lanes running through its orchards.

Conditions: Very muddy, waterlogged and rocky in the green lanes.

Distance: 3-4 miles.

Starting point: SY 095994, Feniton Station. There is a plaque on the outside wall of the tiny booking office, which opened in 1867 and closed in 1965 when Dr Beeching, the Minister of Transport, decided to close down a quarter of the 17,000 miles of the railway network and half the stations. Luckily this station stayed open and just changed its name, all in the same year.

(1) Leave the station by a side entrance and go over the level crossing, turning sharp right into Station Road passing a small row of shops to your right (it's strange that station-side shop parades are nearly always single-storey). Go straight through the estates, passing the school on your left.

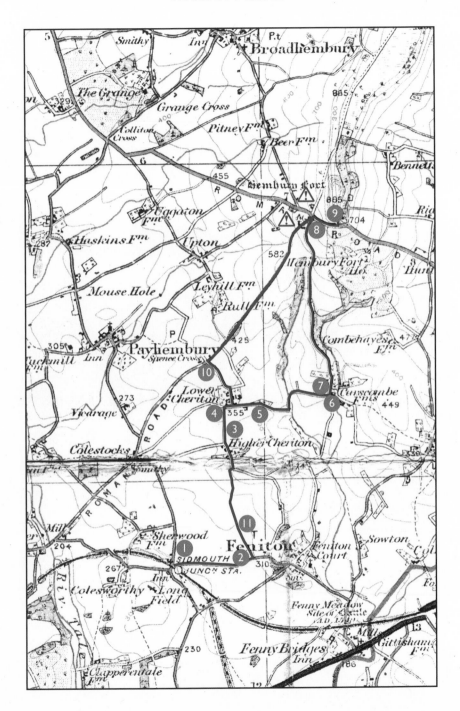

Lovingey Close on your right marks the end of the built-up area. You are in a narrow lane – be careful.

(2) Just past The Old Rectory at Rutts Cross, turn left into a lane marked 'Unsuitable for Long Vehicles'. The lane runs up through sunken outcrops of yellow sandstone with interesting mammal holes at various levels. As you reach a plateau, the lane to the right has a double boundary bank and there are views down to the Church of St Andrews nestling in the Fenny Bridges valley. This lies close to the meeting-place of some prehistoric trackways. As you proceed along this minor road you are soon treading on grass at its centre. There are good views over to the left, and a pine marker tree along the way. When you reach the settlement of Cheriton walk straight through to Court Barton.

(3) Here at Court Cross is a fingerpost indicating one and a half miles to Hembury Fort. Go straight across, and under the pylons.

(4) You reach another junction and turn right towards the hillfort again.

(5) On the bend there is another 'Unsuitable for Motors' sign and a public bridleway post. Go straight across, and you are in Owl's or Cheriton Lane. Gays Cottage is the last habitation to your right as you plunge down into a very muddy and long lane. A stream runs alongside it, giving a 'goyle'-like feel as you descend. (A goyle is a small ravine.) One section has a wall made of yellow sandstone bricks and fringed with Hart's Tongue ferns and pennywort. Pignut grows along the mossy banks, and bluebells grow under holly and hazel coppice. Where the lane disappears into a watery crevice to your right take the marked-off path round the field edge to your left. Pause on the bend here: in spring there are early purple orchids and wood anemones to enjoy. There is another muddy stretch to get through (take the footpath to the right if necessary).

(6) You emerge at Curscombe Farm buildings.

(7) Keep to the left up a well-surfaced, wide green lane. This has a ridgeway feel to it as it climbs steadily towards the hillfort. There are flints, concrete slabs and chunky red mud blocks to clamber over as you work slowly upwards. A break in the hedge gives far-reaching views over the plains towards Dartmoor. The end is heralded by a tall hedge holly to the left, and you emerge at the end of this unmetalled road by a heap of road burnings.

(8) Turn right and up to Hembury Fort Cross and the A373. Notice the Edward VII Post Box to your right here. This is a rarity as, unlike Queen Victoria who had over 60 years to have boxes initialled to her, Edward VII only had nine.

(9) There is a footpath up into the hillfort, and a small lay-by from which the view opens out over this chequered landscape. The hillfort was probably unoccupied when the Romans came here about AD 50. They built a workshop here and some rectangular timber buildings. It is the same date as the legionary fortress at Exeter, and may have had some connection with iron working in the Blackdowns on the Kentisbeare Route. Retrace your steps to the crossroads, and follow the sign down to the left to Feniton (marked on the 1919 map as a Roman road).

(10) At Spence Cross turn left towards the Cheritons once more. The lane is greening in the centre and has some salt and pepper surfacing (typical of the roads in this area) still visible.

(11) On your left as you go down Cheriton Hill is a footpath which will take you to the original settlement of Feniton and the Church of St Andrews, before returning back to the station.

By the way

There is much history to be discovered in this valley. There are the Roman roads which run into Exeter and out along the east coast from here as shown in the maps. This is what Sheldon had to say about the horses that the Romans used:

> *The horses of the native Damnonian breed are described by Roman writers as diminutive, but quick in their movements. For fast travel the Romans used a light two-wheeled carriage called a cisium, drawn by mules. Cisia were kept on hire at the posting-stations along the great roads. Their average pace seems to have been from five to six miles an hour, including stops. According to Gibbon, by the help of relays it was easy to travel a hundred miles in a day along the Roman roads, for houses were everywhere erected at the distance of five or six miles, each of them constantly provided with forty horses.*

On the 1919 map, by Fenny Bridges in a field known as 'Bloody Meadow', is written "Site of Battle 1549". This was another battle fought during the Prayer Book Rebellion which began in Sampford Courtenay. (See Route 48 in *Exploring Green Lanes in North and North-West Devon*).

Unrest in the area continued into the seventeenth century, when after the Civil War the Puritans continued to persecute Church of England parsons.

The parson at Payhembury was driven from his pulpit on Christmas Day, losing his corn, cattle, Christmas dinner and 'plum pudding'.

Other green lanes in the area

The Green Lane street sign here will take you to many lanes in the Ottery area. There are lanes leading into Payhembury too. Another circuit can be made from here to include Tuckmill at SY 077013. Here, Stanes tells us:

> *In the adjoining Rackhay fields, cloth was fulled and stretched on racks and sold to Exeter merchants.*

Links

The railway line from Exeter.
Dunkeswell (no. 4) and Kentisbeare (no. 9) Routes.

Question

On the station you will find its former name. What was it?

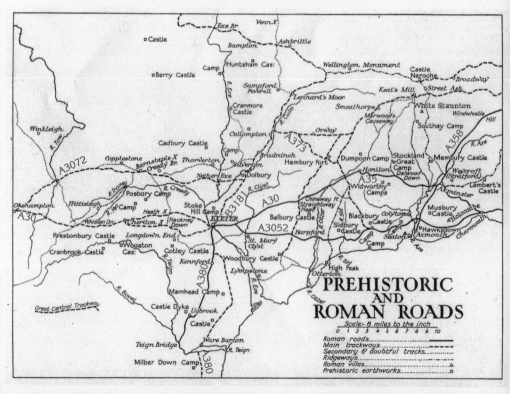

BICKLEIGH to BUTTERLEIGH

In the footsteps of Bampfylde Moore Carew, the Beggar King

OS Explorer 114

Here is a walk which takes you from the Exe Valley and over onto a ridgeway, looking up towards the Cadbury hillfort and down to the sea. As far back as Domesday, Butterleigh was famous for its rich butter-producing meadows. (Route 13 contains information concerning 'Utterleigh Butterleigh', produced in east Devon). This walk shows you what induced the son of a priest to side with the poor who were invariably deprived of the fat of the land. There is a lot of quiet lane walking on this circuit.

Field Maple leaves and flower

Conditions: Muddy underfoot in the green lanes.

Distance: 5-6 miles.

Starting Point: From Bickleigh Bridge SS 937077. You cannot miss this wonderful bridge and weir, even though it was not where Paul Simon composed *Bridge Over Troubled Water*. Make your way to the village, passing Millhayes on your left. When you come to the first lane on the left, start climbing.

(1) There is a fine mulberry tree on the right by Belle Meadow and some hollyhocks too – this village seems to be full of them. You come to the church of St Mary on the right. Just outside the porch is a tomb dated 1690: the details of the Lovell Charity are laid out on the top, and worth deciphering. But there is no such monument to our Beggar King to be found. Unfortunately

the church is often locked, but its setting is beautiful: protected and cosseted by the thatched cottages which surround it.

(2) On leaving the church, turn right and pass the National School (1841) and Exeland Cottage. You come to Major Cross, which is just a bend without any signpost. Take the green lane to your right. It is packhorse-width, and has a great variety of flowers growing in its hedges and underfoot: water pepper, yellow agrimony and tansy are just a few. Where the lane becomes enclosed by pollarded beeches to your left you may catch a glimpse of red deer stags in the fields here. It drops down to a muddy patch where maple and blackthorns take over in the hedges, and you come to a cob-built barn on the left before dropping down into the minor lane which links Bickleigh with Butterleigh. This connecting green lane which you have just left is cobbled for most of its length, and is one of many in this area which follows ancient manorial boundary patterns as identified by Hoskins – these will always merit a hedge-dating exercise (see page 86). Once out of this kind of lane, you can see in the fields around you its pattern duplicated for as far as the eye can see.

(3) Turn left here by the road triangle and willow tree towards Little Burne Farm. There are patches of hydrangea escapees flowering in the hedgerows, along with the wild *Pimpinella major*, horsetail and wood spurge here – more signs that you are passing through an area which was once all ancient woodland. By the green lane entrance to Underleigh, a Guelder Rose shrub grows. You then start climbing until you reach the sign for Butterleigh.

(4) Turn left, then right towards the church. Opposite the Butterleigh Arms, a Coteleigh brewery, is a delightful village square – a rarity in Devon. There is a well-placed seat here by the Church of St Matthew (a church has stood here since the thirteenth century). This church has been rebuilt, but the tower which appears in various views on this walk has been looking out over the valleys for 700 years. The poor box for alms is made from a piece of 4" by 4" oak, and is dated 1629. Once a year this would be emptied and the contents distributed to the poor on Boxing Day.

Return to (4) and go down past the Forces crossroads (often thought to indicate the site of a gallows) and keep to the left over the bridge, passing the wall of Butterleigh House.

(5) Here on the bend is a public bridleway sign. The lane begins at cart-width, then narrows down to packhorse-width through a woodland edge.

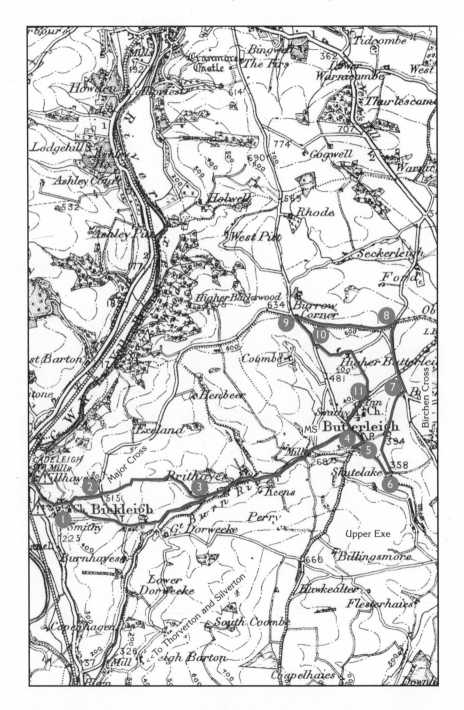

(6) Turn left into what becomes a concreted-over green lane. Notice the field patterns to your left, which have not changed since an ecclesiastical inventory of fields was made in 1680.

(7) Turn right here to have a look at the onion-finialled post at Birchen Oak and see how you are placed between Cullompton-Bradninch and Tiverton. Turn back to where you left the bridleway end, and go on up the hill to the second T-junction.

(8) You pass Butterleigh Saw Mill. Carry on to Burrow Corner and its junction with the Turnpike road, dating back to 1758, which would have been taking traffic from Cullompton through to Crediton or Tiverton.

(9) Take the first on your left.

(10) At Waygate turn left. The lane greens up as you progress, and you go through the farm and the back of the sawmill at Sunnyside Farm. As you descend there are good views over the Exe Valley.

(11) By turning right at the road junction you will come out on the road to the church. You might like to see the milestone, as indicated on the map.

Retrace your steps again to (4) back down to Bickleigh down the Burn Valley Road. As you reach Bickleigh there are three footpaths on the present-day map which you can take to bring you back to the church.

By the way

In the West Country Studies Library in Exeter is a small leather-bound volume entitled *The Life and Adventures of B.M. Carew, the noted Devonshire stroller and dogstealer*, published in 1745. It was written by the self-styled King of the Beggars, who was born in Bickleigh in 1693 and after much travelling and many adventures died there in 1759. It is a great curiosity to handle such a book – as must the man himself have been. The son of the parson at Bickleigh, when he was eighteen, shortly after having been caught with a marked (i.e. poached) deer in his possession, he met up with some gypsies and stayed with them. His skill in hunting seemed to stem from his ability to charm dogs. Written in the first person, it tells of how he lived on his wits both locally and elsewhere. He had some acting talent: in London he went around with various women and groups of children, claiming them all to be his own and begging for money to support them. He tricked the Duke of Bolton into giving him money by posing as a sailor who had just returned from sea and who had lost his trunk and all his worldly goods. In Stoke Gabriel he said that he was collecting money to provide for a crew whom he knew would soon be brought ashore shipwrecked in a forthcoming storm. The book contains a glossary of cant or thieves' slang, some unprintable and others quite sweet: a 'wordpecker' is someone good with words, 'ogles' are eyes, and a 'ferret' is a pawnbroker. The hidden lanes in this area must have been home for Mr Carew and his cronies, and as you go remember the words of the folk song *Raggle Taggle Gypsies* – there is always something compelling about gypsy rovers.

Other green lanes in the area

Bradninch, Thorverton and Cadbury, Halberton.

Links

There are buses which run along the Exe Valley from Tiverton and Exeter. National Cycle Route 3/The Exe Valley Way.

Question

Which monarch was kind enough to ensure that poor boxes were put in every parish church?

BRADNINCH to CULLOMPTON

Following the paper trail

OS Explorer 115

With some careful bus-timetable planning, you can visit these two ancient towns in the Culm Valley using green lanes and minor roads without having to double back upon yourself – a true green lanes circuit. Bradninch's paper mill is still important in the area, but once the town was also a legal centre, especially for villages on the edge of Exmoor. The old Portway, going through Bradninch and linking the Exe Valley ports with the north and east towards Bath, fell out of use

as a main way from Exeter in 1816. This large route gives you the option of exploring both Bradninch and Cullompton, and the valleys and woodland around them. It's up to you how you achieve this, but here is a blueprint of varied and beautiful green lanes to follow. Enjoy your paper chase.

Conditions: Some steep climbs, muddy in parts.

Distance: One route 4 miles; as two routes, nearer 7 miles.

Starting point: ST001022. This is Hele Cross on the B3181, once the busy turnpike from Exeter through to Bradninch and Cullompton in 1846.

(1) From Fagin's Antiques on the corner here cross over and follow the sign to Plymtree and Clyst Hydon. You pass a National Trust reserve gate at Pounds Pit Cross on the right. Go past another two houses.

(2) At Pottshayes cross, turn right into a minor lane which as you climb gives views over White Down Copse, Crow and Ashclyst reserves. At first

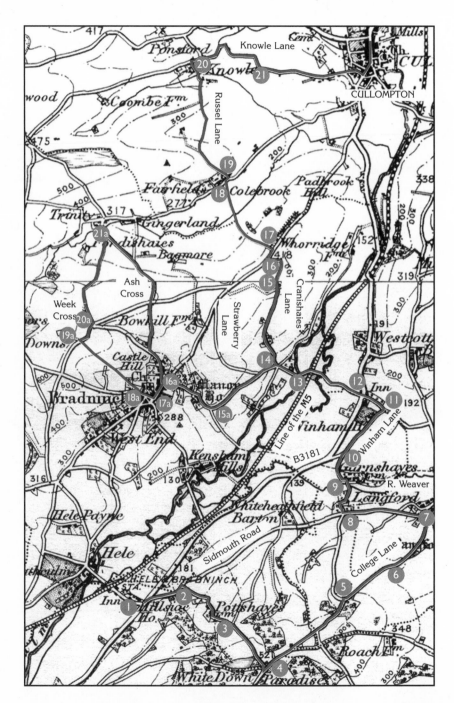

you are flanked by high hedges containing a lot of maple, and the soil at the lane edges reddens. You pass Whiley Cottage, High Hayne Farm (which straddles the road), and Pottshayes Farm. Remember that Hayes means hedge, and all these hedges can be hedge-dated as you go counting the hardwood species in a thirty-yard length on one side.

(3) Keep climbing until you reach the mast in the field to the left, where you will get good views over towards Bradninch and Blackborough.

(4) You enter a beech canopy beside woodland where there is a fingerpost. Keep left here, passing a parking place for Paradise Copse to your right.

(5) Turn hard left by a big pollarded oak festooned with honeysuckle. You are in College Lane. There is a lot of honeysuckle on the right here and an unusual dog rose with double petals, *Rosa micanthra*, at the beginning on the right. The tarmac comes and goes. There are good compact hedges here. The lane sinks and narrows, and you are walking through a predominantly ash woodland.

(6) There is a distinct green lanes junction here. Keep to your right. Notice the Bradninch and Cullompton boundary here, marked by a fox run. The scent is strong, but will soon be replaced by the chicken farms around you.

The green lane becomes more cobbled, but towards the end the grass takes over again and you are walking through thick maple-dominated hedgerows. Towards the end glimpses of Langford Barton break through the rows of fine pollarded oaks which are such a feature of this lane.

(7) At Langford Cross turn left, following the sign to Hele Cross. You are walking along the old Sidmouth road. There is a turn on the left for fishermen to take, but you carry straight on.

(8) By the crossroads at Piper's Farm, turn sharp right. The tower of the not-so-distant Cullompton church appears. This lane, like so many in this landscape, retains a lot of its sinuousness, formed by the headlands created when oxen or heavy horses turned round. The hedgerows have been enriched by cattle passing along these winding lanes, as Hoskins states:

> *I am quite sure that if you ask yourself how our old roads origi-*
> *nated, you can start off with a cattle track. But cattle do not walk in*
> *straight lines, they mooch from side to side, eating as they go, and*
> *they trample out a path which naturally human beings follow.*

(9) But it is neither oxen nor shire horses which come into view just before the bridge over the River Weaver at Garlandhayes Farm (Gurnshayes

on the old map) – it is deer, a lot of them very curious at your arrival. This little river began its life near Dulford as the Higher Weaver, and there is no doubt that it would have served many involved in the cloth trade as it is so close to Cullompton's great church, built by John Lane through woollen wealth.

(10) At this junction turn right into Winham Lane and walk towards the line of poplars which is often visible on this route. It may well have been a group planted under sub-contract to Bryant & May, as this is the tree from which matches are made and the acquisition of small stands of these trees was common in the 1930s.

(11) At Cornerways turn left into a fairly busy road. The smell of the many chicken farms in the area will hit you now. You pass 'The Park and Lodge' accommodation, and come to The Merry Harriers at the crossroads.

(12) Go straight over here towards the weak bridge (nothing over three tons) sign. You will see from the map (dated 1888) that the railway was well established, with a station at Hele Bradninch to serve the mills and the village. The section of the M5 which you cross dates back to 1975-77.

(13) You come to the bridge over the River Culm, where granite parapets to your left carry a familiar sign as well as some mason's marks and initials. The red bricks are used in the farmhouse and buildings which you pass on your right at Champerhayes with a date of 1835. To your left is an industrial estate where Silvanus, an organisation for the preservation of woodland, is based.

(14) From here you must decide whether your journey will take you to the legal centre at Bradninch or towards the wool-rich town of Cullompton. If you choose the latter, then turn right here into the green lane marked 'Unsuitable for Motor Vehicles'. This is Cranishaies Lane. There are cobbles, tarmac and a stream to negotiate here as you climb up through this sunken lane.

(15) At the top just before Highdown you go through two farm gates. Walk up to the road taken by the Cullompton to Exeter buses, the old turnpike of 1813.

(16) Take care as you turn right here. The milestone shown on your present-day OS map has disappeared. Remember that this road was one of the main ways out of Exeter towards the east. Traffic through Cullompton was not diverted until 1969, when a bypass was built which eventually became incorporated into the M5.

(17) The bridleway lane is to your left on the opposite side of the road. It leads down through overhanging hedges to Colebrook. It is narrow and

damp, with water pepper growing up in clumps, and rocky too. Towards the bottom there is a very muddy patch through which a stream struggles to escape. To the right here you might catch a glimpse of the golfers at Padrook Park. Carry straight on over into a lane carpeted with fool's watercress, brooklime and water forget-me-not plants. Continue straight on over the carpet of water plants. In summer, towards the end of the lane you are given a guard of honour by the foxgloves.

(18) Turn right for a short stretch along this minor road.

(19) Another bridleway sign appears to the left through some farm buildings and houses, which brings you out into Russel Lane, a pebble-lined wide running track through lush meadows. You are in command of great views again. Look out for the public bridleway sign to your right, which will take you sharply down into a narrow way which widens out onto a muddy, straight stretch where willows and alders grow in the fields. You pass by Knowle, a house on the green lane, and follow round to the top, passing other houses.

Turn right at the top, then right again into Knowle lane. This is a very winding lane, and there is a footpath to take you across the fields if you prefer; but if so, you will miss seeing the stretches of horizontal wire and bar fencing on the corners. These were often put up to keep men employed between the two world wars; as wages they were offered ten shillings a day or a food parcel. You come out into Swallow Way. Turn left towards the town, keep left at Manitoba Gardens and pass to the right of Willowhayes Primary School to get to Cullompton High Street. Think of how yet another industry, basket-making, must have drawn travellers to this town; without

The evolution of the 1970s Devon County emblem finial sign.

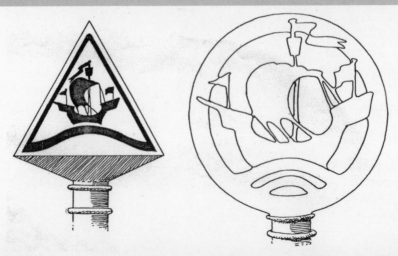

baskets no trade could have been carried out. Take time to explore the town especially the church which is as spectacular inside as out.

Alternative Route to Bradninch

(15a) You come up a road known as The Avenue, planted in 1832 mainly with maples by a William Mathews from the other paper mill at Kensham, which was also a fulling mill. In 1855 there was still a weaver living in Bradninch, in the first cottage on the right up Cullompton Hill; William Tucker was his name – one associated with the woollen industry for centuries.

(16a) As Kensham Avenue becomes Millway, turn left by the playground and take the green lane footpath which crosses over a stile and into a field giving views of the Hele Paper Mill and Killerton Park (see *By the way* below). Go over another stile and into a short stretch of lane where there is a bridge over a stream going down to the Culm. This brings you out into a minor road.

(17a) Cross over, and follow the road through this small estate with, to the right, some houses especially built for the paper-mill workers.

(18a) At the top turn right at the T-junction, and just along the road take a sharp left over the road onto a footpath which goes up and around a field edge.

(19a) This will bring you into a minor road, Back Lane. Turn right and keep climbing and admiring the views.

(20a) At Peakfield Crossways, turn left into an unsigned green lane which leads to Beacon Cross. You are still climbing. There is some stone walling here and lots of holly and spindle. A cobbled surface emerges from the grass one. This once well-maintained way must have been an important link for those travelling towards the north or south.

(21a) At the end of the lane you can turn right and go down to Ash Cross and then back into Bradninch for a good look around the town, including the church of St Dissen, named after an Irish monk in the seventh century. The impressive coat of arms showing a black spread-eagle belonged to Richard Plantagenet, son of King John. Alternatively, turning left towards Trinity and keeping right you can rejoin the route to Cullompton at (19).

By the way

The Borough of Bradninch was once far more important than Cullompton, and was on the King's Highway from Exeter to Taunton. The first paper mill here was ·set up at Hele in 1822; it belonged to the descendants of Forde Abbey near Chard. The Dewdneys perfected the process in the 1820s, and introduced machine-driven power. They manufactured coloured papers, especially blue, which was glazed. This process was a first in the industry. They looked after their employees, building a model village, parts of which you see at (3), and a school in 1823. Paper, once made from rags and then from esparto grass, was eventually made from wood fibre, and the process was electrified in 1891. It seems impossible to believe that until the coming of the railway here in 1844, everything was transported overland to Topsham.

Question 1

We are in cob-building country. Which modern public building pays homage to this?

Question 2

What type of ship is carved on the exterior walls of Cullompton church?

The TIVERTON area

To the east along the Tiverton Canal

OS Explorer 114

This walk will bring you in contact with items of transport and agricultural history in east Devon. You walk along the level path by the canal, and all around you are the ups and downs of the rolling hills looking out towards Exmoor, with glimpses of Dartmoor to the west. You begin by the canal and end up by the waterwheel of the excellent Tiverton Museum.

JAMES ASCOTT,
BUILDER, CONTRACTOR, WHEELWRIGHT, AND MILLWRIGHT,

AGRICULTURAL IMPLEMENT MANUFACTURER, & AGENT FOR ALL THE BEST MAKERS,
HALBERTON.

Conditions: Stony underfoot and fairly steep in places.

Distance: 4-5 miles.

Starting point: SS964122. Begin at the beginning of the Grand Western Canal basin, now known as a country park. The main reason for the construction of the canal was to transport lime into the area as fertiliser.

(1) Take the path to your left for a very pleasant stretch of this canal begun in 1810 by Rennie, who built the Plymouth Breakwater too. The canal was to have formed part of a great canal system running from Topsham to Taunton, then on to branches at Cullompton, Tiverton and Wellington. But just look at the year in which it was started! *'In old England very hard times'*, runs the folk song belonging to these times, and these were indeed dark days throughout England. The Napoleonic Wars had moved into the Spanish phase led by Arthur Wellesley, who became the Duke of Wellington for his heroic deeds.

(2) Here leave the towpath and go up onto the road to look for the mason's marks on the bridge parapets. These were put here for a practical,

disciplinary purpose: so that the overseers could find out who had constructed this section and make sure the work was up to scratch. Now that you have left the canal path, take the minor road to your right. The hedgerows here are thick with the delicate pinky-red flowers and geranium-shaped leaves of Herb Robert. On the left you pass a distant view of Manley, with an 1882 build date on its façade.

(3) At Thurlescombe Cross, go straight on and into a green lane ahead on the bend. There are some cobbles, flint chippings and tarmac remnants as you climb up. But the most distinctive feature to your right is a double hedgebank, which is the boundary between Halberton Parish and Tiverton. The hardships which hit the rural community in times of war went on for a long time afterwards, causing the Reverend Griddlestone of Halberton to encourage his parishioners to revolt:

> In addressing a large body of labourers at a meeting of a Parochial Friendly Society, I enumerated the various rates of pay for agricultural labourers which prevail in other parts of England and advised my hearers to seek something like an approximation to them, not by uniting against their masters, or by any other means likely to produce a bad feeling between master and servant, but by respectful representation; and failing this, by emigration of the young and strong, either to the colonies or those parts of the U.K. in which better wages are given . . .

Thornes Park is to the left. 'Park' indicates that deer would have been contained in this completely wooded area; they are still here. There are sweeping views to your left. You enter into the dappled light of the wooded area of this lane, where there is a series of steps to the right and a small quarry too. These steps could have been used to transport limestone to the canal or to where such grand houses as Manley were built close to it. There are a few pollarded oaks in the area fronting a small group of larches.

(4) The lane emerges abruptly onto a minor road. Keep to your right and go down to White Down Cross (5) and turn right into Newrie's Hill Road. Notice the onion-finialed and plate crossroads sign opposite. There is a line of cherry trees along this stretch of road at the top, with Warnicombe House drive on your right.

(6) Turn into a minor road marked with a wooden Public Footpath sign.

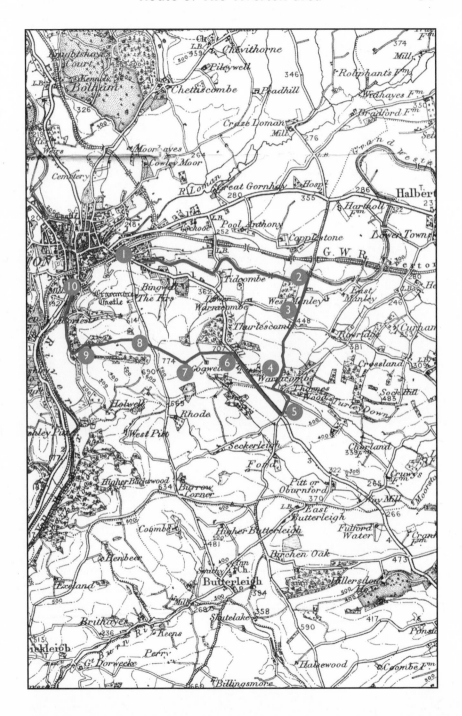

There are quite a few Scots pines in this area, often used to denote a drovers' way.

(7) Just after where the tarmac road ceases and becomes scarified, take a deep oak- and beech-lined footpath to your right at Gogwell.

(8) Cross the minor road carefully and turn right. In front of you on the left a wooden fingerpost sign takes you through one of the first of four gates over lush meadows, full of lady's smock flowers in spring. To your left is 'guoil', another spelling of the famous Exmoor goyles not so far away. Ahead are the hills of Cruwys Morchard and a glimpse of west Dartmoor. The lane is concreted as you descend. Look out for early purple orchids. You come out by a linhay (an open-fronted barn).

(9) Turn right at Woodcote along the minor road back into Tiverton. The landmass which looms to your right is Cranmore Castle, an ancient British hillfort upon which a wooden castle once stood. It was also the scene of a fierce battle concerning whether a child should be baptised a Protestant or a Catholic in that turbulent year 1549. There are some big estate horse chestnuts along the road and leading back into the grounds of Colliprest, home to local hero Peter Blundell, made good through the woollen trade.

(10) At the next road junction follow the Exe Valley signs back to St Andrew's Street behind the Museum.

By the way

The construction of the canal was principally to provide lime as a boost to agriculture. But climate change was conspiring against the poor agricultural labourer even then. Look at this extract from *The Real Oliver Twist* by John Waller:

> *In 1815 the Tambora volcano in the Dutch East Indies erupted, sending immense quantities of sulphur dioxide into the air and creating a canopy right across the northern hemisphere. For several years there were brilliant sunsets, but crops were starved of sunlight and grew stunted, if at all. As bread prices reached intolerable levels, the Corn Law stopped imports coming in. Long before corn had reached 80 shillings a bushel, bread or blood riots broke out, resulting in five executions (the Treasury referred to them as Statutory). Philanthropy alone kept tons of thousands of labouring families alive. Then on top of a terrible harvest came a trade depression.*

No wonder the Reverend Griddlestone of Halberton spoke out as he did. We will never know exactly who was moved to leave farming on his advice – but we know that many did.

Other green lanes in the area

Thorverton Route (no. 1), Butterleigh Route (no. 6) and Bradninch Route (no. 7).

Links

The cycle way out of Tiverton along the old railway line as indicated. The Exe Valley Way/The Grand Western Canal.

Question

What do you call the path which runs beside a canal?

Masons' marks on Manley Bridge.

KENTISBEARE to BLACKBOROUGH

Devon red earth banks and transitory Italianate splendour

OS Explorer 115

This walk takes you up into the foothills of the Blackboroughs through lanes held by east Devon earth banks, a very regional style of hedging. You are walking along the paths of a once heavy and important industry, trod by local as well as foreign miners. At Feniton you look down across the plains of the Exe Valley and beyond. You can make the route a straight up and down, or link back to other small towns nearby.

Conditions: Muddy and wet in places.

Distance: 4 miles straight up and down, but can be extended to 6.

Starting point: The narrow chequered tower of St Mary's, Kentisbeare with squares of alternating Beer stone and a cinnamon-brown variety of new red sandstone at ST 082068. Inside there are two particular items of interest at the top of the Beer stone columns. One is decorated with a woolpack, and another shows a Tudor ship belonging to the London Merchant Adventurers. Along with nearby Cullompton's great cathedral-like church, this shows again how wool-based fortunes were made in this valley.

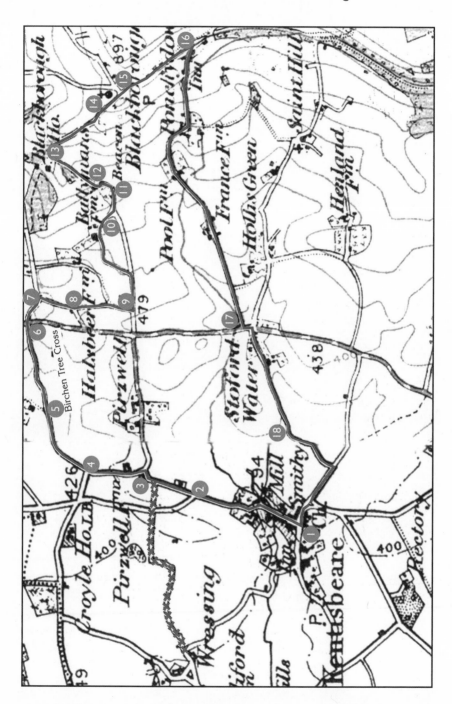

(1) Leaving the church, go straight across up into Fore Street at Kentisbeare Square, with both the post office and store to your right. There is a Reading Room to your left. You pass the school further up on the same side; opposite there is a well, dedicated to George V in 1911, which hasn't run dry since it was opened.

(2) Keep to the right here, then pass a green lane entrance on your left. This leads down to Wressing. There is a cottage here which has a very ornate Bible Cupboard. (I doubt that any of the volumes in this secret private place were brought down to share with others in the Reading Room.)

(3) On the corner veer left and you will pass Pirzwell Manor on the right, which has a fine cob-walled enclosure at the back. You climb up to Yew Wood Cross (there are no signs of this wood nowadays). Going back to the churchyard I see that Arthur Mee, as lyrical as ever, says of the Yews there:

In the churchyard are three generations of yews, a grandfather of perhaps a 1000 years, a father half as old, and a little son not yet a centenarian.

(4) Turn right, passing Hardwick House to your right. This is a wide, sandy lane with Devon turf banks on both sides, typical of arable access lanes in the area. At the footpath sign to your left, one bank disappears. Keep on to your right with big arable fields all around you.

(5) On the left there are some farm buildings and another footpath sign. Ignore both and take the green lane (unsigned) which goes through grassy banks to your right. There are wild Welsh leeks here aplenty, to complement the leeks growing in the fields around. There are some fine examples of pollarded and coppiced beeches both on top of and set into the banks of this long and well cared-for lane. There are heaps of yellowish sandstone pebbles towards the end.

(6) You come out onto a very minor road with a directional fingerpost to your right at Birchen Tree Cross. Go straight over here.

(7) On the bend, opposite a barn on the right, turn right into another

minor road. There are good views in front of you with hills in the distance and on both sides as you descend.

(8) On the bend there is an unsigned lane to the left which has a good grassy surface. It becomes sunken with some large oaks and beeches atop the red sandstone banks.

(9) At this green lane junction, notice the large greensand pillars to the left then drop left into a gully-lined lane.

(10) At Mortimer's Farm, which on our map appears as Ballyman's Farm (used by smugglers in the 18th century because of its remoteness), take the footpath to the right. This is very damp and stony, but by (11) it does become more firmly cobbled as you progress. You come to a short section of stone walling to your left, and then there is a stile in front of you.

(12) Cross over and keep to the left of this rolling field. I saw deer and foxes here when I crossed, and I disturbed a buzzard as it flew away heavily laden with a rabbit in its talons. But this haven of wildlife and rurality will suddenly change as you come over the brow of the hill to Blackborough House surrounded by the workings of the Blackborough Motor Salvage Company workings. The position and sheer size of this great house will surprise you.

(13) Go through the gate, then turn right along the drive of the house.

(14) Notice the quarry to your left, from which the stone for this building and others up on the Blackboroughs must have been taken.

(15) At the end of the lane you reach Blackborough Cross, where there is an information board about the Whetstone miners and a fingerpost which indicates Kentisbeare to be two miles away, Cullompton five and Sheldon two. Notice the small graveyard to your left, where the church once stood. This was built by Lord Egremont to provide a place of worship for the miners. (See the Staverton to Penn Recca Walk, Route 39, where similar motives led to a church being built.) It was demolished in 1994 when the miners and others stopped attending. Cross over, climb up and take a look at the huge mounds which are what remains of the scythestone industry of this area. The views from here are very impressive, and in winter both Beacon and House can be seen through the trees. Follow the road along the ridge to the right from here; see page 23 for a sketch and details of the Cadbury Tree, for which trees here were alleged to be the inspiration.

(16) Turn right down towards Kentisbeare at the T-junction here and notice the former Ponchydown Inn, once used extensively by the miners, on your left. The minor roads will now take you back down to Kentisbeare unless you wish to carry straight on and link up with the Dunkeswell route.

(17) At Stoford Water you may want to go back towards Uffculme via Ashill. The Quaker connections are strong here.

(18) Watch out for the llamas to your left here. Then you can take a footpath to your right which ends in a short stretch of green lane, or you may want to follow the lane round. Either way you will end up at Honest Heart Cross, where there was once a pub. There are some stirring names in this village, such as Silver Street and Golden Cottages. Another good thing is that although it seems to be losing its splendours in the hills, it still has its post office and village stores.

By the way

Although the lanes here are now very quiet, they must have seen a lot of traffic coming from the Exe and going up towards Wellington and beyond. The miners who produced the sharpening stones were said to have come from far away, maybe from Wales, and spoke their own dialect which could, of course, just have been Welsh. The connection with the Quakers from Uffculme is very strong here, and it is said that the tree pictured on Cadbury's early chocolate bars was modelled on one which grew atop the Beacon at Blackborough. The house was allegedly used by the Quakers as a safe haven for refugees from the Nazi regime until they could find 'ordinary' work, and also by conscientious objectors who worked on farms in the area. Between 1943 and 1947 it was taken over by the YHA movement and called Spiceland Hostel, another reference to Uffculme. The house was built by the last Lord of Egremont, from Cumbria, between 1838 and 1840. There was said to be a replica of a ship's galley in one room, and the Great Hall was three stories high. This Grade II-listed building was valued at £1 million when put on the market in 2003, but it remains unsold.

So here it now stands, still surprising many who approach it on foot, as it must have done in Victorian times and as it did the YHA visitors – and me too. Many miners, polishers and sanders must have coughed their way past it on their way to work. They would have seen it as they returned from selling their scythestones, with provisions and sometimes soil in their carts to help them cultivate the barren sandstone terraces here. The halls would have heard their coughing, which was brought about from the 'smech' of the powdery stone, and led to TB and silicosis. Maybe they stood aside for the fine carriages which they would have seen coming down the drive, bearing no resemblance to those which lie grounded all around it now. Surely this must be a place where the ghostly pounding of horses' hooves down the drive can still be heard at midnight!

Other green lanes in the area

There are more around the Sainthill area.

Links

Cook's Buses run in and out of Kentisbeare on certain days from Cullompton and Honiton.

Question

One of the Blackborough churchyard pillars carries a special mark. What is it, and what authority put it there?

Postcard dated 1944. *Courtesy of the YHA.*

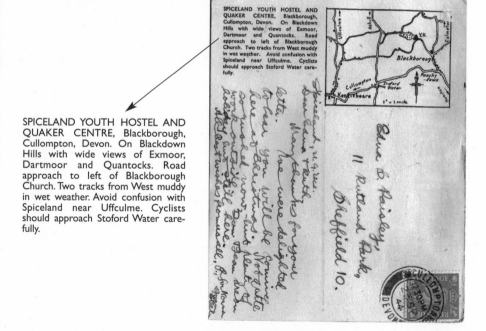

SPICELAND YOUTH HOSTEL AND QUAKER CENTRE, Blackborough, Cullompton, Devon. On Blackdown Hills with wide views of Exmoor, Dartmoor and Quantocks. Road approach to left of Blackborough Church. Two tracks from West muddy in wet weather. Avoid confusion with Spiceland near Uffculme. Cyclists should approach Stoford Water carefully.

UFFCULME to SPICELAND

Sweet news from the east
for the weavers of the west

OS Explorer 128

This walk takes you from a village with an industrial past up into a beautiful wood, along elm-lined lanes and through lush riverside meadows where weavers once worshipped. Cistercian monks first manufactured woollen garments in this

area. We are in an area where wool was once king: although Honiton is said to be the first place where wool was manufactured into cloth (in 1225), Uffculme wins hands down for longevity of production.

Conditions: Some standing water.

Distance: 4-5 miles.

Starting point: ST 068128. This is the centre of the village. Coldharbour Mill has been working as a woollen (worsted) mill for over 200 years and has shaped the development of the village over two centuries. It was one of the first in the 1790s to use water power, as was its neighbour Bradninch, which produced paper later on, in 1822. There is much to see in this unspoilt Culm Valley village, so take your time before starting off.

(1) The Ostler Public House, in the centre of Uffculme, is an old horse and coaching inn. Its name is that of a profession which speaks of betrayal, as recorded in Alfred Noyes' poem 'The Highwayman'.

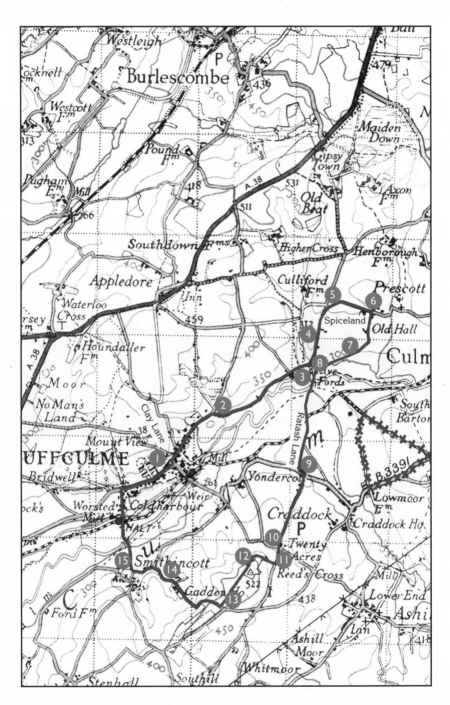

And dark in the old inn-yard a stable wicket creaked
Where Tim the ostler listened, his face was white and peaked.

But there is no such great tale of misadventure to pursue on this walk – just the discovery of some hidden places in the Culm Valley which once were alive with the traffic of different industries, and worshippers walking to and fro. Pass along the road leading to the church. Keep to the left, making for the magnificent red-brick tower of the brewery. You pass the library and primary school on your right, and Clay Lane to your left. Where the new housing developments cease, take the road to your right opposite Ashley Close.

(2) This is a narrow minor road with views towards the Blackdown Hills and the Culm Valley to your right. There is plenty of maple, elm and spindle in the hedges here. Willows gather in clumps as you get close to Five Fords.

(3) To your right on the bend is a public footpath to Hunkin Wood, formerly known as Culm Ham Meadow and now managed by the Woodland Trust. Enter and admire the towering twin trunks of a rare poplar tree to your right. Take a walk round so that you can pass through the arch into the 21st century to admire the leys, one of which in spring is full of the delicate ferny tops of the pignut, a great delicacy for badgers. From here you can follow the footpath signs along the river, but by so doing you will miss passing the Quaker Meeting House at Spiceland. This is done by leaving the wood and continuing up the road before coming to a sign to your right.

(4) A Quaker Meeting House has stood here since the 17th century, and this one, part of a private house, carries the date 1671 over its door. It is said that the founder of the Quakers, George Fox, preached in an orchard here in a field called Spisan when he last visited Devon in 1668. Look out for some names with sweet rather than spicy connotations here (see *By the way*).

(5) Carry on up the lane and turn right at Lower Cross. You pass Prescott, a reminder of turbulent religious differences, and Rackhay, a reminder of the wool trade. Racks were laid out for the woven wool in the open countryside before it was collected by jobbers and loaded up onto their packhorses. As you progress towards Culmstock, think of the many people – over 400 recorded here – who were involved locally in wool-spinning in the 14th century. Before you take the footpath at (6) to your right, proceed a little further to just beyond Silver Street Farm, belonging to the Hunkin family. There is a Baptist cemetery on the corner, and then a chapel bearing the dates of when it was built (1715), rebuilt (1781) and restored (between 1892 and 1898).

(6) Turn back from here and take the footpath on your left at Woodbine Farm, which begins as a sunken lane then veers right and goes over open fields to Five Fords.

You will find yourself in the Millennium Wood. From here you can go back along the minor roads to Uffculme between numbers (3) and (2). Alternatively you can return along the watery footpaths to Uffculme (7) or along a green lane, depending on weather conditions. Both will take you to Coldharbour Mill. The route to the mill through Five Fords is described from here.

Pass along the side of the wood with the black poplars to your right and go through a series of narrow gates, through a stile and over a bridge to the beginning of Ratash Lane (8). The name 'Ratash' comes from clinker used as a lane's surface. You may have to go through into the meadow by your side, as this unmetalled road is also very undrained.

There is another green lane to your left, which is more of a tunnel than the open one upon which you are now walking, and was obviously a short cut for those going to the big house and settlement of Craddock. This area belonged to the Manley family. In the 1820s they were responsible for the re-alignment of the village roads.

(9) You will come out at a crossroads. Bear left, then go straight over and into a greening-over lane marked 'Unsuitable for Motor Vehicles', shown on maps as The Portway – another indicator of how so many routes in east Devon took trade towards the sea and not back up directly over the hinter-land towards Exeter, as is now the case. This Portway was also part of one which connected Cullompton to Wellington in coaching days. It was an ancient route across the Westcountry, linking the Severn Estuary at Bridgwater to the sea at Ottermouth, and can still be traced.

(10) At Twenty Acres crossroads go straight over and you will soon come to a bridleway sign. Sir Thomas Fairfax led the Parliamentary army from Honiton to Tiverton in October 1645 via the Drove Road, and camped on Gaddon Down. Locals are wary of going there at dusk in October, as the screams of Royalist spies are reputed to be sometimes heard as this is where they were executed (more probably the sound of foxes looking for mates).

(11) Turn right into the bridleway, and you will be walking through woodlands which have good views down over towards Uffculme. Towards the top, the lane is lined with drovers' road indicators: tall Scots pine trees. The lane is called the Drift Road, also meaning drovers' road. There are

sweet chestnut trees in these woods too. At the top you come to a signpost indicating various rights of way.

(12) You take the footpath to the left on the corner which opens out into a lane with layered beech trees. There are woods to the left. The lane narrows towards the bottom and veers right, where you pass by the cob walls of the long gardens of Gaddon House and Farm. This big collection of buildings is one of many in the parish which in the 1841 census revealed that the largest group of workers were domestic servants: 184 were thus employed. Next came agricultural labourers, a close 164. It is not surprising that there were 22 shoemakers employed here, given the amount of walking to work in the valley, as well as being on your feet all day.

(13) You come out at a road triangle with a lime tree growing at its centre. Turn right into a minor road. (14) Turn left at the T-junction here.

(15) At the end of this short section of lane there is a gatepost made out of brown sandstone. Turn right here and go straight on for Coldharbour Mill, where there is much to see and good food to be savoured.

By the way

The mill was opened by Thomas Fox, a Quaker who had been apprenticed to his grandfather, a woollen merchant from Wellington. Much traffic must have passed along the ways which lead north and eastwards out of Uffculme. They exported their goods via the ports on the Exe Estuary before the coming of the railway in 1876. As well as exports to the Low Countries and Spain, some Uffculme 'long ells' were sent to China, with blue, purple and scarlet being the favourite colours. As there was already contact with the Dutch wool merchants in the seventeenth century, it is no surprise that their religious ideas should be readily accepted in this area of east Devon. Ironically, given these connections with pacifism, the mill became famous for producing Fox's puttees which were used on the First World War battlefields.

George Fox, the founder of the Quakers, in the 1740s, was himself the son of a weaver. The chapel at Spiceland was the only place where 'dissenters' in the area could come to be married. Peter Holway, a thatcher, married Susanna Lutley, widow of Uffculme on 30th June 1692 at Spiceland; and Ann Smith married Thomas Hayle of Wellington in October 1762 at Spiceland.

They would have suffered persecution in other ways too, as they were not tithe-payers, unlike the rest of the community. It is recorded that George Russell, a woolcomber from Burlescombe, died in Exeter prison in 1682 at the age of eighty, where he was put for preaching against the imposition of tithes. The hundred or so mill workers (at its busiest), were mainly married women. The men were the weavers, the women the spinners. Children were also employed, and thought to be better off here than "in their close, dirty Cottages at home". Hours were long, but people seldom worked after nine o'clock. Thomas Fox, in a letter dated 1813, shows an awareness of the economic climate during the Napoleonic Wars:

> *The distress of the Labouring Classes in this Nation calls for much sympathy and the united exertions of all who are able and willing to espouse their Cause.*

And this he did.

The mill continued to work until 1978, with a remaining workforce of forty, and shortly after its closure the Friends of the Mill bought the site from the Fox Company and kept it alive as you see it today.

Thanks to Mr John Bell of Ashill for helpful local information given in for the Uffculme-based walks.

Other green lanes in the area

Many along the Culm Valley.

Links

There are buses to Uffculme from Tiverton, one from Exeter and another from Taunton.

Question

What kind of poplar tree can you see at Five Fords and elsewhere in this area?

ASHILL

Between Culmstock and Uffculme

OS Explorer 128

One of the green lanes in this route (see the photograph on page 76) has always been difficult to walk down – so be warned. You will be walking along some deep minor lanes, with great views of Blackborough and Hackpen hill around you. In the 1920s there was a candle-lit delivery van serving this area, which ran through Craddock, Ashill, Hayne, Blackborough, Allhallows and Sheldon.

Conditions: Muddy in places.

Distance: 3-4 miles.

Starting point: Culmstock Church, where the tree growing out of the tower as recorded by Arthur Mee in 1938 can still be seen, and the pub once known as The Ilminster Stage, referring to the busy Chard-bound coach road, which ran through here. Let's hope that the private house it is to become will retain the name. Incidentally, the word 'stage' is still with us when talking about fares, just as the word 'shift' is still in our vocabulary. This originally referred to a shift, i.e. a thirty-mile length of journey covered by a coachman. He was paid a shilling a shift, and often got a tip if he had urged his horses on in record time.

(1) ST 101134. Leaving the church turn left, and climb up the High Street and take the first left at Haringay Cross. Turn sharp left again and you are in a straight road flanked by large fields.

(2) Go straight over at Park Cross, named after the deer park of the Coggans.

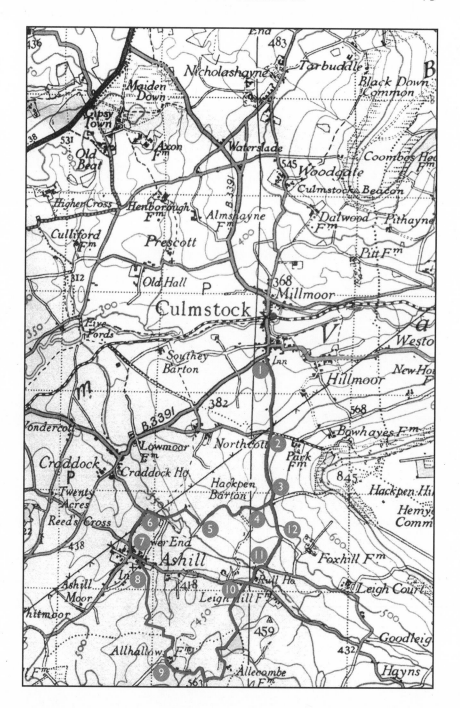

(3) At the next (unnamed) crossroads take the dead-end road to the right. You pass Briar Croft on the left. There are plenty of signs of the Culm valley wetlands along the way. In midsummer, clouds of water dropwort line both sides of this lane. This plant was once known as the devil's-foot. It is very poisonous, and where cattle grazed in the wetlands and churned up the roots, the poison would enter their systems through their hooves.

(5) You pass Hackpen Barton (the Manor was first recorded in 1249) and continue down the wide flint-surfaced lane indicated by the footpath sign to the left as an 'Unmetalled Road'. Behind you are views of the hill. Hackpen is composed of the Welsh element 'pen' meaning *hill* and 'hack' meaning *hook*. This is a very wide lane with sweeping curves, obviously once of great importance for taking and collecting of produce to and from the mill below. There are large pollarded oaks here and, on one bend, a fine sweep of a thick beech hedge. The mill itself belonged to the Duchy of Lancaster, and his resistance partly explains how it kept free of the Enclosure Act.

(5) Take the first footpath to the right (the second is often waterlogged) over the stile round the field edge. Go over a gate and cut diagonally across to the field gate opposite.

(6) You come out onto a lane leading down to a small bridge and the brick-built mill which was once a corn mill, used for fulling (the process of washing cloth). Tear yourself away from this idyllic spot, and go up onto the road and turn left passing Millstone Farm and the waterlogged footpath. There is a drainage channel running by the side of the lane. This was good news for the potatoes, which became a corn substitute for all after the Napoleonic Wars. There are records of the varieties once grown in Uffculme parish: Dalhousay, Devonshire Apples, Thurston's Conqueror, Pilot's Flower Ball, and Sharpe's.

(7) You come to a crossroads with St Stephens Church, Ashill to your left. Turn right and cross over to the sycamore tree standing in a triangle.

(8) Opposite Batt's Farm turn right and take the left round the houses to an 'Unmetalled Road' sign. From the gate on the corner there is a view of the old school at the end of the row of houses. This lane has been cut through sandstone, which has its share of graffiti, some of which is believed to have been carved by those who made their way from Ashill to work up at Blackborough House. Inevitably there is talk of it being known as Lovers' Lane too. It soon reaches a plateau, and it becomes difficult to squeeze through the encroaching hedgerows. Wetland plants such as water pepper shine bright in the gullys. You

pass a woodland to the right, and the sandstone sides appear again. Some graffiti (such as "Linda 1904") stand out because of their antiquity, but there are other more recent-looking additions. You come to a muddy patch, and there are a lot of elder trees in the hedgerows. You swing round some curves made by the Saxon ploughing patterns in the adjacent fields. Turn right through the gate where the hedgerows disappear. Seek out the lane to the left again, and follow a short muddy section which will take you out behind Allhallows Farm. There are records of a medieval chapel and graveyard here; perhaps this is the original reason for the lane being made. There is no sign at this end.

(9) Turn left and pass the large farm and house, which will give you some indication of the importance of this lane. It is possible that the Allhallows school in Honiton, once a chapel and then a school, could have collected road tolls to support a teacher in the old grammar school, as was sometimes the case on an important route. Follow this winding lane down and around, keeping to your left at the next junction and resisting the pull towards Blackborough, always in view.

(10) At this crossroads there stands a square-ended swinging arm cast-iron fingerpost with a 'Tiverton R.D.' annular finial. Go straight over to Hayne and Sheldon, passing Rull House on your right.

(11) Keep to the left at Leigh Cross.

(12) Keep to the left at Foxhill Cross. You will soon find yourself back at (3) again, where your descent into this hidden valley began and where the roads and fields are wider. Having been so close to Hackpen Hill, standing high at 236 metres, and reached by a walk along the wide enclosure lanes here, why not extend your explorations by paying it a visit?

By the way

Just after Waterloo the local landowners here set about enlarging and enclosing fields in the Culm Valley. But as you can see, this affected the land to the north-east of this route far more. In the excellent book on Uffculme from the Local History Group (see Bibliography) there is a chapter devoted to Ashill by Mr John Bell. He has become an expert on the field patterns in this area, and gives a full account of them here. Uffculme's Enclosure Act was in 1815. He also states that any beech in the hedges here indicates that they were planted after 1800.

Other green lanes in the area

Those which go out towards Kentisbeare.

Links

There is a bus service to Culmstock from Honiton and one to Uffculme from Exeter and Tiverton.

The adjacent routes here at **(10)** and **(12)** on the map, linking up at the crossroads, which has the relics of an Anglo-Saxon plural ending clinging to it still: Birchen Tree Cross.

Question

Which nationality is well represented in the Allhallows Lane graffiti?

Worker in Allhallows Lane, circa 1900.

CULMSTOCK to CULM DAVY

Closer to heaven as you climb

OS Explorer 128

This walk gives you an opportunity to enjoy both the highs and the lows of the Culm Valley. The rich meadows in this valley still cradle this farming community, and indeed it was here where the successful dairy industry began at the end of the nineteenth century. The streams also provided the power for some of the earliest fulling mills in Devon. You are safe along these minor roads as they are wider than most Devon lanes, having been created by the enclosures of commons in the eighteenth century. There are many nonconformist chapels in the area, but high above them all has been the steadfast presence of one little Church of England chapel set close to its farming community for centuries.

Conditions: Some muddy surfaces and gentle climbs.

Distance: 3-4 miles.

Starting point: ST 102135. Begin at the church in Culmstock. From here turn back onto the B3391 in a north-westerly direction and cross over the River Culm by the Railway Inn. It is named after the Culm Valley Light Railway which ran between Hemyock and Tiverton Junction from 1876 until 1975.

(1) At the junction where the school stands, take Blackwater Road to your left opposite at the head of which is a K2 telephone box. You soon pass the Old Mill on your right with the leat running close by, for Culmstock was

once an important woollen town. You are now walking on one of the wide minor roads created by various Enclosure Acts in the parish from 1815 onwards. There are views of Culmstock Beacon to your left. After the footpaths which cross the road in both directions you can make out the line of the dismantled railway to your left, which was specifically constructed to run to the milk factory at Millhayes near Hemyock. There are views of Hackpen Hill to your right before you reach the dead-end sign on your left.

(2) Turn left here up a semi-tarmacked lane towards Clement's Farm. There is a fine farmhouse here, and when I passed by there were some interesting bits of old farm machinery: root cutters, and old harrows lying in the fields. This farm obviously benefited from having access to Clement's Common, as the route of this green lane indicates.

(3) Here to the left is another footpath leading towards Culmstock Beacon, but your way lies to the right.

(4) At the top you come to a green lanes junction, where you continue to climb upwards along a sunken lane which rises as you do and emerges onto a minor road.

(5) Turn left here towards Culm Davy Farm. This farm dates back to 1133 AD, when William Widworth gave it to his son David during the reign of Henry II.

(6) Here you are presented with a further choice, and can climb up onto Clement's Common. But by keeping straight on for this route you will come to a T-junction.

(7) Here turn sharp right back down the valley.

(8) On the bend here stands a beautiful little chapel with foundations going back to the fifteenth century. See if you can find the following inscription:

In memory of Anne ye Wife of William Garvis of Ashculm who died 25th October 1705 and was inter'd in ye west end of this chapel.

(9) Continue down the lane, passing a turning to your right and then another to your left. (From here you can take a further tour of the farmland of the area if you so wish.) Towards the end of the lane a drainage channel appears to your right, leading you down to the junction.

(10) In front of you is a fine example of a square-ended arm cast-iron fingerpost. It seems to shelter against the cottage here, surrounded by the dark red flowers of a trained quince. You may choose to return to your right back to Culmstock, or carry on further to the left towards Hemyock.

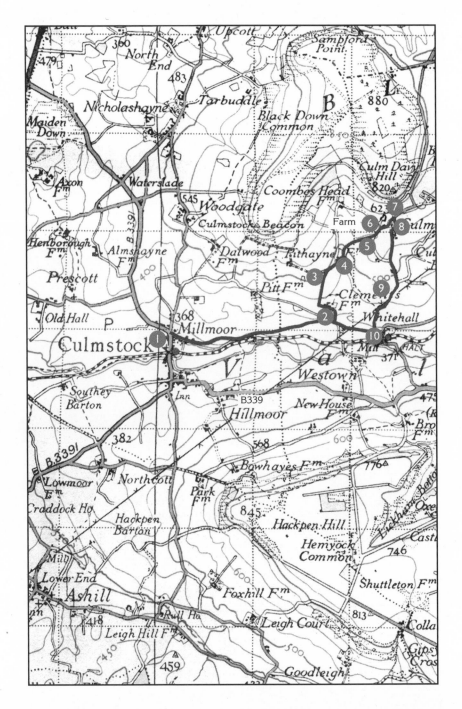

By the way

In this area, close to the Somerset and Dorset borders, we are close to the area where the Tolpuddle Martyrs came from. They were famous for banding together to form a union of agricultural labourers seeking a fair wage in 1834 (see Route 15, Stockland). Many such societies had been formed at a local level, and the fate of the Tolpuddle Martyrs was meant to act as a warning to them. One such was the Society of Weavers and Combers of Cullompton, Bradninch, Silverton and Thorverton. Between 1720 and 1730 they were great supporters of their fellow society in Uffculme, Culmstock and Hemyock, known as The Tradition of Old Men. They were constantly campaigning for a fair day's pay for a fair day's work. Although the wool market was prosperous, it was not always stable: it relied a lot on the whims of fashion, and who was going to war with whom, and so stability was difficult. Like many other places, although today this is an area of rural tranquility, it has seen troubled times in its past. The folk song entitled *In Old England Very Hard Times*, written about the post-Napoleonic period, applies to many periods in the history of the labouring rural class.

Other green lanes in the area

Route 11, Ashill and Route 13, Hemyock.

Links

There is a bus service from Wellington and Honiton to Culmstock.

Question

What is a turbary?

Square-ended cast-iron fingerpost with DCC round finial.

TOWARDS SOMERSET

HEMYOCK

From Peterloo to peat, and more peaceful dairy days in the turbaries

OS Explorer 128

This route can take you back and forth through history, as you criss-cross the valley once walked by thirteenth-century Cistercian monks from Forde Abbey. There are stunning views all around you on this walk. Should you venture towards Clayhidon and Rosemary Lane, you will also find a wayside monument to a surveyor murdered there in 1853. In so many areas where our routes go, there are many stories to be told.

Conditions: Beware of the peat marsh, and also of swift traffic approaching on the minor roads.

Monument shaped like the bayonets used at the Battle of Waterloo, 1815.

Distance: 3-4 miles, but, as you see from the map, a complete circuit of a similar length is possible around Clayhidon.

Starting point: ST 139139 at Millhayes, site of the old milk factory and terminus for the specially-built railway. Why not begin at St Ivel house, now the head office for the Blackdown Hills Area of Outstanding Natural Beauty? Although there had been a local initiative backed by the local priest in Hemyock from the early eighteenth century onwards, it was not until the opening of the factory in 1886, employing 3,000 people, that the fortunes of farmers here became established. The factory at Millhayes opened in 1897. This is where you are standing now, and which saw the closure of the milk industries in 1999. The mill which stood here was once a corn mill, and possibly a wool mill before that. Milk had always been sent here to be skimmed and fed to cattle, but then butter was produced, which became very popular and it was sent up to London when the train line opened here in 1876 (it closed in 1975). During the First World War margarine was sold to the public, and this affected the production of butter: after the 1920s it was no longer made here. Milk was sent to London from here in glass-lined containers, with lorries coming out from Hemyock to collect it. Milk for the catering company of Lyons was bought here, as well as that which went into the making of the Mars bar. During the Second World War the Ministry of Food commissioned the factory to produce dried eggs, amongst other things. It had retained a fleet of seventeen lorries to cover an area of 100 square miles. After the 1960s, bulk tankers were in operation from the nearby dual carriageway. Unigate (an earlier amalgamation of Cow & Gate) ceased to trade in 1975, but it reopened in 1977 and went on to produce St Ivel Gold, Low Fat Gold and the aforementioned Utterly Butterly until 1999. The owners received a grant to take the factory up to Liverpool, an area where many people were out of work, thus leaving many locals here without jobs.

(1) Turn right off the main road just by the cast-iron fingerpost, and go into Higher Millhayes Road.

(2) After a few yards, cut up to the left towards the hill and you will find a footpath sign by a field gate. You go through a boardwalked stream and up and over into a meadow where cottongrass grows. There are extensive views over towards Devon, although you are so close to Somerset at this point.

(3) Turn right onto the fairly busy road again for a matter of yards.

(4) Just past Dixcroft turn right again into a green lane indicated by a dead-end sign. You pass Maidengreen House on the right, and you are in a wide, well used green lane – surely this was one of the medieval ways up to the peat fields of Clayhidon and Ashculme. Towards the flinty end of this lane you walk next to a stream. The hedge contains elm and sallow.

(5) You come out just below Tanhouse Farm. When you get into the turbaries later you will see some slender oaks which have been pollarded quite low down. On Dartmoor this indicates that the oak bark was used in the tanning trade, and there is no reason to doubt that it may have been so here too. The name Hemyock means 'low-lying watery place of the oaks'.

(6) Turn right at these crossroads and you are in Black Lane, an obvious

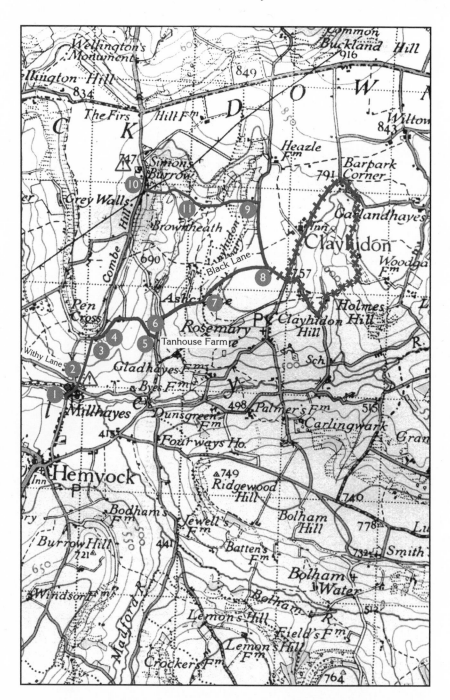

name for such a peaty district. This area of peat fields or turbaries supplied fuel that was created by its poor drainage. The traditional way of managing the land was by grazing and burning, and the area also provided bracken as bedding, mulch and thatching. Bracken ash was used in glass- and soap-making too. The slabs were cut in rectangles and set in dry mounds known as 'ruckles' or 'mumps'.

The individual peat blocks were 7" x 2", the standard size. The cutter was paid half-a-crown a journey – this would have been one turf-barrowload, which was transferred to carts for easier handling on the lanes. A journey will make a good cartload, and thirty to forty loads are required to supply a farmhouse for a year. Today the area is managed by Stockland Parish Council, and much of the heathland diversity has returned: sundew, marsh St John's Wort, pied flycatchers and redstarts have returned.

(7) This is a good point of entry for exploring the turbaries. Although the lands around were enclosed in the years following Waterloo and the commoners often lost valuable land, the Hemyock enclosures spared five separate areas for the turbaries, amounting to sixteen acres. Purple Molinia (*Molinia caerulea*) grass is what you will find here; it flowers late in August and in September. It is named after a Spanish botanist who wrote about these plants, which were first identified in Chile. They are tall and graceful but strong, and capable of being plaited into rope. The habitat here is one of moorland, permanent pasture, wet woodland and chert-heath. Sometimes the paths here are closed to allow ponies in for grazing purposes.

One of England's oldest war veterans, Harry Patch, a Somerset man who fought in the First World War and was 115 in June 2008, when asked what he thought had made the most difference to him in this life, replied that it was the coming of electricity. He said that his mother was pleased to have an end to the constant battle involving peat, coal, wood and anything else which might be burned to generate heat.

(8) At this point there is an alternative route to the right, along the lanes around Clayhidon.

(9) Staying on the main route, continue up this minor road, gaining glimpses of the Wellington Monument as you go, and drop down into the bridleway to the left by Jennings Farm. This valley is full of holly, birch, sallow and willow.

(10) You come out to face a steep climb back onto a minor road with The Old Chapel to your right.

(11) Return to this point in order to avoid walking down the main road, unless you are going straight up for a view of the monument.

By the way

The Militia Act of 1757 laid out plans for the evacuation of this area onto Dartmoor in the event of a French invasion. There are detailed lists of the people, goods, chattels, riding horses and drafthorses, the cattle and waggons which were to go. The occupations and religious beliefs of those who were to go were also listed. Their route was to be through Kentisbeare, Bradninch, Thorverton, Creedy Bridge, Barnstaple Cross, Bow, North Tawton and then down to South Tawton, West Zeal and out onto the Moor. How relieved they must have been when Napoleon was finally defeated at Waterloo! The monument you see today, standing 175 feet high, formed with three sides and in the shape of a bayonet, was not completed until 1892. It was meant to be surrounded by cannons taken from Waterloo, but it seems that they never arrived. Pausing here, by chance on the anniversary of the battle, the 18th June, I wondered how long the news took to get through to the villagers below, and how long it was before the wounded started limping their way back into these enfolding hills.

Other green lanes in the area

There are those around Clayhidon as indicated.

Links

There is a bus from Honiton to Hemyock and on to Taunton.
Another bus runs through Uffculme and up to Appledore, then on to Wellington close to the monument.
Culm Davy, Route 12.

Question

There is a boundary stone at the beginning of this route which provides a clue to its milky past. What is inscribed there?

Hedge-dating theory

First put forward by Dr Max Hooper and Dr E. Pollard: count the number of different hardwood species of tree growing on one side of the hedge in a 30-metre stretch. Each species represents 100 years. Briar should be included in this exercise, but not ivy.

Peat-cutting tool.

MEMBURY

Thomas Wakeley, founder of *The Lancet* and sabre-rattler against injustice

OS Explorer 116

Conditions: Steep and rocky in places.

Distance: 4-5 miles, but can be extended.

This route takes us through countryside which was once familiar to a local landowner's son, Thomas Wakeley. The visual rewards of walking through this country are great,

but the sudden climbs and flinty nature of the land, although a little difficult today, must have been harder in the past for those who had to walk every day to their workplaces. There are records within living memory of limestone being hauled about this area on three-wheeled trucks with one wheel at the front and two at the back, all having wide iron tyres. The Yarcombe Valley is a magical place, which was once famous for its cheese, known in Exeter as Membury cheese.

As your present-day OS map indicates, there are many ways here to choose from, which date back to those times when walking was the only way to travel.

Starting point: **(1)** SY 267985. There is a public bridleway sign northwards off the A35 here, on the Axminster-bound bus-shelter side of the road.

(2) You soon come out in a minor road crossroads. Go straight over into a lane marked 'Unsuitable for Wide Vehicles' and carry on down to a junction by a large oak tree to the right. Carry straight on to a small bridge and up and over. There is a cottage on the left with a good flint wall and, as you climb, the hedgerow maples become taller.

(3) At this junction turn left into Nower Road. Dogwood joins the maples here. Dulshayes Farm ('Dulcis' on the present-day map) is to your left. You pass a footpath to your left and one to your right. Nower Farm itself is one of those which straddles the road as well as in the many buildings either side.

(4) On your left is a footpath to Naishe's Lane. Pass it by, and once on the ridge by Dane's Hill you have a good view to the left down over the tower of Dalwood church to your right and the bell turret of the Quaker Loughwood Chapel to your left. Here is a good place to pause and think of one of Wakeley's Reforms. There was a Law of Deodands which stated that if you were involved in a carriage accident and, say, the wheels of your cart were damaged, the guilty party had to pay – not you, but the church – a compensatory fee so that the monks might pray for your soul. You received no other compensation or help. After the Reformation this fee went to the state, and continued to do so. The fee only considered the physical damage to the vehicle, and not any physical injuries of a traveller. Wakeley changed this law to deal with the real consequences of a traffic accident.

(5) Take the unmetalled road marked 'Unfit for Motors', which is Dalwood Lane. It begins in grass and, after Thorne Cleave Cottage to your left, turns a sharp right under pylons where the surface breaks up into flint hogging. It both widens and narrows as it descends. When it veers left by Bray's Farm it runs through a dark tunnel before emerging at Beckford Bridge crossroads.

(6) Go straight over here for a look at this now disconnected old bridge with a cobbled surface, possibly part of an old drovers' road. If cattle were driven, they would have gone through the river. However, the existence of a Pig Street in nearby Axminster points to another animal which might have been driven over this little hump-backed and cobbled bridge.

(7) Go over the modern bridge with a metal parapet, and follow the road to the left with Yarty House appearing high above you.

(8) Go left towards Yarty House. Just past an orchard to your right and Lea Hatch to your left, by an iron-gated drive entrance there is an unmetalled road fingerpost sign to the right by a clump of delicate meadow crane's-bill.

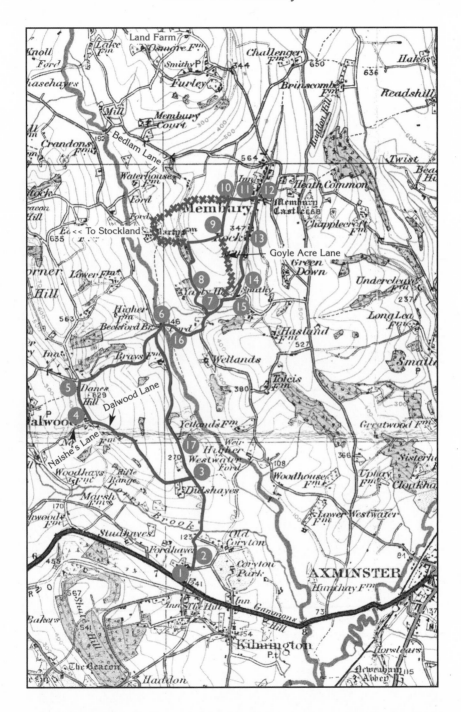

You are now entering one of the many green lanes in this area. Often they are quite narrow. This one begins with some tall cherry trees bordering it to the left. If you have time ascend this one, passing Yarty Farm.

(9) At a holly copse take the next footpath sign to your right over a stile alongside Yarty Wood. Go over another two stiles, then at the end of the field follow its edge round to the right. It was here one June morning that I thought I was looking at the rusty handles of an old harrow, which suddenly stiffened and turned towards me. It was a family of red deer which had just emerged from the wood. They let me advance towards them before spring-heeling off back under cover. Turn right along the hedge line here towards the lane at the top and go through the gate.

(10) You come out into Goyle Acre Lane (a goyle is a local word for a gully or valley and, like the red deer, mostly seen on maps in the Exmoor area). Turn left over a muddy patch.

(11) You will come to a T-junction for these 'county roads', as it says on the posts here. Turn right down a slippery lane which will soon give you a dramatic view of the tower of the church of St John the Baptist in Membury. Enter in and on the far wall to your left at the back of the church look for the following memorial:

In memory of
Thomas Wakeley
Surgeon and Coroner
Medical and Social
Reformer
Member of Parliament
Founder and First
Editor of
The Lancet
Born at Land Farm
Membury Devon 1795
Died in Madeira 1862

Outside, the castellated parts of the church are made from that rich brown stone to be seen in the Kilmington Stone.

(12) Come out through the lych gate and turn right along an interesting section of road. One side is constructed from large concrete blocks with air holes along one end. Concrete as a road-building material was popular in the 1950s.

(13) As you descend away from the village there is a lovely sign warning you of Overhanging Buildings to watch out for at Rock: here there are Peppercorn Cottage and Wild Thyme Cottage to avoid. There are horsetail, bogbean and fool's watercress in the hedges as you approach the Mill where, a little further on, the leat has been made part of a trout farm.

(14) There is a sign by the entrance to Lea Mill Hotel (Lea Mill Farm on the map) indicating an unmetalled road. Go along here and if you do not wish to take a cream tea or stay a while, follow the footpath down to the left which will bring you out back onto the lane again.

(15) Veer right at the junction here, and on your right you will pass another set of rights of way signs giving you yet another way through to the Goyle Acre's lane complex.

(16) Once over Bickford Bridge again keep left passing Bray's Farm to your right.

(17) Here by the flint-covered farm on your left called Chantry Wood I met a local who told me in a fine east Devon accent that it looked as if a storm were brewing, but not over us. This is often the case in areas of east Devon which are so close to the sea. Further down the lane, when I passed the sign for Dulcis Farmhouse and Longhouse I noticed that on the old map it was called Dulshayes, a change brought about by 800 years of local speech patterns. But why was there no Chantry Wood on the older map at all?

By the way

In the great 'nature or nurture' debates, there are always cases of people being so affected by something which they experienced in infancy that they were inspired to put right the wrongs they had seen. This has been true of many great social reformers (see Route 1 in *Exploring Green Lanes: North and North-West Devon*, the story of Ernest Bevin, once a farm labourer), Wakeley's friend Charles Dickens being a famous example. Contemporary with Wakeley were Cobbett's *Rural Rides*, as well as Dickens' novels. Many of Wakeley's reforms were reactions to the generally debilitating nature of working and living in the countryside in the mid-1800s which he had witnessed. His father was a wealthy landowner with eleven children. He was involved in the new enclosure of wastelands movement. His father made sure that his sons had experience of the land and, at age six, Wakeley was working alongside the agricultural labourers of Land Farm. In later life he defended labourers threatened with transportation for refusing to take a reduction in their wages when times were hard. He served a time at sea, and later was instrumental in banning the practice of flogging in the Navy. He studied to become an apothecary in Taunton, and then went on to study surgery at St Thomas's and Guy's in London. He was desperate to return to Devon and practice here, but no vacancy arose. As the plaque in the church shows, he was an active reformer in many fields.

As a boy in Devon he had walked six miles to school in Chard, then further afield to Honiton. When studying in London he walked there and back from Devon on a regular basis. What he saw along the way would have given him a basis for the many changes he made in what Coleridge, his local poet, not so far away in Ottery, referred to as "a community of subordination".

There were Utilitarians at Ford Abbey, and Jeremy Bentham went to live there on the Somerset border near Chard, in 1814. He was visited there by many of his friends, and a lot of walking in the fields and byways was indulged in – I wonder if they ever met up with Wakeley there.

Other green lanes in the area

You may wish to extend your walk by delaying your return to the A35. After taking tea at Lea Mill Hotel you could take Naishe's Lane just by **(4)**. Or at **(3)** keep to the left and pay a visit to Miller's Farm Shop.

Links

There is a regular bus service from Axminster to Exeter along the A35.

Question

There is quite a lot of dogwood growing in the hedges in this area. Do you know what its slender branches were used for in medieval times?

STOCKLAND

A bridge to Transportation – not if Wakeley was around

OS Explorer 116

The road from Chard to Honiton by way of Stockland was always hard. It followed the course of the old medieval post-road and then went forward from Chard, instead of bending down to Axminster. The gradients were so severe on the Stockland road, however, that a good deal of the traffic between Crewkerne and Honiton avoided the steep gradient by making the long circuit through Axminster.

On the present-day map you will find a section of minor road just north of Uplyme called Coach Road (SY 325947). When you see where it was placed, it is no wonder they kept changing the route. However, this route is not too harsh as long as you keep your hands off the bridges (see the text below). The distance covered on this walk is small, but the variety of scenery and the historical periods through which you pass are great.

Conditions: Some minor-lane walking and steep climbs.

Distance: 3-4 miles, but extendable if linked to Membury.

Starting point: Stockland village, with its flint and thatch cottages, is a delight to explore. But we are brought up sharp as we descend towards the bridge at the bottom of the village which gives a clue as to the deprivation, hardship and separations once suffered.

(1) ST 244047. As you descend, on the right-hand parapet of the bridge is a sign reading:

DORSET
Any person wilfully injuring
Any part of this COUNTY BRIDGE
will be guilty of FELONY and
upon conviction liable to be
TRANSPORTED FOR LIFE
7& 8 GEO. 4 C30 S15

So why would people have risked such a fate? The years given here are the seventh and eighth years of the reign of George IV, 1827-8. See *By the way* on page 96 for what was happening in this countryside then. Climb up away from the bridge.

(2) You reach Hornshayes Knap Cross. The presence of horn in a place name can indicate a drovers' route. There is a house called Larkrise to your left. Pass a very waterlogged lane to your right.

(3) Turn right here. At the next junction keep right, passing Higher Seavington Farm as you descend into the valley. You'll have to climb up again.

(4) Here is a road triangle; go straight over. You pass a footpath sign and come to Mayes Cottage on your right. There's a welcome wayside seat here.

(5) Turn right into the footpath here and you are turning into a way which has been made by generations making their way to Stockland's Little Castle settlement since prehistoric times. You come to a three-way footpath signpost; carry straight over. The lane is wide, with chalky ruts underfoot. Behind you are views opening out in all directions. You reach two gates here. To the right are the rounded contours of Little Castle. Go through the gate to your left along to another gate by a wood. Go through and along the field edge again. Watch out for deer here.

(6) You come out into Shrubbery Lane. Turn left and follow the wood edge along.

(7) You soon reach Mount Pleasant Farm. Go straight down into the woods here to your right. This is a byway through the woods. There is some laurel here, and some fine examples of oaks with the classic stag-head-shaped tops. You are close to the squatters' settlement of Shore Bottom, dating from the eighteenth century. As you come out of the woods, there are views coastwards and the light changes whatever the weather. You go into a

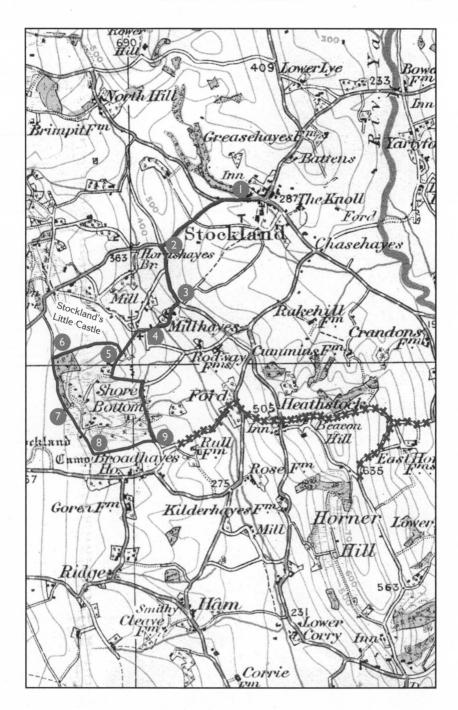

narrow high-banked lane which suddenly opens out with greensward at your feet. It has a magical feel to it.

(8) There is a footpath sign to your right on the bend, but just keep following the lane. This section will reward a hedge-dating count. However, I am reminded of Rackham's warning when dealing with dating hedges around here which were once part of the great Neroche Forest, the biggest in the south-west. When these woods were enclosed in the eighteenth century, hedge-planting took place with many species which were then at hand. He gives us this advice:

> *The encroachment hedges and post-1833 hedges have averages of 6.7 and 6.3 species; in this respect they are statistically indistinguishable from the medieval hedges. But the species are not the same. Elm and hazel are specially characteristic of the old hedges; furze of those of intermediate age; sallow, privet, and oak of the post-1833 hedges.*

Towards the end there is certainly a lot of holly here, and the lane becomes stonier. The lane may also be called Firs Lane. The planting of such trees meant that you were on King James's side during the Monmouth rebellion era. If limes were planted, it meant you were for the return of William, the Prince of Orange.

(9) In order to return to Stockland, turn left here and work your way back to (4). However, if you wish to link back to Membury via Ford turn right and follow the lanes as indicated in order to arrive. There is another version of this link further north along Marsh and Mill Lane.

By the way

As we have seen in the case of Wakeley and the Deodands Laws, there were many others in a similar vein, and some with severe punishments, such as being hung for the stealing of a sheep or a lamb or for injuring a bridge, were common if not always practised. Before these laws were reformed, one way of dealing with criminals was to send them over the water to Australia. Transportation began in 1787 and continued until 1850. But it was not only criminals who were leaving rural Devon. Between 1851 and 1901, 371,000 folk left for the north of England or other countries. This well-known

Devonshire folk song refers to these migrations:

All around my hat I will wear the green willow
All around my hat for a twelve month and a day
And if anyone ask me the reason I am wearing it
It's oh that my true love is far, far away.

Other green lanes in the area

As indicated, to Membury.

Links

There is a bus service along the A35 from Exeter to Axminster.
Routes 14 and 16 on the same present-day OS map.
There is a leaflet published by Devon County Council giving details of walks around the village.

Question

Which country would you have been transported to if you had damaged the bridge in Stockland?

The beginning of Firs Lane.

HAWKCHURCH

Drovers' ways that failed to lead Monmouth's supporters to safety

OS Explorer 116

This walk is set in a village placed on routes run-ning along a north-west to south-east axis: a once-busy one, leading from the coast up towards towns over into Somerset and Dorset. This is a circular route, mainly through lush meadows and woodlands, a fact which those fleeing towards Sedgemoor in support of Monmouth in 1685 would not have had time to notice.

Conditions: Mainly on the level; some damp patches in the green lanes and meadows.

Distance: 4-5 miles.

Starting point: ST 344004. The village of Hawkchurch, which has only been part of Devon since 1896, has its centre by the church and The Old Inn oppo-site. If you visit in June, you will notice the scent of the roses. A vicar at the end of the 19th century planted roses round the doors of the cottages. As the illustration shows, they are still a feature by the church. There is also a Scots pine in the churchyard, and we are to meet more of these drovers' road indi-cators along the way. Inside the church there are some interesting decora-tions, including green men and a goat playing the violin. Perhaps the prox-imity and open nature of the churchyard led to clashes between secular and ecclesiastical members of the community. The Old Inn was burnt down

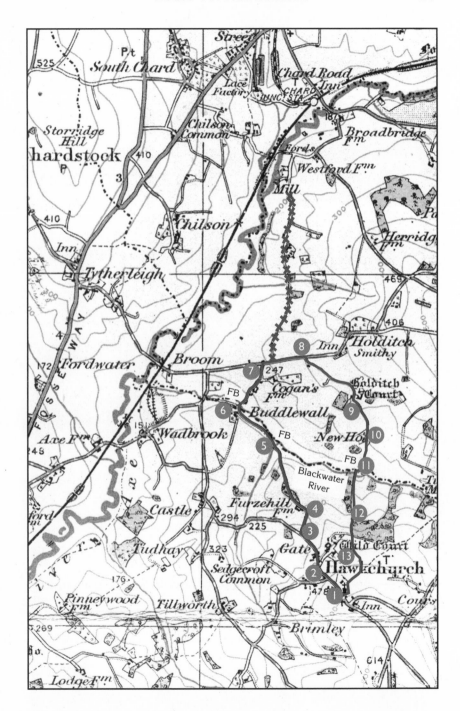

deliberately in 1543, along with the poorhouse and four cottages.

(1) Leaving the church, turn right down towards the green where the war memorial stands. Three families in particular suffered great losses here in the First World War.

(2) Keep to the right, passing the entrance to Wyld Court on your right. Large pollarded oaks line the lane as you descend.

(3) Turn right down towards Furzehill Farm. The thatched farmhouse stands to your left.

(4) Go through the farmyard on the road and look out for the pines ahead as you enter a wide, flinty-surfaced green lane. This was once an important route, and features on early maps of Devon. On the bend go straight across into a narrow grassy lane where, as it widens once again, you will be walking over fool's watercress, brook lime and water forget-me-not down towards the ford.

(5) This is the Blackwater River, forming the boundary between Dorset and Devon on the old map. Keep to the right through a gate. There is a fine meadow to your left, and the hedge line on the right has dropped away.

(6) Go through another gate and you will be by Buddlewall Farm. A 'buddle' is a Devonshire dialect word for drainage channel, not to be confused with a 'biddle', which is a large wooden mallet. Enjoy the well-kept lawns here, and rest a while on the seat. Turn right across two footbridges; tarmac gradually emerges as you reach the houses at the top. Opposite the farm you pass on the right, with a black-faced clock on its wall, is a clump of Scots pines and a drinking trough, further evidence of drovers.

(7) Turn right at the top into a minor lane, having passed two footpath signs to your right. This stretch of lane has some good views out towards Somerset. You pass Brimble Cottage where they sell alpines – we surely haven't climbed that much!

(8) You soon come to an attractive wooden sign on the right for Holditch; follow this to the right. As you walk between three counties today you pass many farms with settlements around them; remember that at the time of the Monmouth Rebellion, eighty percent of the population lived in villages and hamlets.

(9) Just past Holditch Court keep to the left (although like the fleeing rebels there is a temptation to go towards the woodland); follow the signs to the left to Newhouse, passing an ivy-clad ruined tower on your left. The flints give way to a grassy and hop trefoil-lined lane.

(10) You pass the idyllically placed thatched farmhouse of Newhouse. It is suggested that the sandstone pillars here which lead out onto the meadow were built to intimidate and to stand as a fortification. Go straight down over the meadow towards the woodland.

(11) Here there is another footbridge over the Blackwater. Keep to the right, making for the large tree-stump gateposts ahead on the rise.

(12) Keep following the footpath signs straight ahead.

(13) These go along the woodland edge and take you into a meadow as the church and the lone Scots pine appear. You go down a dark tunnel up against a flint wall joined with lime mortar, which brings you out into the expansive green all around the church once more.

By the way

Those who supported the return of Monmouth in the 1680s in this area were not just disgruntled agricultural peasants. Amongst their leaders were tradesmen, craftsmen and dissenting ministers, as well as unemployed cloth-workers. They were fighting for toleration of different religious beliefs and other freedoms which belonged to the Commonwealth. Thirteen rebels from this area were executed, and the sufferings of those who survived but were treated badly can only be imagined as we walk along. Robin Stanes rightly celebrates the importance of these rebels:

> *Monmouth's rising was the last English rebellion, and also the last occasion on which Devonshire people were directly involved in deciding national history.*

Other green lanes in the area

Those leading back to link up with the Colyton, Route 18.

Links

There is a weekly bus in and out of the village from Axminster.
Your present-day map will show you how close we are to Chard and the long Drift, a drovers' road shown on the modern map.

Question

Where was the clock at Middle Holditch made?

KILMINGTON to SHUTE

A Roman road with rebellious beginnings

OS Explorer 116

This is a very straightforward walk, perhaps due in part to the presence of the Roman road. But the beauty of the countryside through which you pass is underpinned by some physical reminders of the very hard times which led to the Monmouth Rebellion and the punishments meted out to those rebels who took part.

Shute Piers

Conditions: Mainly on the level, but muddy in some places in the winter months.

Distance: 4-5 miles.

Starting point: This is quite a big village, and merits a walk round before you start off. Outside the village hall there is a brown block of Kilmington Stone of great antiquity. Just below the church is a collection of buildings dating from the time of the Old School, which must have been the centre of activity supplemented by traffic coming off the A35 at the Old Inn.

(1) SY 274984. This is just before the Inn, where you take the Whitford Road at Allways back into the village.

(2) Just beyond the junction with the lane called The Street is the post office.

(3) Turn back to the junction and turn right by a large stone-built house on the corner called Koppers. There is a stream running to your right, and on the left a plaque to tell you what wild flowers you may meet along the way.

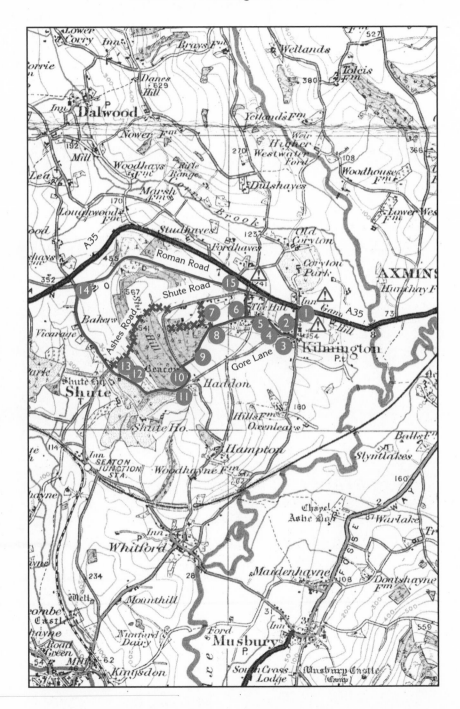

(4) Follow the lane down to the junction with Gore Lane, where there is a green with two tall willows – not leaning, but growing ever upwards. Carry on up the hill.

(5) At the junction with Silver Street carry straight on, passing Arch and Well Cottages. The Well in the village is known as Kate's Well, and comes not from a well source but from an underground stream. It is named after St Katherine. Other wells on these routes blessed by saints with healing powers for eye complaints can be found at St Dunstan, just outside Yealmpton, and St Gudula outside Ashburton.

(6) At the junction with The Hill, go straight over. Before entering Springhead Lane, the green lane with a dead-end sign in front of you, go down to the left to see the collection of delightful cottages in this sunken lane space before it joins up with Bimbon Lane.

(7) Go straight over into Springhead Lane. You pass a house called Labley Brook, and the lane soon picks up grass at its centre as you descend.

(8) At Spring Head there is a sign for a public byway to your right – a diversion if you wish. However, for this route carry on, taking the bridleway straight ahead to the right of the house drive. You climb up through patches of rhododendrons and tall Scots pines. There is a dank, woody smell as you twist your way along; it's a perfect place to hide from any pursuers. Veer sharp right on the corner of the woodlands where an upended silver birch plate stands. These trees have such shallow root systems that when they go over they bring everything up with them.

(9) There is a sign here into a private wood with public access named Hester's Gate; but more tellingly, on the map the area is known as Mount Hungary, surely originally spelt 'hungry'.

(10) You emerge into a minor road. Turn left where there are views out towards Uplyme, Dorset and the sea.

(11) You soon reach Haddon Corner, where you turn right down a tree-lined minor lane with an 'ER' post box on your right (see the Feniton Route) and a cottage called Sea View to your right. There is an orchard to your right as you descend and pass the parking place for Shute Hill.

(12) Turn left into the church of St Michael here. It is placed at the back of Shute House's imposing gatehouse. The old church door mentioned by Mee is still there, with its sanctuary ring in place. There is a very informative Parish Map in the porch, and after having seen Sir William Pole's lifelike statue in the church it is heartening to see that another Pole, Sir Frederick,

requested, more humbly, that his body be taken for burial in an ordinary farm cart. The board tells you that when you used Ashes Road you said you were "going up Ashes and coming down cinders", and that Shute Piers are haunted by a coachman who fell from a carriage on its way to Shute House. However, see (14) below for another theory. The gatehouse of the Poles' Shute House which faces the road here dates from 1570. The house belongs to the National Trust, and can be visited on certain days during the summer.

(13) From the telephone booth you may want to return 'up Ashes', which has an 'Unsuitable for Motor Vehicles' sign at its entrance. But to take the Roman road, turn right into a fairly busy road towards Shute, passing The Old Post Office, The Old Vicarage and a collection of houses known as Bakers. From here you will see a column on the horizon.

(14) You come to what is known as Shute Piers, although there is only one of them here. As mentioned above, it is thought that the area around here is haunted, as a coachman fell from his postillion position and was killed here. However, there is probably a more grim truth that points to the origin of its haunting. After the rebels supporting Monmouth had been executed by judgements passed by bloody Judge Jefferies, their hung, drawn and quartered remains were hung up at crossroads and junctions for all to see.

Turn right into the Roman road here. You enter a lane which is at least twenty feet wide and bounded by ancient banks. You pass a new building development and then go through woodlands. At the point where public access to the woods is given to the right there is a monkey puzzle tree growing and other signs of a once-cultivated area. You pass into a space to the right which has had its conifers felled. Think of the Romans exiled from their sunny country, as W. H. Auden wrote in his poem 'Roman Wall Blues':

Over the heather the wet wind blows
I've lice in my tunic and a cold in my nose.

(15) This was the road which went through to London via Salisbury. It later became the busy turnpike road to Lyme, the sounds from which will follow you all the way along on your left as you march along this straight lane.

At the end of the lane, make your way to The New Inn. We are in an area once involved in lace-making, so it is not surprising to hear that the car park here was once a lace room where lace was repaired and sorted, an activity suggesting making-do and mending before sending goods further up the road towards the fine London markets. The roads from here to Axminster were once drovers' roads as well. It was not just cattle that were driven, as the presence of Pig Street in the nearby town of Axminster proves this.

By the way

Shute Piers, a Grade II scheduled construction, stands high up on a corner at the beginning of the Roman road and could have borne such aforementioned grisly remains. Lately there has been a notice attached, saying that it is to be repaired, but work cannot take place until the owner of the pier is identified.

Robin Stanes, in his book *A History of Devon*, has a picture of a pillar identical to Shute Piers, used for a similar purpose at Escot; it was originally at Fairmile on the old A30. Maybe the Highways Authority need look no further than the Crown for origins of ownership.

Other green lanes in the area

Through to Colyton below, or up to Stockland and Membury above.

Links

There is a bus which goes along the A35 from Exeter to Axminster. If you do not make the walk circular, you can link back down into the next walk at Colyton along another green lane as indicated, perhaps once more following in the fleeing footsteps of the seventeenth-century rebels.

Question

How old is the block of stone outside Kilmington Village Hall?

COLYTON

Taking to the hills with the rebels
to avoid a good tanning

OS Explorer 116

This walk starts close to the famous school
and takes you up and over rolling hills which
must have been hard going for those involved
in Monmouth's Rebellion. But don't let this
restrict your musings, as a former vicar of
Colyton once said: *"Peditatio Totum
Meditatio Totum* – I walk Everywhere, I think
of Everything!"*

There is certainly every opportunity to do
this around Colyton, as there are so many routes to enjoy.

Conditions: Flinty, with some puddles of standing water.

Distance: 4-5 miles.

Starting point: SY 247924. At the top of Harepath Hill (meaning 'route of the
army'), at the bus stop go over the Exeter to Lyme turnpike road.

(1) Turn right into Fairview Lane and go straight on up, passing a footpath sign to your right and a narrow green lane entrance too.

(2) This brings you to the junction of Four Cross Elms at Hillhead by a
wayside seat. Go straight over and you will see that this narrow lane still
does have some elms in the hedgerows.

(3) There are some large oaks here bringing you to the next junction
over the Old Sidmouth Road, where you go straight over again. You descend
and there is a walled orchard on your left.

(4) Veer left here, then straight over and up the hill. On the stone pillars

of a house on the left is inscribed 'Ridgway House' and the initials 'ECH'.

(5) Be careful how you cross here, with the house Little Acre to your right as you descend to another junction and another wayside seat. You turn left here.

(6) At a roadside triangle marked Heathayne Cross keep right and go down to the footpath towards the house, where rescued battery hens are brought for a happy retirement. The façade of the house is very beautiful, with stone windows and a centrally placed external chimney-breast – just right for coddling. Go to the right here through a gate into another green lane which leads down to the swift-flowing willow-girthed Coly. Turn left and go over the bridge. (Turn briefly left for another wayside seat.)

(7) Turn right, then left again by the hedge and follow the bridleway over a stile into a lane with plenty of flints and a distinct camber.

(8) You come out onto the road again and turn left to Gittshayne Cross, where the farm advertises its beef and free-range eggs. Just before the entrance there is a green lane to your left.

(9) It begins fairly steeply and narrowly, and winds with whitish flints underfoot up to wonderful sea views framed by Seaton Down and Fort and the hills surrounding. Towards the top, ruby-tinted flints surface.

(10) There is a grass triangle here. Keep to the left and join the minor road at Red Cross. There is no post here, but could this have been a directional point for those who were to be transported, or does it refer to the red flints, or does it mean something altogether more bloody?

(11) Take the grassy green lane running up to your right here into Downhayne Brake Road. Although called a road, this long green lane is hardly that now. It gives sweeping views in all directions and you definitely feel that you are in the heart of the countryside. As Michael Dower once described these lanes:

> *The key: Take a green lane as your route to traverse the country-side, and you will have both a way and a means of penetrating the character of the place.*

> *The lock: Each green lane is a precious package of nature and culture . . .*

(12) Turn left into Yardbury Hill Road towards the eerily-named Watchcombe Moor. This map shows that there were very few trees there in

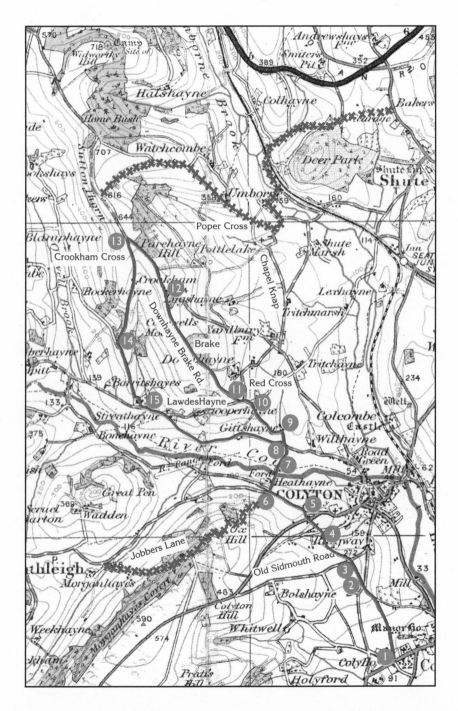

1946. Today the wood is full of primroses, bluebells and Devonshire violets.

(13) At Crookham Cross, just past the main entrance to the wood, turn left and down into another long, delightful lane which takes you into a deciduous wooded valley, over a gate by some ruins and by another wood.

(14) Keep to the left here through some muddy patches and a towering fragment of a holly hedge.

(15) Go through Lawdeshayne Farm. If you want to join the East Devon Way further upstream, then turn right or continue left passing two junctions to your left which will bring you back to Gittshayne Farm at (9). Follow the signs back into Colyton, where there is so much to see. You come into the town over the 600-year-old bridge. Keep right here, and there through the garden centre is an industry still in operation after 400 years.

To return to Four Elms Bus Stop, take the road opposite the library which will bring you out at Hillhead (2) and then back down to (1).

By the way

When Charles II's illegitimate son, the Duke of Monmouth, set up a bid for power against his father in 1685, he was backed by many for different reasons. Eighty-eight men came from Colyton: some were Dissenters fearful of the Catholic Church; others were lawyers, tradesmen and craftsmen. There had been a downturn in the cloth trade, and these weavers and spinners were fearful for their future.

The unsuccessful outcome of the Battle of Sedgemoor saw the rebels suppressed, and those who survived from Dorset and east Devon were cruelly used, their lands confiscated, some transported to the West Indies and others executed.

Other green lanes in the area

Jobber's Way Lane, as indicated. ('Jobber' is the term given in east Devon to a trader who used packhorses to transport his goods. Also, as Sheldon tells us:

> Persons well-known as pig-jobbers, who constantly drove herds of them into Dorsetshire and elsewhere have regular halting-places, where the animals were either fed with horse-beans in the street, or made to halt for the night, as the case might be. At Axminster the spot where the droves were habitually fed is marked by the name of Pig Street.

Links

The Jurassic Coast Bus which runs from Exeter to Pool stops at Four Elms
Cross **(1)** where you can pick it up again as many hours later as you like.
The East Devon Way.
The Beer and Axmouth Routes.

Question

What is the traditional industry here (which is still in operation) called?

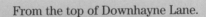

From the top of Downhayne Lane.

AXMOUTH

Transported to another world – Captain Swing speaks out

OS Explorer 116

This walk takes you away from the coastline, still showing evidence of the landslip on Christmas Day and Boxing Day of 1839. You walk into the hinterland, where big fields support a thriving agricultural community; but of course it was not always so. As you look down over the expansive Axe Estuary, with its lack of big ships and docks now, it is hard to believe that it was once a busy port, especially during Roman times.

FIFTY POUNDS *Reward.*

Whereas, on Saturday last, Letters signed **"SWING"** were sent to Mr. Hawkings, and Mr. D. Symes, Farmers of Axmouth, threatening to destroy their premises by FIRE; whosoever will give information leading to the discovery and conviction of the writer, SHALL RECEIVE A REWARD OF **50 POUNDS**

All Communications to be addressed to the *Church Wardens and Overseers of Axmouth.*

N. B. The above Letters passed through the Colyton Post Office, & bear the Axminster post mark. Dated December the 6th 1830.

T. Ham, Printer, Bookbinder, and Stationer, Lyme and Axminster.

Conditions: One or two steepish climbs, some straightforward minor road walking.

Distance: 3-4 miles.

Starting point: SY 254899, Seaton Bridge.

(1) This is the old concrete bridge built in the nineteenth century, which has been closed to traffic since 1990. Although manufactured in concrete, the arches, piers and parapets are scored as if made of old-fashioned masonry. The designer, Philip Brown, built the bridge for the Lord of the

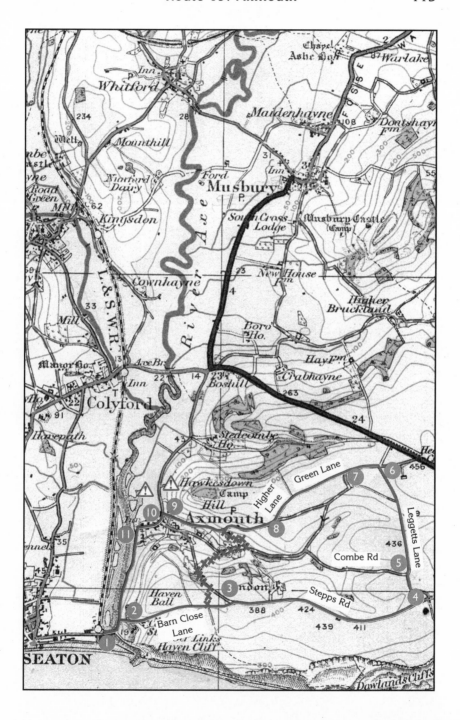

Manor, Sir Walter Trevelyan, to replace the ferry across the mouth of the Axe. Yet he continued to collect the 'ferry' tolls by putting up the bow-fronted concrete tollhouse on the road upstream. The tolls were collected up until 1907.

(2) Just along from the bridge on the right is a public bridleway sign to the Axe Cliff golf course. Climb up the road here, then go straight over the course into a green lane marked as the Coast Path. There is a lot of field maple in the hedge here, and breaks by gates to the left give you good views of Axmouth and the hills above Colyton.

(3) At the junction follow this minor road along to the right; Stepps Road follows the 400' contour on the old map. You are in Devon-Dorset border country now, and there is a great variety of hedgerow flowers thriving on the chalk here; every inch is covered with parsleys and vetches.

(4) Just before Dowlands, at Dowlands Cross, there is a T-junction which takes you to the left past a wayside stand of large Monterey pines.

(5) On the corner in front of you is Leggett's Lane. The surface of this public bridleway brightens from brown flints to chalk as you progress. There are patches of elm in the hedgerows, and sweeping views towards the white cliffs of Seaton Hole and distant lands on the other side of the Axe estuary. The lane widens to a carriage-width towards the end.

(6) Turn left along a short stretch of minor road flanked on the right by a line of marker beeches, which lead you to another bend.

(7) The road turns to the left, but it is obvious that the green lane you are to follow is directly in front of you. Here begins Axmouth's very own 'Green Lane'. It is wide, in a drover-like way, and sheep-rearing was, and still is, important here.

(8) Turn left down towards Axmouth on this minor road.

(9) Turn left again, which will lead you through some interesting back streets.

(10) Here is the relatively busy A3172 and the Church of St Michael's where, in 1938, Arthur Mee records having seen the following:

On a garden wall by the churchyard rests a shallow bowl with a hole in the bottom, brought here from a deserted farm and thought to be one of the old standard measures for corn once kept in church porches.

This must have been used in the allotment of tithes for the church, or possibly for dole payments for the poor. But where is it now? There are good footways to take you across to the estuary edge.

(11) There are shelducks, curlews, herons, cormorants and other species of birds to be seen. This is the estuary where the Romans built a spur of causeway to link the once important port of Axmouth to the Fosse Way. To your left looms the wooded Hawkesdown Hill, one of a chain of Iron Age forts built along the river to protect it from, initially, invaders from Dorset.

In 1989 some Roman lead sling bullets were found, dating back to the first century AD.

By the way

The bill dated December 6th 1830 is reproduced on page 112 as an example of the unrest which once swept through the countryside along with new, labour-saving devices such as threshing machines. Labour definitely did not want to be saved in this way. At this time the protestors would also have been rioting against corn prices. They kept their anonymity by using a fictitious name, *Captain Swing*, as leader of their cause. A Mr D. Symes, one of the farmers threatened by the 'swing' rioters here, belonged to a family which held important positions in the church and the judiciary. If the rioters were discovered, he could have recommended them for transportation to Australia. Between 1787 and 1850 over 500 'swing' protestors were 'sent away' – there were 2,000 arrests and nineteen executions. On the Dorset border here we are close to Tolpuddle Martyr country. The martyrs were deported to Australia in 1834 because they had come together to form a union to fix the wages of agricultural workers.

Other green lanes in the area

Beer (no. 21), Colyton (no. 18), Rousdon and Combpyne (no. 20) and Stockland (no. 15).

Links

The Seaton Tramway, Combpyne and Rousdon and Colyton.
The Transportation Bridge walk in Stockland.

Question

What year was the concrete bridge at Seaton built?

ROUSDON to COMBPYNE

Green lane and grand drive survivors, once everyone's cup of tea

OS Explorer 116

This is a short circuit which passes through open countryside all around but also gives you glimpses of the sea close by. There is some minor-lane walking on this route, and a fast coast road to watch out for. By using the Jurassic Link bus between Exeter and Poole you can make this walk as circular as you wish, extending the diameter as far as you like.

Conditions: Some standing water and cattle dung in lanes.

Distance: Short circuit 2-3 miles, extended circuit 5-6 miles.

Starting point: SY 295913 at Rousdon. However you arrive, you begin this walk from the A3052 along the Roman route which runs along the coast from Exeter to Lyme Regis. It began as a ridgeway, set back from the perils of the coast. SY 296914 is the bus stop for Rousdon Garage. You alight at the stone bus shelter, built for the Festival of Britain in 1951.

(1) Turn right down past the Orchard, now a Country House Hotel. There is some stone walling to your left which marks the boundary of the Old Dower House.

(2) Go straight over the crossroads into Combpyne Road and notice the clump of larch leaning uphill over to your right. Further along at Rose Coombe there is a line of tall elms which have reached a disease-free height of fifteen feet or more in this lane which leads you up into The Square. If you want to make a day-long circuit, then it is from here that you can extend your walk to take in the many 'hayeses' (hedges) on the map and Musbury House.

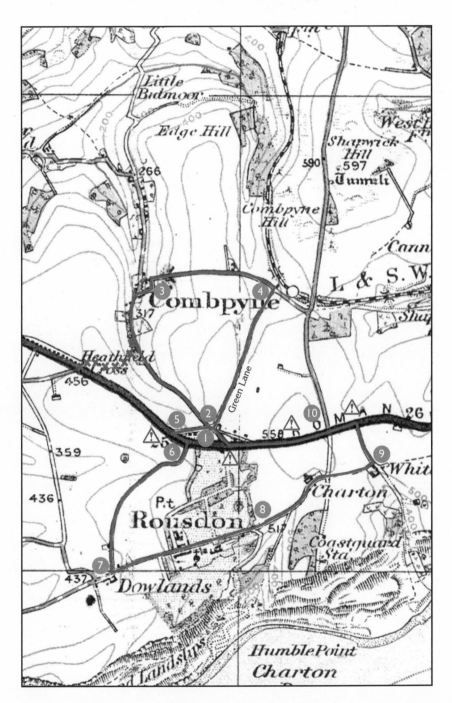

(3) If not, then turn right here towards Shapwick, which rises slightly then levels out with a mixture of grass and exposed chalk at its centre; high banks of maple and elm hem you in. Then in front of you is a viaduct, packed with straw, over which the Axminster to Lyme Regis train once ran. As is to be expected there are a lot of chalk quarries in the area – the place name Charlton tells us this. But this has been sheep-rearing country for centuries.

(4) Take the public bridleway to your right at the bottom of the slope. Almost immediately it becomes a wide drover-type lane with some tall old oaks to mark it out in the landscape. There are a lot of elder bushes here too. Stand still and listen to the birdlife all around you: the greenfinches wheezing in the branches overhead, swallows and swifts aerialing above, along with larks out of sight over the tall hedgebank, and far away sea birds cry. The lane's surface is mainly cobbles of a chalky nature and some patches of large bright red bricks too, maybe taken from an old building which is no more. At its end you come to Green Lane Farm with an impressive arch at its entrance and a bungalow by its side, but neither feel as old as the lane from which you have just emerged. You have now returned to (2), so go straight across at this crossroads and walk along the back of the Dower House Hotel with patches of wild comfrey in the verges.

(5) Turn left onto the main road for a short stretch.

(6) Cross and take the minor lane to your right down towards Dowlands. In the hedge gaps there are views of the beeches on the other named 'Green Lane' in Route 19.

(7) Turn left at the phone box, passing St Anthony's on your left, and go through the gates into what was once Sir Henry Peek's (of Peek Frean's biscuits) very own estate. Having made his fortune in tea, his subsequent business success led him into taking the biscuit as well, in this case the whole parish of Rousdon which he bought in the 1860s. Yet this public bridleway has survived. You walk along the grand drive, without trespassing; there is much to see along the way, including your first glimpse of the sea by a house called The Paddocks.

(8) The drive runs out as you pass through under the arch of a gatehouse, through the yard and into a narrow, elm- and sloe-lined bridleway. Suddenly it opens out into the yard of Charton Farm, with its stern grey pebbled façade. Go through to the road junction.

(9) Here in front of you is another piece of farming reality far removed from the new apartments of Home Farm: the huge navy blue doors of a farm-

ing storage tank, which seems to be rusting away. Just on the corner here over the gate there are stunning views out to the Isle of Portland twenty-five miles away, and further to the west to your right Start Point can be seen. Turn back to the main road from here to

(10) Charton Cross, from where you turn left back to Rousdon along a road which has successively been used as a ridgeway, a Roman road, a turn-pike, and carried motorised vehicles. It has survived any attempts at diversion, and has never been neglected. This sense of continuity is well expressed in the opening lines of the poem 'The Road Goes On':

Faint from far downs, where age-old trackways ravel
Turf, wind-swept, rain-washed for unnumbered years,
Comes to us still the stir of ancient travel,
Of men who knew not they were pioneers:
The trader by his customed landmarks bounded,
The huntsman his obscurer paths upon –
By heel and hoof the highway first was founded,
To tire and tractor-belt the road goes on.

by C.W. Scott-Giles, 1946. (See Bibliography for his invaluable book on highway history).

Back at Rousdon there is the milestone to examine, which is also part of Peek's Victorian legacy.

By the way

All Hallows School and Home Farm buildings which you pass between **(7)** and **(8)** have a big story to tell, which can only be summarised here. The buildings, apart from Home Farm and the original site of a chapel at St Pancras' church, have been here for only about 125 years. Sir Henry Peek, although building himself an ivory tower together with a billiard room and observatory crowned by a truly magnificent-looking gryphon, also thought of his estate workers whom he had purchased along with Rousdon Manor. He built a school here with facilities for hot meals for the pupils – unheard of at the time. He also had a tramway built for the removal of muck from the farmyard. The history of the school of All Hallows, which came here in 1938 (and lasted until its closure in 1998) after five centuries in Honiton, is well documented. There must always have been a sense of community here, feudal or otherwise, which has now been replaced by the silent solitude of individual living requirements – and maybe the silent blessing of the shepherds who once walked this way to keep their flocks from straying too far seawards.

Other green lanes in the area

Axmouth (no. 19), Membury (no. 14) and Colyton (no. 18).

Links

The Jurassic Coast bus, the X53, passes along here.
The South West Coast Path and The East Devon Way.

Question

You are walking along one of the oldest roads in the county. When was it established as a turnpike?

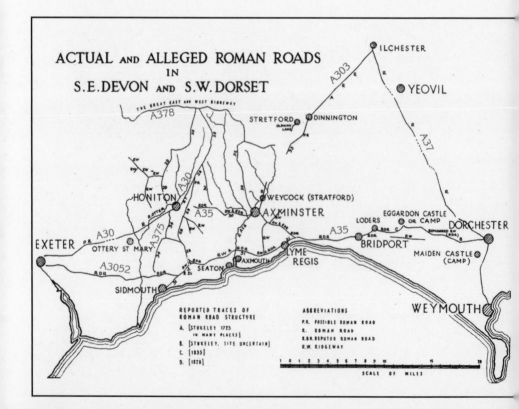

BEER

No small Beer for quarry workers

OS Explorer 116

If there were any liquid refreshment for the quarry men, then it would probably have been in the form of cider rather than Beer. These quarry workers,
who worked underground in smelly, damp, dark conditions for up to four-
teen hours a day, must have emerged with quite a thirst. Still, they had a nice
walk home to look forward to, as you shall see. This walk confirms what is
only to be expected of most green lanes: they are old routes to and from
work. In this case the workers were quarrymen, fishermen and maybe jobbers involved in the lace trade centred in Honiton and Branscombe. Of
course we must not forget the usual mainstay of agricultural workers, one of
which is immortalised in the Hangman's Stone, the point on the A3052 where
you turn off in order to begin this walk.

Conditions: Steep in places.

Distance: 5 miles if going on into Seaton.

Starting point: SY 212903. When you step off the bus here and turn right,
notice on your right the façade of Bovey House. This had been the home of
the Waldrons since the thirteenth century. The chimneys which you see here
are said to be hiding holes for priests and contraband, for we are in Jack
Rattenbury country. This famous smuggler was born in Beer.

(1) Take the public bridleway to your left, Bovey Lane, which has been
cut through a larch plantation. There are many faceted flints beneath your
feet, and the sea breezes murmur in the larch needles above.

(2) You descend gently through the dappled light, then pass through deciduous woodland which opens out to rolling hills with chalk outcrops showing

through. Throughout the descent there is a series of high humps placed at regular intervals for drainage purposes, and alongside them are little patches of flints laid out like votive gifts to the water which chalk readily yields up.

(3) You are now well below the field level. At the end of the lane turn sharply left to a road junction.

(4) Then turn left and right by a wooden sign reading Public Right of Way, Paizen Lane. The surface of this lane becomes whiter as you ascend. Surely this is one of the old ways into and out of the 2,000-year-old quarries. Maybe an example of an early one-way system. There is silver weed at your feet, and dogwood and holly by your side. The lane's camber is firmed up by light brown flints.

(5) Turn left at the top, and descend a fairly wide lane where you will find Beer Caves to visit on your left.

(6) Now descend towards (3), passing some fine chalk-faced houses as you meet the Causeway, an important route from water to high ground.

(7) Stay a while on the beach here. When the Reverend Kilvert came here with his family in 1871, he saw a collier discharging coal barges onto carts hauled up the beach by six horses. No doubt a lot of the load ran up Bovey Lane to Bovey House and left in smoke through those chimneys we saw at the beginning of this walk.

With a shout, plunge and a struggle the cart was dragged up the steep shingle bank, ploughing deep into the loose shale and rattling pebbles. When the cart had been emptied at the wharf, to save time the five horses were unhooked and the shaft horse sent galloping down the beach to the barge entirely alone, and going full split through the thongs of holiday folk, scattering them right and left in the widest dismay.

The only load carted up the beach nowadays, maybe, is seaweed and sand as fertiliser for the fine set of allotments above the chalky Beer stone cliffs.

(8) Take the Coastal Footpath to Seaton Hole through the Jubilee Memorial gardens. From here there are good views of England's most southerly outcrop of white rock, and the quarry that you walked round by the green lanes. Samphire grows here and, ravens build their nests here too.

(9) From Seaton Hole walk along the fine shingle beach into Seaton and take a return trip to Beer by bus, or continue eastwards to explore more green lanes in the Axmouth area.

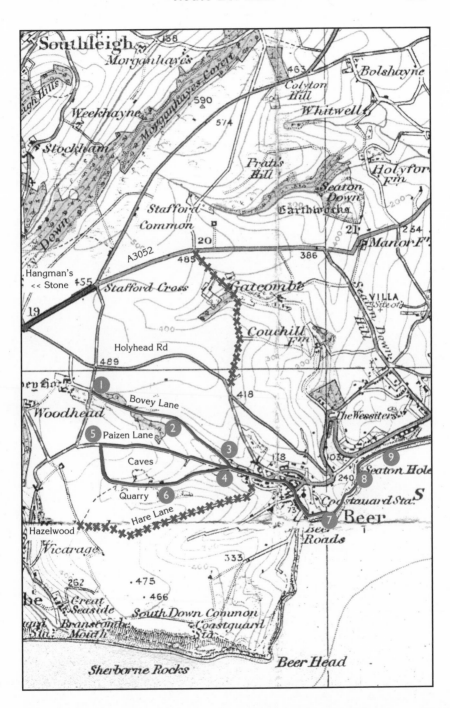

By the way

Seaton stands on a branch of the Icknield Way, now the A3052, that linked Seaton and Beer quarries with the rest of Roman Britain.

One could ponder long on just how some churches in Devon, graced with Beer stone (formed 92 million years ago), received their loads and so write a new history of communications based on these routes, given that the church was the centre of all communities. It was used in the construction of twenty-four cathedrals in all, including a very famous and enduring one in London (see Question below). The stone was extracted by candlelight with pickaxes and saws, and transported to the beach using the horse-drawn waggons as illustrated. These caves were also familiar to local smugglers such as the famous Jack Rattenbury, a bit of a local hero (see Bibliography). They were also used to hide Catholics persecuted after the Reformation.

As in many of the quarries and mines in this selection of walks, you will find hibernating bats have taken up residence in these quieter, non-industrial (and more religiously tolerant) days.

Other green lanes in the area

Those linking back to Honiton.

Links

The South West Way. The Jurassic Bus Link provides an regular hourly service along this coastline.

Question

In which famous London building is Beer stone to be seen?

Eighteenth-century stone quarry workers.

BRANSCOMBE

Lace, smugglers and modern 'swag'

OS Explorer 115

This walk takes you close to one of the most spectacular stretches of coast in east Devon – but don't feel that you are missing out, as the lanes here are magical too. They have long been connected with pirates and revenue men, but also with the lace and wool jobbers of the area. There is some minor-lane walking here which is quite safe.

"SMUGGLERS RUNNING SPIRITS." 1807.

Conditions: Very wet and muddy in places.

Distance: 4-5 miles.

Starting point: SY 174907. Branscombe Cross on the A3052.

(1) Take the lane signposted to Branscombe and soon you will see the sea on the horizon.

(2) Go left and you soon reach a farm and a group of houses.

(3) Follow the road round, passing the newly converted Edge Farm on the right looking out across to the sea. You descend with patches of furze appearing on the steep hills around you. You pass through pillars leading to Edge Barton, a house occupied since Norman times and taken over by Bishop Branscombe in the thirteenth century. You join the ridgeway on a bend just as you reach the main entrance. (4) Go straight across and into a meadow, passing two ponds on your right. Make for the corner, then go through a gate and take the green lane to your right which climbs up into ash and hazel woodland. There are good views of Edge Barton here, and the lane

is full of horsetail, a plant indicating the ancient woodland nature of the area. Towards the end the lane is cobbled and there is a leat to the left.

(5) You emerge with Hole House to your left. Veer to the right and go through two columns planted up with miniature cypresses. There are more views of the sea here and you go through another set of columns – mind how you go. The lane is bordered by intriguing groups of pollarded ash trees. They seem too young to be another example of the work of William Leigh of Leigh's Weston, a lime-burning merchant from Salcombe Regis in the 1770s. Competition to obtain the culm coal (imported from Wales and used to burn the lime) was so great that he built a ship of his own to run his own culm in and out. He was in such a hurry that he cut down thirty oaks and three crooked trees in Salcombe Manor in order to do so, and was fined £40. Go through a hunting gate (indicating a bridleway) and descend towards the village, passing the old school house and then the school on your right.

(6) Keep to your right for a visit to the church, passing cottages made of local yellow stone and the beautifully named Church Livings opposite the church. Go back towards the road and keep straight on passing (or of course visiting) the National Trust properties of The Forge, the Bakery and Manor Mill.

(7) Turn up left before you reach The Mason's Arms pub and follow the road up. You pass a footpath sign on the left.

(8) Take the next lane to your left towards Gay's Farms. There is a walnut tree on the road triangle here. Pass along the front and round the back into a green lane with good views back towards the sea again. Large lumps of limestone appear on the surface, and the course of the road is very twisty. On one of the bends to the left there is an outcrop of flints running under tree roots.

(9) The lane narrows and takes a long sweep to the right, lined by dogwood, a tree favoured by archers for making arrows.

(10) The lane is gated at the end here, and immediately to your right is another gated byway into which you plunge on your way to Higher Watercombe.

(11) Veer left up another stretch of green lane of packhorse width and out through a gate into a crossroads.

(12) Cross over here towards Elverway Farm. Could this be the way that elvers, young eels, were transported from Somerset?

(13) The footpath comes out close to the once-busy Three Horseshoes Inn. Sadly it is no longer functioning as the busy hostelry it once must have been on the Lyme turnpike road of 1758. Hutchinson records that he found

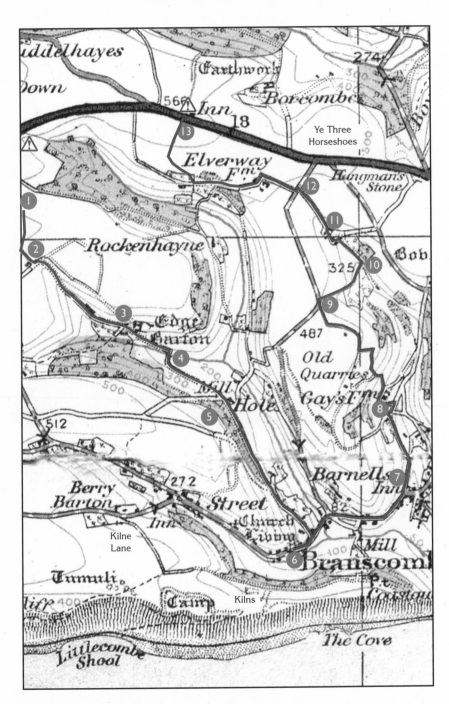

the foundations of a chapel in a field opposite and traced a bank behind the Inn which looked like the west side of a square Roman camp.

By the way

Although you can see from the number of quarries in the area that lime-burning and its transportation was a big industry here, its lace-making produced some of the finest work in the country. At Barnwell and Trafalgar Cottage in 1851 John Tucker, a lace dealer, employed 500 people. They were not all working here, but would bring in their piece-work from the area. They were earning a shilling a day at a time when agricultural workers were earning 7s a week. Berry Barton was also a centre for lace-making and trading. The lace barons also owned shops involved in the system of payment in goods from their shops, known as 'truck'. Lady Trevelyan in Seaton took up the cause of the workers, but by 1870 the boom in lace fashions was over and the lace-makers had to turn their hand to other trades.

The Hangman's Stone (see map) from Hutchinson's entry in his 1857 diary as recorded in from *Travels in Victorian Devon*:

> *The story runs to the effect that a man one night stole a sheep in one of the fields near Branscombe. In order to carry it he tied the forelegs together and then leaning forward he placed its body on his back, with the legs round in front of his forehead. When he got to the top of the lane, feeling tired or wishing to readjust his burden, he sat down with his back against this stone with the sheep resting upon it. The animal now made an effort to get loose, and in its struggles shifted its legs down over the man's face and under his chin. With his back against the stone and unable to extricate himself, the weight of the sheep pressing against his throat soon served to strangle him.*

Given that they might as well be hung for a sheep as for a lamb (the kind of justice that was prevalent in the country), this interpretation of the stone serves as a warning tale for those still involved in poaching.

Other green lanes in the area

Those towards Seaton and Beer.

Links

The Jurassic Coast bus, the X53, runs along the top road here.
National Cycle Network 52.

Question

At **(5)** watch out for some realistic-looking animals which are always a potential hazard for walkers. What are they?

NEWTON POPPLEFORD to SIDMOUTH

Along the raddled lanes

OS Explorer 115

This walk takes you along the old Ottery Road, where very little traffic passes. We are truly walking back in time here, as the farmhouses which flank the road display different styles of buildings reflecting changes in farming fortunes, mainly from mixed, to dairy, and then to arable. There are quite a few green lanes to your left which you cannot negotiate, but the two that you can are quite unique. I have

marked with crosses alternative routes to follow, as this area is full of ways towards the Otter and down to the sea.

Conditions: Steep, rocky and muddy in places.

Distance: 3-4 miles.

Starting point: SY 094895. There is a bus stop on both sides of the road at the entrance to Four Elms Fruit Farm, Bridge End. Negotiate this tricky crossroads.

(1) Here is the first farm, situated on what is known as the Old Ottery Road, the aptly named Northmostown Farm. There is an 'Unmetalled Road' signed here to the left and another two green lanes close by, which you pass.

(2) There are lush meadows to your right bordering the Otter as you walk along the valley bottom.

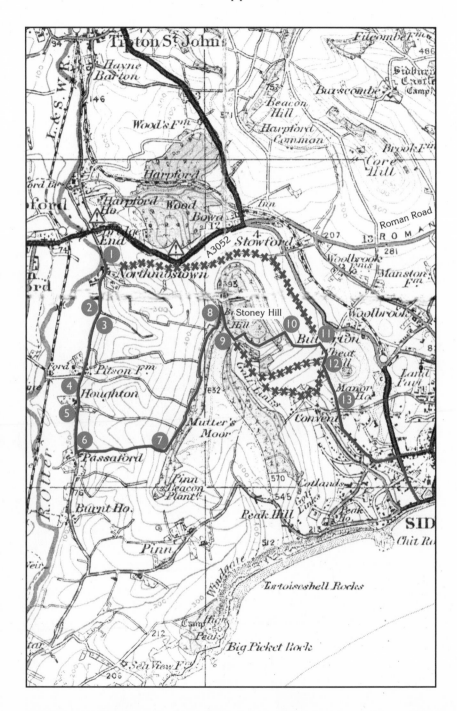

(3) Kitts Cross is unmarked and you can make out a blocked-off lane here. Keep going to Pitson, just before which there is evidence of another neglected lane.

However, at (4) take the lane to the left which runs along the side of the farmhouse. This is not Calm Lane, but does have a very still atmosphere. It is Pitson lane, which is wide and sycamore-lined. It is well used by the farmer, and has another sunken lane paralleling it to the right. There is holly here and gorse on the hillsides. You will have to return to the road again, as the lane becomes impassable, but there is a track going over the fields towards Otterton Ridge.

As you continue along Old Ottery Road you can see the iron bridge which crosses the Otter just by Ashtree Farm, where a beautiful example of the species stands in a triangle by its entrance. There are many legends attached to the sacredness of this tree: one was that if you passed a cripple through a cleft ash, then bound up the tree afterwards, the patient would be cured. Maybe it's time to check the famous folk rhyme:

Oak before the ash, we're in for a splash,
Ash before the oak, we're in for a soak.

(6) Continue along the lane passing Houghton Farm, which has an un-negotiable green lane but a fine collection of cob buildings flanking the road. As you go along, the road becomes increasingly sandy.

Here is Pavers Farmhouse on your right. It stands in an old orchard which stretches across the road by the entrance to Passaford Lane. There is a year 2000 parish boundary marker here, and a wooden fingerpost for the public right of way to Mutter's Moor. It begins at a width of six feet and climbs, gently narrowing as it goes, becoming increasingly sunken as it cuts into the sandstone. There is a welcome stile at the top where you can sit and look down on the Otter Valley and the Hawkerland and Harpford Commons in the distance. This landscape, with its long hills crowned with woodland and bordered by meadows sweeping up to them, is typical of the east Devon landscape.

(7) Crossing over, there is a sign towards Mutter's Moor up through the woods. But we are not going to visit the moor, named after a famous smuggler, so keep left to enjoy the woodlands here. When you reach the main path, turn to the left and enter a well-trodden woodland track along the ridge to the bottom of Bulverton Hill. As you go there is much to see, both within and out of the wood. Sidmouth's nineteenth-century historian Orlando Hutchinson

pointed out that Bulverton was higher than High Peak; he found a cairn of dry flints within Bulverton. Compare the map with the present-day one and you will see that the acreage of woodland has been increased towards the south.

(8) At this footpath crossroads, for those wishing to return to Newton Poppleford I have marked an alternative route to Northmostown which goes down a lane giving stunning views towards Harpford and beyond. For those going on to Sidmouth, keep to the right for a short stretch along the base of the hill where a stony lane widens out.

(9) By a bridleway and footpath post, turn left into Stoney Hill which follows the contour round. A shorter way down (but a little dangerous) can be followed by keeping straight on down – this is one of east Devon's county roads – with the golf course flanking a fine beech-lined way. This has quite a distinct camber, and is lined with large sandstone blocks. The base of the woodlands here reveals banks constructed like a ha-ha to control the movement of deer.

(10) At the end of Stoney Hill, turn right and follow the bridleway signs to the right. You emerge from the woodlands with a good view over the west end of Sidmouth Bay. After a muddy patch, you come out at the base of Greenway Lane. This is another alternative route back to Newton on an alleged Roman road.

(11) Turn right into Bickwell Lane. This is a winding lane flanked with some fine oaks.

(12) You pass the network of green lanes to Bulverton on the right, which must have formed part of an early one-way system.

(13) At the junction with Broadway go straight across down into Convent Lane, in 1883 the home of French nuns but now a school. Another road appears to your left, which is called Cheese Lane and will take you out seawards too. You will know you are in the right lane when Cheddar Cottage and Dairy Cottage appear at the end.

By the way

The farmhouses that you pass along the Ottery Road demonstrate the end of the cross-passage design at the end of the seventeenth century. This is what Peter Beacham has to say about these houses:

> *Another late variant form are houses with unheated central rooms, Burnthouse, Otterton, where along a two-mile stretch of road there*

are seven farmhouses with different plan types either modified or newly built at this period. The cross-passage is still found in all of them but variations include the central unheated dairy at Burnthouse; the inclusion of a staircase in the dairy outshot at Passaford and within, an added parlour wing at Pitson; the insertion of service rooms behind the hall and kitchen but within the main structure of the house, at Pavers; and the placing of the hall stack in the wall facing the cross-passage at Smiths, with a dairy beyond.

To give you some idea of the speeds at which coaches of the time ran, here are a few facts and figures. In the 1790s it took thirty-two hours from Exeter to London. By 1824 there was a coach running from Plymouth to Exeter in seven hours and, by then because of road improvements the journey between Exeter and London only took twenty-four hours. In 1835 this was further reduced to roughly sixteen and a half hours. Duels between the coaches called 'Quicksilver' and 'The Telegraph' were famous.

Other green lanes in the area

As listed in the walk and also in adjoining circuits in the area.

Links

The Coastal Footpath.

Question

A diamond of a lane. Along one of these lanes you will find a diamond in the rock face. Which one?

SIDMOUTH to OTTERTON

A land once lined with mills

OS Explorer 115

This route takes you out of the town and on to Peak Hill, then drops down by the river Otter. This direction of travel from Sidmouth to Exeter was quite common in the 1830s, and follows the old ridgeway pattern. Although hard to imagine now, Otterton and Okehampton were the only two market towns listed for Devon in the Domesday Survey of 1086. Sidmouth became popular with the gentry during the Napoleonic Wars when they could not travel to Europe. The lanes here have quite low, clipped hedges, unusual in any part of Devon.

Conditions: Very muddy through wooded areas. Steep in parts.

Distance: 4-5 miles return trip.

Starting point: Sidmouth's stunning sea front at SY 125873.

(1) Of course you will be drawn to the sea front, so don't resist. Make for Jacob's Ladder, a former lime kiln, on the sea front at the western end of the town. You pass by windblown sandstone cliffs which, although picturesque to us now, would have represented literally the rock face for many quarrymen in the area.

(2) Leave the beach and climb up to the road for a while, but keep to the greensward passing the dedicated seats as you go. There is a beautiful house to your right and an inscribed stone to your left which reads:

On this hill lived R.F. Delderfield whose inspired writings gained him International Fame 1912-1972.

As signposted, you are now going along The Old Road.

(3) Turn left onto the coastal path at Peak Cottage, where the path is

lined with flints. You go through some scrubby birch woods, but always keep to your left for viewpoints which soon give wonderful views over the coast. Once out of the wood you go through a gate and are out in the open. There are big rolling hills to your right.

(4) You soon enter another wooded area, and pass along the lane by its side along the edge of Peak Hill, which is 500 feet above sea level – and not always tree-clad. This becomes the ancient ridgeway route, acquiring the name of Bar's Lane. It is a main trackway along a ridgeway leading up to Dumpoon Camp and Hembury Fort. The lane widens to the width of two carriages as you progress.

(5) You come to a green lane on your right which, despite its narrowness, claims to be a county road. Do not take this, as it is worth continuing along to the red-bricked Sea View Farm and just beyond, before taking the next green lane.

(6) It is well-cobbled, and takes you into the folds of those big fields you saw from afar. The hedges are low and well-clipped. You meet up with the county road again to your right (7), but keep to your left and you will come to a minor road on its way to Sidmouth.

(8) Cross carefully into the Public Right of Way, Rydon Lane.

(9) This is a varied and beautiful lane leading down to the River Otter, which was silted up by 1530. There is some holly in this lane, and it is quite straight in part. There are views to Collaton Raleigh on your right. Then as you descend where the lane narrows by the barn there are good views over towards Bicton College Lodge and its distinctive tree-lined avenue. There is also a good view of the menacing monument to John Coleridge Patterson, Taylor Coleridge's cousin who became a missionary, and was murdered on the Indonesian island of Nukapu. The natives did this in revenge for what had been done to some of their fellows by white slavers.

(10) The river suddenly appears, and you can follow it to Otterton by crossing here or keeping high up over the river. If the latter, you will soon have good views of the church tower before you. This way takes you down into the village green with the mill to your right, the pub to your left and the road to the church in front of you. The 'drang' which runs through the village by the pavement is popular with different species of wagtails.

(11) This church has the most striking grey slate pillars supporting Beer stone arches, under which there are some interesting copies of the register of burials on display. There is also another record of a Sidmouth town receiv-

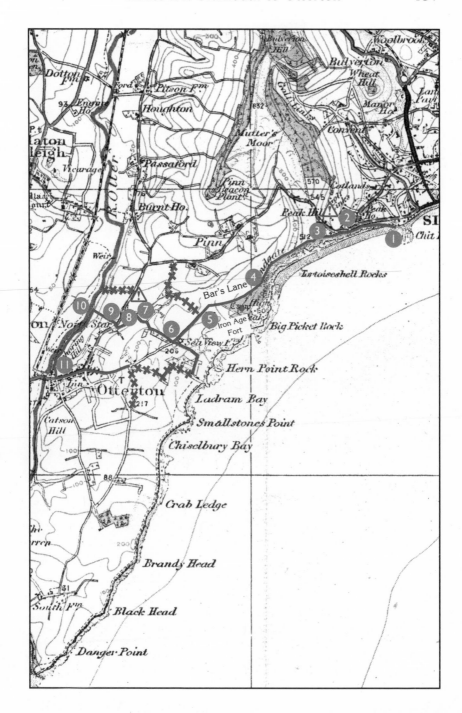

ing alms from property held elsewhere, in this case the Poor's Field at Crediton. You can return by ascending towards Ladram Bay, then following the lanes as indicated back to **(6)** at Seaview Farm.

By the way

There is an interesting piece of highway history to enjoy nearby: the Bicton Scriptural Direction Post. It is a tall, brick-built construction, which you see when leaving Tipton on the B3178, and was erected in 1580 by the Sheriff of Devon, who had to order the burning of a witch. It stands where three parishes met at that time. In 1743 Lady Rolle added plaques naming the places to where each road leads.

Other green lanes in the area

Routes in this book around Sidmouth.

Links

There is a bus every hour from Otterton to take you back to Sidmouth, or take the alternative green lanes back visiting Ladram Bay as you go.
The Coast Path.

Question

What is the name of the trees which line either side of Bicton College drive?

The Old Sidmouth Road.

EAST BUDLEIGH

A heart of oak in Raleigh country
which never went to sea

OS Explorer 115

This route's green lanes are distinguished by the number of very large oak trees lining them. It is natural that we should associate them with the hearts of oak which became ships and thus led to the defeat of the Spanish Armada, and much more besides. But one of the longest-lived oak beams from East Budleigh never went to sea; it is eighty feet long, and runs through five rooms supporting the house where Walter Raleigh was born, Hayes Barton. It is a lasting tribute to man's powers of conservation. Like many a rampaging explorer into the New World, in later life he began to see man's folly of looting the natural world for his own ends. He put it thus:

> *Earth is the stage,*
> *heaven the spectator is,*
> *who doth behold*
> *who'er doth act amiss.*

This route is circular, but can be extended down to the sea or up on to the commons.

Conditions: Muddy in places.

Distance: 2-3 miles.

Starting point: SY 067845. If you enter the village from a northerly direction notice the statue of its most famous son, Sir Walter Raleigh, which did not appear until 2006. Close by is the Church of All Saints, where the beautifully carved bench ends record a whole way of life dating back to medieval times. There is a ship here and some sheep-shearer's shears, which today might be replaced with piglets' tails, as you will see later on in this route. Within the church is the answer to the question on page 142. Go down the High Street, with its attractive leat running alongside, to where Middle Street begins. On the right here stands Wynards Farmhouse, opposite the primary school.

(1) Turn right here and go through the farmyard, one of whose buildings has a plaque which shows that it was built by Mark Rolle in 1879. The green lane ahead marked 'Unsuitable for Motors' is the one you take. It runs neatly below the line of the surrounding hills and has a good sandy surface. You can almost hear the deadened thudding of horse's hooves cutting up to Hayes Barton, but not with news of the Armada – just ordinary concerns of a more domestic nature such as the use of common land hereabouts, or the poaching of deer or rabbits.

(2) You now come to a green lane crossroads and, carefully looking both ways for waggons or horses, go straight across. The surface becomes flintier as you climb, and there are patches of red brick too. The lane sinks more as you ascend.

(3) At the top you reach a footpath crossing with, on your right, sweeping views over to the sea and Sidmouth. (You can see where you took the way to High Peak on Route 24.) Be on the lookout for deer here, which are so well contained within the woodlands around, and were revered by Sir Walter: his coat of arms is supported by two of them.

(4) At the top, pause for the view and go to the left over a stile which brings you out on to Shortwood Common. Keep to the centre path, and enjoy the gorse and many species of butterfly attracted to this dry warm haven. The feathery limbs and tightly-packed cones of larches are all around you until you reach the far side.

(5) Here you go down a green lane, veering to the right along the forest edge where, to your right, there is a large bank with every appearance of a ha-ha. These were constructed to keep deer within their master's grounds and to discourage poaching.

(6) As you turn right here, there are fewer conifers next to the lane, and glades of bluebells under towering pollarded oaks dapple the light on your way straight ahead. This was Raleigh's wildwood paradise, very different from the jungles he explored in South America, and to which he longed to return.

(7) Where the woodland ends you follow a lane, Shortwood Lane, which becomes cobbled and ideal for the timber waggons which must have passed this way.

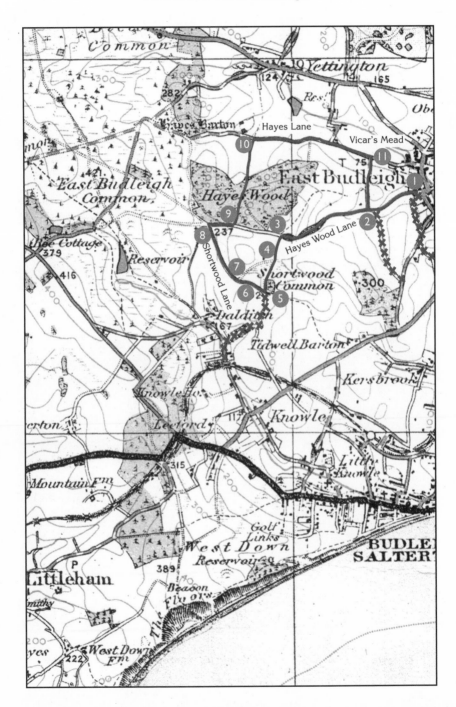

(8) Turn right at another green lane junction and follow along the woodland edge.

(9) There is a footpath sign on your left here which takes you along a darkly wooded ride leading to Hayeswood Cottage at the end. You now come out onto fields, with both sides full of free-range pigs and chickens.

(10) At the end of the footpath take a left to view Raleigh's birthplace, Hayes Barton, built in 1484. It is not open to the public. However, as a grown man (at six feet, quite a tall one for Elizabethan times) he never realised the dream of purchasing his birthplace. Return to (10) Hayes Lane again and then back towards East Budleigh on your right. After Mill Lane to your left you come to Vicar's Mead on your right. It is thought that Raleigh attended school here.

(11) Turn right into the green lane here, and a gentle climb along disintegrating tarmac will take you up to enjoy good views again. Drop down to (2) again, this time turning left back to Wynards Farmhouse again. Whilst on this corner you could turn right to purchase some freshly grown produce from two elderly stallholders here – you will not regret it. They run their wayside market in a merchant adventurers' manner, worthy of the Elizabethans.

By the way

The story of Raleigh is as well known as is the painting which shows him on the seashore close by listening to a sailor's stories. Raleigh was Queen Bess's favourite, and fell out of favour when he married Bessy Throgmorton from Devon. Another of his local connections is to be found in Route 40.

Other green lanes in the area

There are those leading down to Budleigh Salterton, overlooking the Otter.

Links

There is an hourly bus service from Exmouth and Sidmouth.
Routes 23 and 24 in this collection.

Question

In the church you will find the name (an Elizabethan-sounding one) of Raleigh's stepmother, spelt backwards. The primary school is named after her too. What was her name?

Northwards from
NEWTON POPPLEFORD

From Four Elms to fruit farm

OS Explorer 115

This walk is placed in the middle section of the Otter Valley and covers some varying habitats but always with big sweeping views towards the sea. There is some minor road walking but a lot of long-green-lane ('Unmetalled Road') walking too.

Conditions: One or two inclines, but in the main fairly level walking.

Distance: 4-5 miles.

Starting point: As always it is a good idea to visit the local church, in this case St Luke's, where a church has stood since the fourteenth century. Its exterior is made up of Beer stone, sandstone and some local 'pobbles' – for the name Poppleford comes from the presence of these smooth brown pebbles in the area. In terms of highway history, we also have here the oldest tollhouse in Devon, built in 1758 and part of the Lyme Regis Turnpike Trust. Keep to the raised footpath by the church and make your way down to the bridge, passing some interesting thatched houses and an old village pump. Cross over and take the Back Lane at SY 085895. You will pass two footpaths – one to the left and another to the right on the bend, by a splash of purple comfrey.

(1) Ignore these, and take the next footpath to the left, which is wide with purple fumitory on its banks; one of the many orchards in this area peeps through the hedgerow. Go through the metal gate and into a narrow lane through the wood. A hazel tunnel gives way to conifers; here follow the sign of the purple foxglove, the East Devon Way to the left.

(2) Out of the wood, follow the meadow line to the right (notice how large oaks in hedgerows begin to dominate the skyline from now on). Go over the stile and into a narrow low-banked green lane which curves with the contours of the cultivated land surrounding it. You are climbing slightly, without noticing it; elm appears in the hedge.

You come out into (3) a minor road, with a bungalow called Harleston on your right. The road continues to climb and is hewn out of sandstone; carved out is 'love for Clare' – but from whom? All we can say is that he was not a car user, and was able to linger in this minor road for a while.

(4) Through a wood the road widens as it descends into Venn Ottery, a little hamlet where the small church of St Gregory has stood for over 500 years. There are monuments to the Mundys here, who were charitable in Ottery too.

(5) On the bend by the noticeboard go straight up the first of the many unmetalled lanes in this circuit on your way to Fluxton. The lane has a 'pobbled' surface, as do most here. There are views of Tipton St John to the right. There is a slight climb, then at a grass triangle you come to a staggered green lane crossroads.

(6) Turn right, and then sharp left where the bank is covered in a frizz of clipped holly, dwarfed by big oaks along the lane. To the left there is a plantation of rowans, maples and cherries. The lane narrows and drops down to the road at Metcombe.

(7) Go straight over the road here and up by a farm to your right where the lane goes up and over giving views of East Hill rolling back into Ottery. You reach the next road again by passing Perry Cottage with its delightful verandah to your right.

(8) Turn left up another green lane, wide to begin with then narrowing down a little as it descends, flanked by more huge oaks and patches of rosebay willow-herb standing upright in the hedgerows.

(9) You come out onto the road at the thatched Higher Fluxton Farm. Turn left, then take the minor road to your left signed to Metcombe again. Continue along with patches of comfrey either side to the next junction with a grassed road triangle. This seems to be one of the few areas in Devon that does not have an individual name for a junction.

At (10) turn right towards Aylesbeare; there is a footpath along the verge here which will take you to the footpath at (11) on your left along a drive through a beech wood. Keep to the left just before the house and go down

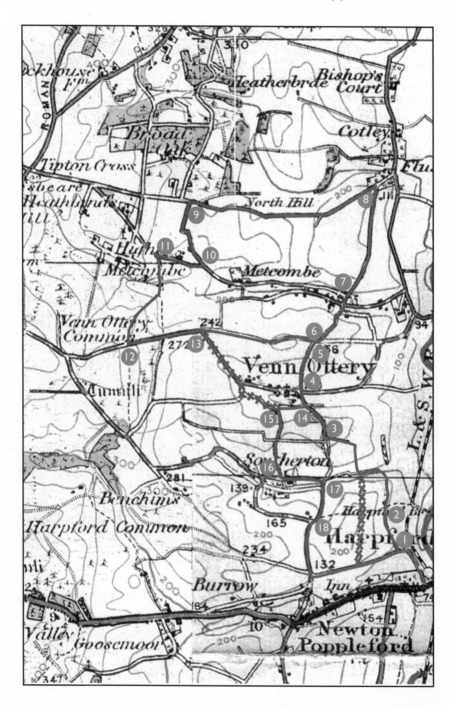

into a magical area by a stream complete with a deserted house. Cross the footbridge with a '34 FP' numbering, then up left into Venn Ottery Common, an RSPB reserve of twenty-four acres of wet and dry heathland with a raised bog area, willow and birch scrub set in the old field patterns of this common land. There are Dartford warblers here – not in sight or sound when I visited in spring, but I did see a bright pair of yellowhammers. Follow the signs up and over to the road.

(12) Turn left and in front of you are more stunning views, this time towards the sea and Sidmouth.

(13) At this signpost take the green lane to your left, which is a Constitutional Boundary and is flanked by magnificent oaks. You now return to numbers (6), (5) and (4). This time at (4) take the unmetalled road to your right with idyllic views of St Gregory framed in field maples to your right.

(14) Where the lane forks you can go straight ahead and extend your walk along yet another unmetalled road to moorland, or turn left passing a cottage called Si. It is sharp and steep, then even and narrow – a packhorse lane used for transporting, amongst other things, fruit harvests from this area.

(15) You come out opposite Harleyford. Turn left by a magnificent group of cob-built barns. At the next un-named junction (16) turn right, then just before the next junction look out on the left, for a foxglove sign at (17). This takes you up and into the orchards divided up by whispering poplars, and a group of five to six foot high elms forming wide hedges, for we are in the valley of the Four Elms Orchards.

(18) You are now walking by rows of apple trees. Keep to the footpath as indicated, then go through a kissing-gate at the bottom and work your way back to the High Street by ways which once would have carried fruit and market-garden produce down to the station at Newton Poppleford.

By the way

Newton Poppleford once had its own railway station, and saw a lot of local produce, such as early peas, along with its apples and cider, being taken up to London. It stands on a ridgeway at the foot of the hills in the north, providing a safe communication highway for feeder lanes from the coast. This village at the foot of the long slope up towards Sidmouth stands at the gateway to east Devon.

Other green lanes in the area

There are so many in the Otter Valley, in particular around Collaton Raleigh and Otterton.

Links

Buses from Exeter to Sidmouth and beyond here pass at least hourly.
The Otterton (no. 24) and Ottery St Mary (no. 27) Routes in this book. The East Devon Way.

Question

How can you tell an elm leaf from a hazel or beech leaf?

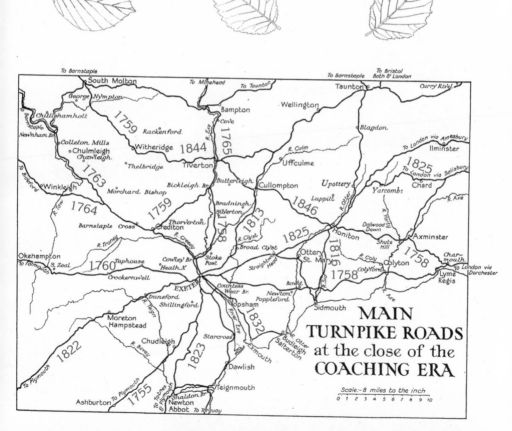

OTTERY ST MARY

A mariner's ancient haunting

OS Explorer 115

This walk takes you along the banks of the River Otter via many valley lanes, woodland views of the Moors and tumbling weirs, as once explored daily by Ottery-born Samuel Taylor Coleridge. In the canon of writing about walking (when considered apart from walking for or to and from work, worship, trade or warfare), Coleridge's writings at the end of the eighteenth century have shaped how generations of walkers approach the countryside. He was a great walker, capable of covering forty miles a day, but don't worry – this circuit is based closely round his home town.

Conditions: Slippery and steep along the river, some minor-road walking.

Distance: 3-4 miles.

Starting point: Of course, you will want to start at the Church (SY 099956) and more particularly at (1), the plaque to Coleridge (1772-1834) in College Street. Proceed up Paternoster's Row. (2) There are some fine eighteenth-century houses built in the year of 1776, when there were riots led by those just wanting bread to eat at a reasonable price. (3) To your right is The Ridgeway; continue down here until you come to a dead-end sign. There is a lot of elm in the hedge to the left here.

(4) At the very end on the left, notice the beautiful cob house built by craftsmen who are bringing back these buildings into the landscape from which they come. Follow the footpath signs along the field edge and down through a gate into a short stretch of green lane lined with pollarded oaks and beeches.You come to a T-junction; take the minor road to your left by Holcombe.

(5) Turn right. This is a gentle climb up to West Gate Hill, at 275 feet, with sessile and pedunculate oaks trimmed back to form the hedges.

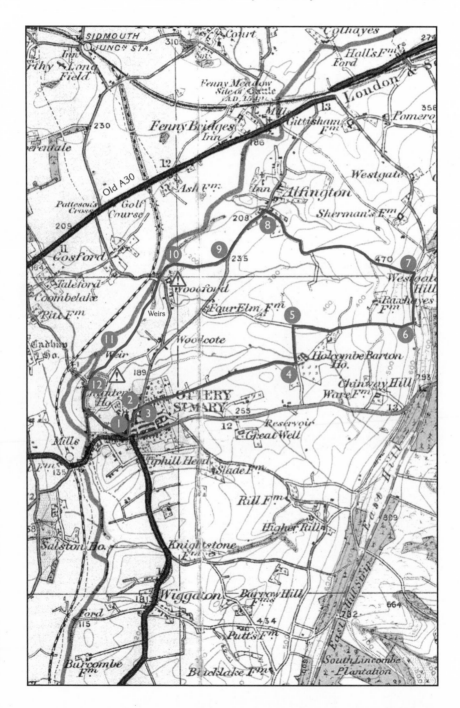

(**6**) Take the third Right of Way sign to your left at the top by East Hill Farm. You pass along the edge of bluebell woodlands with views across the Otter Valley and beyond to Dartmoor and Exmoor.

(**7**) At the end of the woodland you come out onto a wide, drover-like road, which stretches for over a mile before you. There is an open gully running nearly all the way to your left; the surface is dry and paved with flint. Vehicles on the two A30s below slide along as if on wires. Towards its end the lane becomes very sunken and, in spring, passing a large patch of white dead-nettle to the right, you come out by a small bridge into Alfington.

(**8**) Turn left along a short but fairly busy section of a minor road before entering another green lane to your right. (Alternatively you may choose to go north towards Fenny Bridges.)

(**9**) There is no hedge on the right. It finally appears just before the end, formed by masses of intertwined dog roses – delicate but thorny, fragrant and a little frightening should you stumble into them. This is maybe what happened to young Coleridge:

> *I ran away, to a hill at the bottom of which the Otter flows – about*
> *a mile from Ottery. – There I stayed; my rage died away; but my*
> *obstinacy vanquished my fears – & took me by the arm – I expected*
> *a flogging – I ran away – There I stayed.*

Later in life he spoke of how the bellowing of the cows in the fields around him forever haunted him. Being haunted was a big inspiration to the poet, but a distinct handicap in his personal life.

(**10**) At Woodford Bridge you are close to where animals first crossed at Gosford, mentioned in a document of 1249. Cross over the road here and follow the river along to your right. At some point you cross fields above the river. Along the river and at the path's edge are great cave-like hollows of red sandstone – perhaps the inspiration for Coleridge's Pixies' Parlour in his sentimental ode 'Songs of the Pixies'. A Pixie Fair is still held every year. (**11**) You pass the weir to your left with a fine view of Cadhay Bridge to your right, which was washed away in 1801 – some of those rocky caves which heralded 'Kubla Khan's stately pleasure-dome'.

(**12**) You come out by Cadhay Bridge Farm. Follow the road to the left back to the Public Amenity Car Park and Coleridge's church.

By the way

There are many famous sons of Devon who haunt the lanes where they once walked. There is definitely something haunting about Coleridge's lands around Ottery. Although he was sent away to school in London, his memories of his childhood home town remained.

With unclosed lids, already had I dreamt
Of my sweet birth-place, and the old church-tower,
Whose bells, the poor man's only music, rang
From morn to evening, all the hot Fair-day,
So sweetly, that they stirred and haunted me
With a wild pleasure, falling on mine ear
Most like articulate sounds of things to come!

It was recorded that as he walked with others (sometimes including Wordsworth), he would cross from side to side of the footpath as from subject to subject; he appeared to float in air, to glide on ice. He always questioned the place of man in the landscape, and never excluded any he might meet walking in it – after all, he was the author of rebellious pamphlets, supporter of the French Revolution, the inventor of 'pantisocracy', and very much aware of the community of subordination around him. The eighteenth century is a time of strange contrasts: after Ottery Mills' success making common serge, they were to change to the production of silk handkerchiefs and ribbons in 1823, and continued to employ a large number of workers. However, throughout history luxury goods have usually been in fashion for only a short time; then the factories close down, causing significant local unemployment.

Other green lanes in the area

Around Otterton and Whimple.

Links

There are many buses between Exeter and Honiton which go through Ottery. To Route 5 via Fenny Bridges to Feniton.

Question

What kind of animal was driven across the Ford at **(10)**?

TEIGNMOUTH to HOLCOMBE

Diversions, dramas and smugglers
who knew the ropes

OS Explorer 110

This walk takes you back to a time before the railway chuffed its industrial presence along the seafront; a time when the residents of Teignmouth kept as far away as possible from the sea, settling in the hills and valleys above. All the place names around here which contain the elements 'teign' and 'head' refer to the tenth of the produce from a hide of land which was payable to the church. But of course the sea is often within sight and sound, as is the A379. This is a circular walk which links up easily to both bus and train.

Conditions: Steep in places.

Distance: 2-3 miles.

Starting point: SX 947732 in The Triangle where all the buses come and go. Turn left into Regent Street and notice on your left French Street, where there is a plaque to commemorate the French landing here in 1690. 200 great shots were fired at east and west Teignmouth by the French, and 300 houses were destroyed. They moved on to Shaldon, where 116 houses were destroyed; they entered churches and tore up bibles and prayer books.

Turn left into Dawlish Street for a look at the church of St Michael the Archangel, which looks out to sea and dominates any views you may have on circuits which look down upon this old sea port. Go through the church-yard and turn left.

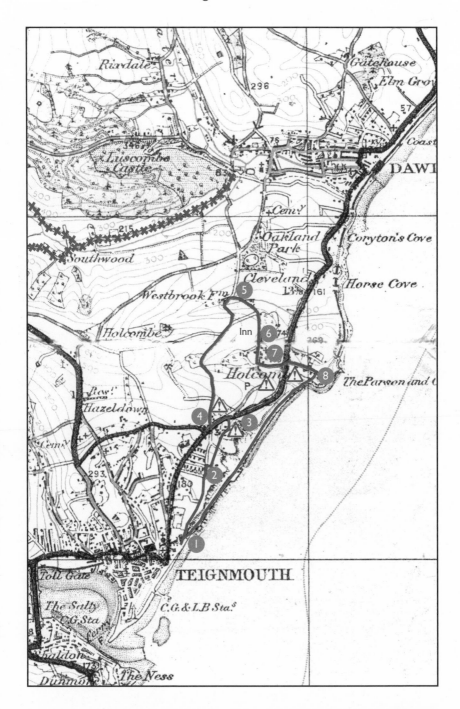

(1) Take the steep path towards the back of the Yacht Club, known as the East Cliff walk. It is a dark path upwards passing over the railway line at first, then walled in by red sandstone. There are patches of white campion and the occasional smell of garden privet as you ascend seawards, following the footpath signs to the right through a gate into a cobbled green lane. At the top by a large house there is a footpath sign pointing to the left through a cast-iron gate made by Burden of Teignmouth, a memory from the port's industrial past.

(2) Ignore this and veer to the right where, on a bend, there is a good view back towards Shaldon. You go over a stile into a meadow with a view of a large building to your left which looks like an abbey. Cross another stile into a green lane crossroads. Keep straight on, following the wall to your right. This continues for some way and feels like a manorial boundary, broken only by intriguing doorways or a sudden lowering of height which reveals the truth that you are in fact passing through a modern housing estate. At its end you come out onto the A379 with a bus stop conveniently to your right.

(3) Turn left here with your eyes on the tall tollhouse opposite, and cross over. This was built by the Teignmouth Trust between 1823 and 1826, and is one of a pair. This one would have caught traffic from Teignmouth going towards Exeter and perhaps still hoping to use the old agricultural service lane into which we now step.

(4) Oak Hill Cross Road soon runs out of houses, and there is a dead-end sign leading you into the green lane on the right. The oaks after which it is named appear at fifty-yard intervals. You pass Middle Holcombe House on the right, then go down over a stream. The elm trees have now risen to some height, but most have grown together to form a dense, uniform hedgerow with a some holly, hazel and elm intruding in places. At the top there is a large elm to your right by a footpath sign and a green lane T-junction. Keep straight on.

(5) Turn right into a well-cobbled lane. As you descend there are views over towards Dawlish Warren and beyond. You come down into the surprising hamlet of Holcombe, once an import point on the through road from the coast up towards Exeter before the turnpike, the railway or the A379. At the crossroads by the Castle Inn, go down Holcombe Road. The former village school (now the Church of St George) is well worth a visit. No doubt when their school closed the children were not too pleased at having to walk over to Dawlish every day. However, this would just have been taken in their stride, literally.

(6) At the next junction by the plane tree turn left along Hall Lane, which

becomes Rope Walk. The making and stretching of rope from locally-grown hemp was once a thriving trade near Teignmouth, providing all the ropes for the boat-building industry. This is a sign that we are nearing the sea again. Cross over the A379, by the bus stops.

(7) Go down into Smuggler's Lane. This is wide and very sunken, with another huge stone wall and a gatehouse at the top. You then go under the railway line, which is exciting, but it may not always be possible to get up onto the South West Coast Path which runs alongside the railway line (constructed in 1844). Here we meet the meshed-in red Devon cliffs sprouting grey and yellow helycrisum, pinks and sea kale.

(8) If you make it on to the Coast Path, turn right and notice the rock formations of Clerk and Parson: the diminished Clerk opposite the Parson – or is it the other way round now, as the seabound rock is diminishing? You come to the Groyne, thought to derive from the French word for snout, and the really impressive patch of tamarisks by the big sign for TEIGNMOUTH that you see from the train. The sea is wild here, and cormorants skim faster than trains along to where the warning flags are placed.

By the way

This section of the coast is probably most familiar as you go by in the train between Newton Abbot and Exeter. The red sandstone cliffs which tower over you are in fact fossilised sand dunes, made of sand from the Permian period, 290 to 206 million years ago. The sand started life at the bottom of the sea on gravelly beds, and was blown up to these heights which tower over you.

Other green lanes in the area

Dawlish (no. 31) and Bishopsteignton (no. 30).

Links

There is a regular bus route running round the coast from Newton Abbot into Exeter. The trains from Exeter often stop at Teignmouth and Dawlish. The South West Coast Path.

Question

You pass through plenty of red seaside hills on this walk, but a small fragment, carefully labelled, comes from other red lands. Which one?

SHALDON to RINGMORE

Farms, firkins and some fishing

OS Explorer 110

This is a walk which takes you along the Teign by Shaldon, then up into some very ancient farming country along some long green lanes (with an undercover story based on smuggling, rather than farming or fishing). There are three significant green lanes on this walk and some minor-lane walking too. Alongside this route, to the west, I have indicated another set of green lanes well worth exploring.

DOG ROSE

In Henry VIII's time, when Leland was writing about the area, he thought that it was 'no great thing'; but Gerard Manley Hopkins, a Victorian Jesuit and poet, thought otherwise. Who will you agree with at the end of this walk?

Conditions: Often steep and muddy in parts.

Distance: 4-5 miles.

Starting point: SY 932724. Begin in Shaldon where the bridge enters the town. This was built around 1827 and collected tolls until 1948. The South Devon railway came to this stretch of the coast in 1844.

(1) Before you set off along Riverside, notice the milestone here which lists the distance from the coastal towns of Torquay, Brixham and Dartmouth in miles, furlongs and poles. The nearest inland town (Totnes) is listed, but not Newton Abbot. Turnpikes were set up with trade in mind, and Newton Abbot was not commercially important then; its connection to the railway in the 1890s brought it into prominence.

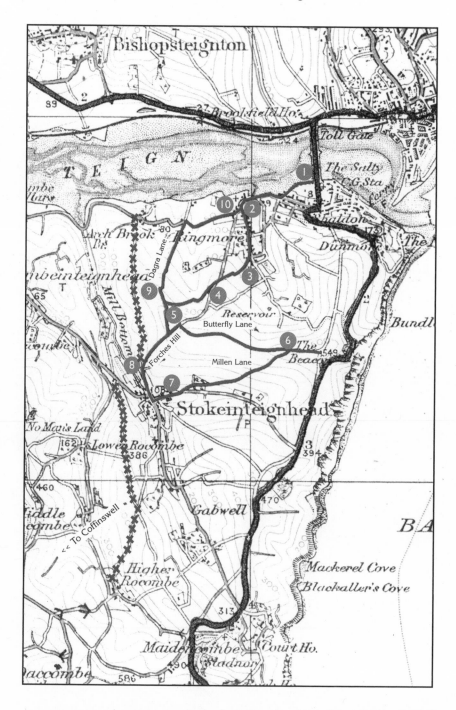

Pass by the rather run-down King George V's Playing Fields (1910-1916) with their royal coat of arms, through an alley to the left following the Templer Way sign, then to your right along the estuary side road. Here you will see cormorants, shelducks and our now permanent exotic residents, little egrets. Pass Salty Lane to your left and climb up, following the road round to the top of the bend.

(2) Take the Higher Ringmore Road to the left. Along here there are some fine examples of how important agriculture was, and still is, to coastal settlements. There is Old Stoke Cottage (watch out for the cattle pound on the right), then there are Home Farm, the Old Cottage, Vine Cottage, Hill House Cottage, Cape Cottage and Teigngrace Farm. As you climb, elm takes over in the hedges and you are entering the lands where agricultural workers have been walking about on foot since Domesday.

(3) Take the first green lane to your right and start to climb up on its broken tarmacked surface towards Ringmore Heights. The lane seems to curve more than is indicated on the map, and there are dogwood, hedge maple, elder and ash here, all festooned with dog roses. A clump of whispering poplars heralds the end of the lane, where the surface becomes cobbled.

(4) Turn to the right and then down into Forches Hill, where you turn left and climb towards the beginning of Butterfly Lane, passing the renamed 'The Palmes' (shown as 'Forches' on the map). This name often refers to the site of a former gallows. Given that the area was known for its smuggling activities, this is not surprising. There are accounts of how the locals became involved in smuggling. Kegs which had been stored in Stoke were taken down to the beach, where the smuggler

HONEYSUCKLE   B,

> *would be met upon the beach by a considerable number of the badly paid labourers of Stoke. Each man took 2 kegs weighing 70lbs in all and proceeded to Coombe Cellars over fields, not lanes.*
>
> (from Thornton, 1840).

Each labourer was given five shillings for his load by the contrabandist – roughly half the weekly wage of an agricultural labourer at the time. Nevertheless, it must have been considered worth risking your neck for.

(5) Turn left into the cobbled Butterfly Lane. It is steep to begin with, but soon becomes level and there are sweeping views: first towards Dartmoor, then down to Shaldon Bridge, then out towards the church of St Michael's looking out towards the sea. On a clear day you might catch a glimpse of the white cliffs of Beer. There are quite a few butterflies here even today, but perhaps the name comes from the fact that the lane 'butts on' to the ancient strip field systems on both sides. There is a muddy patch before the lane links up with Millen. Just after here there is a group of ashes and two elms. Continue along here, and notice how rich and wide the hedgerow is. There are dogwood, maple, elm, elder, dog rose, honeysuckle oak, and patches of the musty-smelling wood sage. Continue along to the Beacon, where there is a trig point up in the hedge. You are standing above Labrador Bay. Until the end of the eighteenth century the Newfoundland fishing industry was very important in this area: 40 to 60 vessels set off from Teignmouth every year between February and April. They would drop off goods in Spain and collect salt for the fish which they would bring back. St John's was the port in Canada where they anchored. They then went out in small boats from June onwards to catch cod with lines. These were salted and spread out to dry. Cod livers were pressed to produce train oil. The race was then on to see who could get back with the fish to the European markets first. The industry declined because of 'bye-boatmen' who did not sail across the Atlantic, but used smaller vessels in local waters. This enterprise, together with our wars with the French and the loss of the American colonies, leaves us today with the legacy of the place names in this area – and communities in Newfoundland with distinct south Devon accents even today.

(6) Return to the beginning of Millen Lane on the left. There are views over towards the Rocombe Valley which are reminiscent of times when the whole of the Teign valley was densely wooded. There are holly and cherry growing in Millen Lane, and the hedgerows all around you are very wide. The lane is cobbled, but its sandstone surface is deeply gullied in parts. The poet Keats must have explored such lanes as these when he was staying in Teignmouth and came to the conclusion that:

You may say what you will of Devonshire, the truth is it is a splashy, misty, snowy, foggy, haily, fluddy, muddy, slipshod County – the hills are very beautiful when you get a sight of 'em. (1818)

(7) Where the curve and the gradient is steepest, note how the large cobbles are used to hold back the stampeding lines of packhorses. Towards the end of the lane you pass a weighbridge next to the farm buildings; then turning sharp left, you come into the road which leads down to Stokeinteignhead with the Church House Inn in front of you. It is worth visiting the Church of St Andrew to notice how stone from Beer Head (which you might have been lucky enough to see when up in Butterfly Lane), forms the capitals of the columns here. They are beautifully decorated, mainly with leaf patterns, and one has two heads with swept-back hair – green men pulled through Ringmore's thick hedgerows backwards. Return to the village and take the road towards Teignmouth.

(8) Turn up into Forches Hill on the right, noticing the coat of arms crowned with what look like elephants on the back of Rock Cottage as you ascend. You pass Teignharvey Road, a green lane to your left, and there are views over the estuary.

(9) Take the next green lane to your left, Dagra Lane. It begins with cobblestones and a row of tall ashes which once must have been layered. Where it joins a lane to the right (which you do not take), it narrows down as it goes straight on. The surface is eroded, and there is a lot of overhanging vegetation. There is some evidence of packhorse ledges here, formed to allow the packs to pass without being damaged. On a bend by a small copse there are holm oak and spindle, and you sense the atmosphere of former users; pause before you turn the corner and see how close the waters of the Teign are below you. The lane erodes underfoot here, and to the right there is evidence of a double hedge-bank, an indication of a parish or manorial boundary. Turn right at the bottom by a cherry tree. You pass by Devon Valley Holidays and down into Ringmore-on-Sea on your way back to Shaldon.

(10) Take time to visit the small church of St Nicholas (a saint associated with the sea), which has stood on the edge of the river since the thirteenth century. If it is closed, then there is always the beautiful cherry tree to sit by and admire, and to remember the thriving fruit farms of this lush area you have just explored.

By the way

The market gardeners of Shaldon go back a long way. In 1741 some 340 individual fields for cultivation, each of a furlong length, were listed; many of these are still discernible in today's field patterns. Remember that the old coaching and droving ways to Exeter from Torquay lay along the coast. Cattle and sheep were driven from Maidencombe: they came over Fuzzy Dee and along Commons Road and across the Salty at low tide.

Other green lanes in the area

There are plenty to choose from here, some of which have been indicated.

Links

The Templer Way. The South West Coast Path. You can walk westwards as indicated towards Coffinswell and the Whilboroughs and Kerswells of Route 33.

Question

How many feet (or metres if you prefer) is The Beacon above sea level?

IDEFORD to BISHOPSTEIGNTON

From Roman road to Bishop's Palace

OS Explorer 110

This is a very satisfying route, as you walk through many different kinds of habitat and in the footsteps of many travellers from across the centuries, from Roman soldiers to postmen. It is a linear walk, which can be done in either direction and linked with other adjacent walks. However, it is always more exciting to walk towards the sea with the anticipation of a glimpse of oceanic blue from a background of rolling hills.

Conditions: Steep and stony.

Distance: 5-6 miles.

Starting point: SX 884779, Waperwell off the A380. This is a great name for a starting point, and one easily accessible off the bus route from Kingsbridge to Exeter. When you double back on yourself to go under the road in the direction of Ideford and Luton, take a detour to the left and there on your right below Waperwell Cottages is a clearly defined section of road which is part of a rare stretch of Roman road in south Devon which runs from Exeter to Teign Bridge. This deeply sunken section of Roman road is distinguishable by its agger, a slightly raised causeway built to cross wet ground, similar to the one on the Dawlish Route (no. 31). It is a fine example of a holloway, which reveals its Roman origins by its width. The Roman road runs on up to Dunscombe Bridge and Beggar's Bush as indicated on the map.

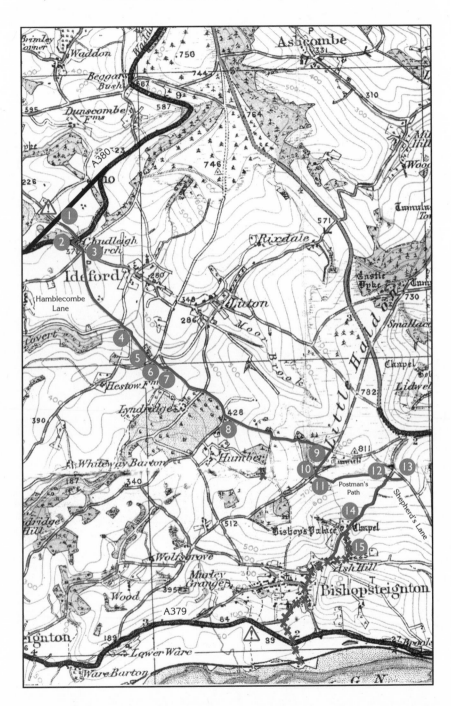

(1) Back on route to the right, you soon come to the impressive Ideford Arch (2). As soon as you are under it you come to the brow of a hill where no fewer than six ways meet by the white pebble face of Longthorne Cottage. Cross over, then take the green lane to your left.

(3) This is the beginning of Hamblecombe Lane. It is a cart-width lane, giving views out to the left over the Ideford valley, whose church tower makes a brief appearance. There is some cobbling and a lot of field maple and holly. Where the lane bends and climbs down there is a lone Scots pine, reminiscent of those giving welcome to drovers who passed along the way, as well as being a route-marker tree. As you descend the tall hedgerow trees disappear, and there are a lot of broken flints at your feet. You come out at the foot of the lane where a triangular barn stands, and a beautiful pond.

(4) Go straight over and into another section of seaward lane. (From this point you can go up to explore the village of Ideford.) Keep to your left at the top, and climb up to a minor road.

(5) Turn left and the sharp right.

(6) This is a short link section of packhorse lane which brings you out on the road to Lyndridge.

(7) Turn right and you soon pass the entrance to a great house, now known as Lindridge Park, once owned by Sir Peter Lear in the eighteenth century and also by members of the Templer family, but burnt down in 1963. It once boasted an impressive elm-tree drive, which has been replaced by beeches (which feature in the landscape all around you). Notice on your right, just past the entrance, a gate with great granite pillars on either side which must have once been topped with lamps and now bears the name Avenue Park Acres. At Lindridge Lodge on the right there is another green lane to the left, which will take you down to Luton.

(8) This is the beginning of Three Tree Lane, leading up to Humber Down and passing through Haldon Park. Notice at least one Scots pine remaining, which gives us this drovers' marker-lane feel again.

(9) Turn right at the end opposite to the golf course and walk down to Gypsy Corner.

(10) Turn left, and almost immediately on your right on the opposite side of the road is White Well Park.

(11) Enter the woods here, and there you have it: the view of the sea for which you have been longing. If you want to go down to the well itself, there is a path running down through the woods which will bring you to this cir-

cular two-metre-deep pool set in limestone rock and famous for curing fevers and for telling fortunes. All along the ridge of Postman's Path (the local name on the map) there are views out towards Shaldon and to the hills traversed in previous walks. There is a lot of birch and oak scrub coppice interspersed with patches of gorse and whortleberry, habitat for the small copper butterfly in late October. To your left there is springy heathland, peat beneath your feet and a deep ditch to your right; you are walking along not only a postman's path but one of the shepherds' ridgeways which eventually leads down into Shepherd's Way at the end. Towards the end of this ridge notice how the steep hill towards you often lies in shadow and yet is subdivided and crossed with hedges and signs of intensive agriculture.

(12) Turn right at the end here, and then sharp right again.

(13) This leads into Old Walls Hill, leading to Bishop Grandisson's Summer Palace built in 1332. This is a very steep way down which twists and turns; you pass through a small copse with an enclosed stream almost cascading down into the road. The old walls emerge to your right, built from red sandstone; the tallest of them is the back wall of the Bishop's Palace. It is said of this Bishop that he rose from layman to Bishop in five days (one wonders whether he fell from favour just as quickly). This is also the site of the remains of the Chapel of St John. Just past the Palace is Bishopsteignton Vineyard, a viticultural enterprise which would have been applauded by the Bishop.

(14) Take the footpath to your left along a wide lane which brings you to a farm. Carry straight on, well under the lee of the ridge hill now, and plunge into a green lane indicated through a signposted gate.

(15) You come out onto a minor road to Ashill, where you turn right for Bishopsteignton.

Continue along to the crossroads signed with Radway Street, Ashill and Old Walls Hill. From here you can pursue your way to the estuary via Combe Lane, looking out for the footpath which will take you down over the A379 to Trinity Point on the estuary.

If you go straight back to the Teignmouth Road, then make sure you visit the church of St John's and especially Bishop Grandisson's Sanctuary Chapel in the grounds of St John's and some tombstones going back to the fourteenth century. Here wrongdoers were granted sanctuary before they fled over the water.

By the way

The ruined Bishop's Palace, the White Well and the Sanctuary Chapel bring to mind these words of the Venerable Bede:

> *And one of the king's chief men presently said:*
>
> *'It is as if thou wert sitting at a feast with thy chief men and thy thanes in the winter-time: and the hall is warmed, and outside it rains and snows and storms. Comes a sparrow and flies swiftly through one door and goes out another. So is the life of man revealed for a brief space, but what went before, and what follows after, we know not.'*

from the Venerable Bede's *Ecclesiastical History of Britain* (c.673-735)

Other green lanes in the area

There are some leading back towards Kingsteignton.

Links

Buses pass here from Newton Abbot and Torquay.
The station at Teignmouth.

Question

What is the name of the high headland visible on the other side of the estuary?

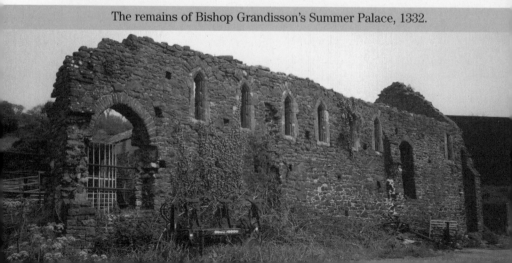

The remains of Bishop Grandisson's Summer Palace, 1332.

Dawdling above DAWLISH

Sweet-scented memories still here today

OS Explorer 110

It is always difficult to step back from the sea, but this route takes you up to sights and scents that match the red-fringed sea below. There is some footpath and minor-lane walking, as well as plenty of green lanes to explore. This is a beautiful hidden area, where the scents of the flower industry still dominate.

VIOLET

Conditions: Muddy underfoot.

Distance: 3-4/5 miles if extended towards Mamhead.

Starting point: SX 965785. Whatever you do, don't miss the black swans in The Lawn area in front of the sea at Dawlish. Turn westwards, climbing up towards Teignmouth on the A379 along West Cliff.

(1) You come to a footpath sign near the top to the right along Barton Lane. There are some fine Monterey pines along here, you pass along the backs of the many opulent villas in this area of the town – opulence brought through the railways and the growing tourist, market-garden and flower trade. Nicholas Nickleby was born in a farm in this area, and Dickens loved the place, as did his readers. You go over a road banjo marked out in yellow lines, and, ignoring the footpath sign to the left, come out **(2)** into West Close. Turn right here, and be careful as you cross the road towards the foot-path leading to the huge parish church of St Gregory. Notice as you enter another railway connection here. To the left is a screen stone construction with gothic arches by Sir Gilbert Scott, who also designed the red K2 telephone box and reached his pinnacle by designing St Pancras Station in London.

(3) Turn left through the lychgate and into a public park, keeping to the left along the top by the waterfalls and over a small bridge.

(4) Turn right into a minor road, passing Stocklands and Emperans Hill on your right and staying on the road which climbs to your left leading to Long Lane. As you progress there are views of the impressive cedars and beeches to your left which form part of Luscombe Park. In the hedgerows there are maple, hazel, elm and beech trees. The perfumes begin as you brush by clumps of lemon balm. You pass the entrance to Fairfield House – now Oakwood Court College – on your left. There is a magnificent black poplar standing high in the garden of Littleton where there is an intriguing notice for the Holiday Fellowship. There is a well in the wall on the right, and a group of cottages at Dawlish Water. The Old Mill House is to your right and on the left Weston Farm buildings stretch out along the valley. However, there is a lane to the left leading down to the Linhay, a Veterinary Rehabilitation Centre, which carries the only traffic you are likely to encounter along this long minor road.

(5) At the junction, pause a while and take a deep breath before you start to climb to the right, for in front of you are the greenhouses and the fragrant scent of Whetman pinks. Climb up through the hazel-tunnelled lane which gives you views of Starcross and beyond to Warboro Plantation.

(6) Turn left along a short stretch of lane lined with oak trees planted equidistantly along the horizon to mark out the way.

(7) This brings you to Five Lanes Cross. Go over the minor road and up into the green lane to your left. It has a sandy surface, and is hemmed in by bracken. On the right there are wide views over to Kenton, Starcross and Exmouth.

(8) At a junction with a footpath sign to your left, pause to see how tired you are, and whether you want to go forward along this green lane. If not, then turn sharp right into a ruddy green lane which twists down into Pitt Farm. This is one of the most beautiful and well-used lanes in all of south Devon.

(9) Turn right into a minor road with grass growing in its centre and a fine holm oak tree on its rise. The hedgerows in summer are full of blue scabious. (10) At Five Lanes, cross over towards (6) again.

(11) Continue down into Long Lane to your left. It is cobbled, and lined with oaks. There are views out towards the plant nurseries on the plains flowing down to the sea and one named after the famous Devon Violets. You enter a muddier, narrow stretch of the lane which passes through woodland

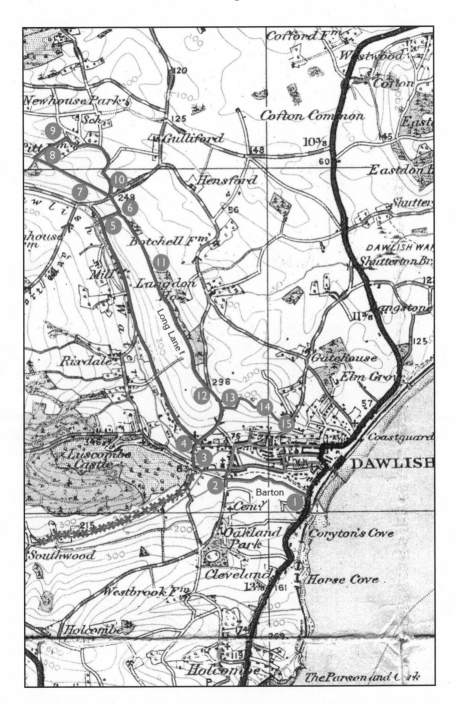

where there are some conifers, holly and sweet chestnuts growing tall.

(12) Leaving the green lane you come out briefly onto a minor lane and cross over taking the footpath sign.

(13) There is a footpath sign on the left. This goes down into a green lane, which continues to your left, but you cross over the stile and out into a meadow with more sweeping views of the coastline towards Portland Bill.

(14) At the end of the meadow go straight over, and by a seated area there are coastal views to the west towards Berry Head. You go down through a small length of green lane tunnel and then through a housing estate, keeping straight on.

(15) Take the footpath to the right; here are the Monterey pines again, and a leaning stone wall which takes you out almost to the sea. It joins a deeply sunken red-cliffed road, Stockton Hill, where you turn right and cross over by the South Devon Inn and come out opposite the Tourist Information Centre (something the first Victorian visitors to Dawlish seemed to manage quite well without, maybe preferring to keep this beautiful place as secret as their own bathing habits. This is the home of the first bathing-machine in the country!)

By the way

Before the flower industry developed here, hemp was grown in these valleys to provide the ship-building industries with the ropes they needed. In 1891 the first batch of violets was sent to Covent Garden from Crofton (see the Starcross Route 32), and by 1938 it was estimated that over 200 acres were grown locally. The variety favoured was the 'Princess of Wales'. Over a hundred people were employed, and sixty varieties developed. It was said that the railways and the extant coaching services would slow down in order for the travellers to breathe in the scented air as they passed through.

Other green lanes in the area

The Starcross (no. 32) and the Teignmouth (no. 28).

Links

Buses and trains run from Exeter to Dawlish. The South West Coastal Path.

Question

There is a farm above Dawlish which dates back to the signing of the Magna Carta. How do you know?

STARCROSS

On the waterfront no more

OS Explorer 110

This is a circular walk which takes in the exhilarating waterfront of Starcross, once a lot more involved with trade along its waterfront, and the low common lands of Haldon. There is some minor-lane walking involved.

Conditions: Most of the green lanes here are unsigned, and are steep and overgrown in places.

Distance: 2-3 miles.

Starting point: The railway station on the estuary at SX 977818.

(1) Cross over the A379 from the station, and make your way to the post office on the Strand to your left. Take the first right up Warboro Road and take a detour along here to visit the church of St Paul. Not unsurprisingly you will notice that there are quite a few sea captains buried here.

(2) On the bend take Brickyard Lane to the right and follow it through until you reach a 30 m.p.h. restriction sign at Heywood Drive to the right. Go straight along here, and be amazed by the acres of Starcross allotments to your right.

(3) You will come to a T-junction and a triangle (with a felled tree stump) with Derwent Cottage on the left. Go left here and follow the lane up towards Warboro Plantation. The lane soon becomes potholed and ever greener in the centre. It rises slightly where there is a fully grown elm tree to the right.

(4) There are breaks in the hedge here to the left where you can look down over the Warren, as the view – across fields where square hay bales are stacked in late summer – is clear down to the sea. Toadflax, mallow, tansy and fleabane grow in the hedges, and there are clumps of blue fleabane in the

standing corn. There are views across to Mamhead Mansion. You start to double back on yourself here down the lane and turn to the right into a green lane.

(5) This is a narrow lane with some cobbling. On the first sharp bend you can see an older small field pattern gradually disappearing from the area. Large oaks appear in the hedges, and there is a narrow drainage gully along one side. The lane narrows towards the end and is taken over by tangly blackthorns, honeysuckle, briars and brambles. There are flintstones underfoot now.

(6) Turn left into a rapidly greening minor road, which takes you down to (7) where a tollhouse dated 1839 (restored in 1974) stands at the junction. Directly opposite is an overgrown stretch of green lane which you can take to get up onto the Cofford group of lanes. However, it is easier to turn left here towards the coast and take the next green lane.

(8) You turn right into an ascending lane, wide and semi-metalled, lined with sweet chestnut trees to the right and well worth the climb. Once at the top keep to the right where more elms appear and keep straight on.

(9) This lane contains holly and dogwood and more and more wildflowers as you descend: thale cress, coltsfoot, white campion and yarrow are just a few. Before you the Roman agger banks up to the left of the lane. There are views towards Mamhead, and its church stands out clearly in the distance.

(10) There is a muddy patch to negotiate here, and you can either choose to descend and make a loop around Westlake Farm, or return up to (9) and then turn right into an overgrown and rapidly descending green lane with willow-herb and water pepper growing at its end. This is a reminder that Cofton Creek once stretched out for a mile inland. Just before Cofford Cottages a big marker oak tree appears to the right.

(11) You pass a big MOT centre on the right and cross over the A379 at the crossroads. The cross itself stands high up on the right of the bank. Go past the farm and holiday camp.

(12) On the right is the church of St Mary's. This ancient chapel was first rescued in the fourteenth century, then fell into a ruinous state. It was restored by the Courtenays in 1839. Follow the road and you come to Cockwood Marsh on the left.

At (13) go straight up Westwood Street to the top and into a green lane. Keep to the right through woodlands with some limes and hornbeams.

(14) Turn left into the road at the top and down into Cockwood. There

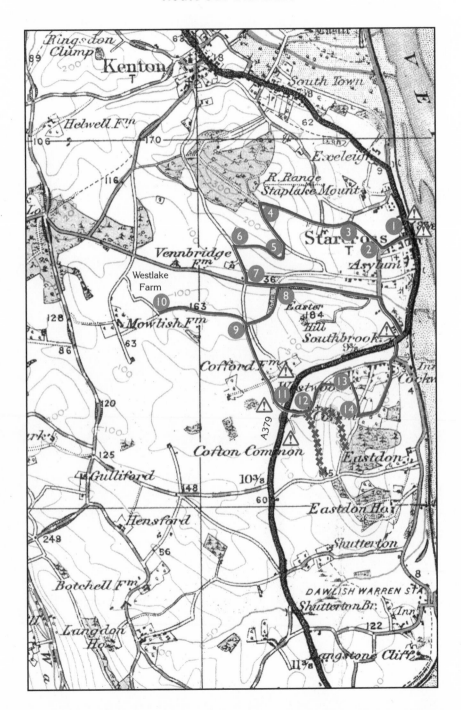

are some fine views over the estuary and up as far as The Blackdown Hills to your left as you descend. Here behind the railway track and by their own stretch of the Exe estuary are the pubs which you glimpse from the train. Be sure to pay them a visit before following the coastal footpath signs back to Starcross. An annual strawberry fair was held "on the sod" at nearby Coften at the end of June. Baskets of strawberries were laid out along the sea wall and visitors came to eat as many as they could, washed down with cider.

By the way

The estuary crossing here gets its name from the stairs which were built by the Bishop of Sherborne in the twelfth century; travellers and pilgrims moving between the abbeys of Buckfast and Sherborne were given free passage on the ferry. This free passage continued under the licence of the City of Exeter until 1846 when it was sold to the South Devon Railway. As a port, although it never really fitted that definition, it first developed in the seventeenth century. Coal from Newcastle was brought in here in 1632 on canal lighters to Woolcomb's Island, now gone. This was where canal lighters left their loads for the bigger ships to collect and take up to Topsham. When Celia Fiennes visited in 1698 she wrote of the channel "where the great shippes ride".

In those times everything was cheaper by sea, as the eight miles from here to Exeter (then over difficult roads) would have cost twenty shillings a ton, whereas by sea it was only three shillings and fourpence. There was always a small trade in corn, coal and cider and oysters too, which are still harvested here today.

Other green lanes in the area

Dawlish (no. 31), Teignmouth (no. 28) and Bishopsteignton (no. 30).

Links

There are buses and trains which run between Exeter and Newton Abbot and pass along here. The RSPB Exe Estuary Reserve. The South West Coast Path.

Question

There are some industrial archaeological remains here not connected to the former quay. Where are they?

The WHILBOROUGHS and KINGSKERSWELL

Fine flour and rum for naval captains and the birth of an artisan industry

OS Explorer 110

This walk is perilously close to Torquay, and yet if you were taken blindfold to Compton Castle where the walk begins, you would believe yourself to be in the heart of the countryside. The Whilboroughs and Kingskerswell remain rural thanks to the rolling landscape in which they have developed, but, as you will find, they are criss-crossed with former busy ways. There are many routes here which reach out to and  from the coast, along which goods were hauled by packhorses. Throughout the walk you will catch glimpses of Long Burrow Windmill, constructed maybe with a view to providing more bread for the troops in Torquay who were ready and waiting for Napoleon.

Conditions: Steep and rocky in places, with some standing water.

Distance: 4-5 miles.

Starting point: SX 867648. You may wish to visit Compton Castle before setting off. Facing the castle entrance on the right are the beginnings of a green lane with a double boundary defensive bank. Take time to enjoy the swifts and swallows wheeling up and down the leat which runs by the road.

(1) The footpath begins steeply opposite the Old Farmhouse, and it is not long before you can stand back and admire the views of Compton Castle below you. Its imposing defensive façade was an addition to a manor house dating back to 1520. It was home to Sir Humphrey Gilbert, Walter Raleigh's half-brother, and is still lived in by the Gilbert family.

(2) There is a high stone stile to climb, which takes you into another level. The pollarded oak tree to your right must be at least 200 years old. The route of the footpath is well signposted, and runs along the field edge and then across to the back of West End Nurseries with its many greenhouses. Turn left into a minor (but busy) lane, and notice the double row of oaks which mark the parish boundary between Kingskerswell and Ipplepen.

(3) Turn left into Windmill Lane, bearing the sign 'Unsuitable for vehicles'. Here is the converted Long Burrow Windmill, North Whilborough. Originally built of red sandstone, it stands 450' (137 metres) high in a position which commands impressive views over Dartmoor to Haytor. Before setting off into the lane, look back towards Moles Cross and you will get a good clear view of St Mary Church, Torquay.

Steep and muddy in places, and very narrow and overgrown, it does not seem possible that residents of Ipplepen once used this lane as part of a regular short cut to Torquay – sometimes on bicycles! However, it does have a cobbled surface in parts and traces of tarmac towards the Whilborough end. Glimpses of North Whilborough appear to the right. In this section it forms part of the parish boundary. Test out the hedge-dating theory on page 86 here.

(4) The lane emerges sharply onto the road, where you can see from the map that further mills of the water-driven variety are traceable to the left; but this walk lies to the right down into North Whilborough. This hamlet, like Compton, retains open leats by the road, much loved by birds. There are some fine houses and cottages here. At the crossroads, go past Mill Lane and Whilborough House to your left. Try not to disturb the geese opposite.

(5) Follow the signs round to Long Barn Holiday Cottages and the John Musgrave Heritage Trail. This lane is in part tarmacked, but where it joins the footpath sign to the left it breaks up again.

(6) Turn left onto the limestone surface revealing itself in both pink and startlingly white chunks. This lane is lined by a stone wall and leads towards Whilborough Common. It is well paved too, and has a causeway feel to it. First you go through a mysterious, ivy-festooned ash copse with some large hawthorns too. You are close to prehistoric settlements here, and the field

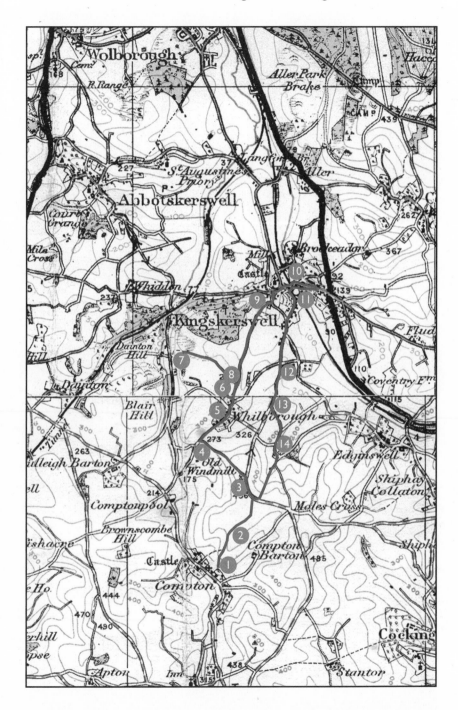

patterns were established during that period.

(7) Once out onto the common there are views over into Bickleigh Quarry, worked for its limestone. Retrace your steps from here and notice the square field patterns and the towering oaks in the lane. Turn to your left at (6) into a well-used lane. On your left at Kerswell Down Hill is the site of a Roman coin hoard which was discovered in 1838. On the right is the entrance to a small wood owned by the Woodland Trust. After this the lane descends in a very zigzag pattern until you emerge by Beechwood House and the 'Unsuitable for Motor Vehicles' sign.

(8) Turn left, then over Greenhill Road and down into Church End Road.

(9) The fifteenth-century church of St Mary, with a leat running by its entrance and sometimes full of the King's cress, present in the Kingskerswell place name, is to the left here. This is the way that traffic to the Aller Potteries would have gone.

(10) Keep to the right here passing The Tors as you go, and cross over the railway bridge leading to the bottom of Rose Hill. Notice here just one of many old pressed aluminium green-and-white street signs around the village. Look out for Daccabridge Road on the right over the road. This is a detour well worth taking, as it will lead you to a small packhorse bridge. On the left parapet on the stream side of the bridge you will see a plaque which gives its date. You end up in Kingskerswell playing fields. Before this level, seven-acre area was generously given to the public by Mr Adams in 1952, it was where cattle were kept overnight before moving on to Newton Bushell market or being driven down to the coast. This area was known as the oxen fields. Retrace your steps and cross over the railway bridge again.

(11) On the corner turn left into Yon Street, passing Station Cottage on your right. Go past the junction with Greenhill Road and notice the number of Scots pines in the area, a sign of welcome for drovers. The way is white-lined for the safety of pedestrians as you climb up, passing Edginswell Lane to the left. You enter Huxnor Road and pass a United Reform Chapel with a 1930s-style back window made from rich bottle-green glass. Could this be the work of the Kingskerswell Cottage Art School, established in the 1880s by John Phillips, the great craft educator? At the top there is a crossroads with a telephone box, Gourders Lane to the left and a sign to Whilborough to the right. Go straight over here and continue for some distance.

(12) On your left here take the sharp turn into a very well managed short section of green lane with some dramatic hedge-laying on the right-hand side.

(13) You come out at the junction with Saturday Lane to your left. Keep on down into South Whilborough with the fine farmhouse to your left. There are many limestone buildings here. Keep to your left and notice the number of apple trees around you – so many in fact that in 1888 Mr Hill made a huge pie from the fruit and carried it to St Marychurch annual fair at Torquay. When this fair ceased, the tradition of the pie continued in Marldon, with some interruptions. Today it is celebrated during the last weekend in July where you can see the pie cut ceremoniously by the Apple Pie Fair Princess.

Left: Coffee pot in early Kerswell Daisy pattern with rough 'orange peel' finish. White clay. Potter's Mark 'T'. *c.* 1888.

Right: Early kettle delicately decorated in Persian pattern. White clay. Unmarked. *c.* 1885.

South Whilborough is an isolated hamlet which lies hidden behind the Torquay to Newton Abbot bypass. At the bottom of the lane to the left stands a farm with a hand-pump still in place by the wall.

(14) As you proceed down to your right, there stands a row of cottages which may have been useful because of their isolated position: under one of them runs a passage sixteen metres long with a small chamber, all hewn from the red sandstone of the area. Given the proximity of Ye Olde Smoky House, a public house in Marldon famed for its smuggling activities, perhaps this little still-forgotten hamlet provided a convenient resting-place between Paignton and Newton Abbot for storing contraband.

(15) Opposite the Colliers Barton, turn right up Woodpark Lane with its typical sunken lane appeal and red earth and stones underfoot. You must labour on upward until you emerge by Moles Cross.

(16) Turn right at the top of Woodpark Lane, passing Style Park Gardens and take up the return footpath on the left again and (2) and (1) back to Compton Castle.

By the way

The Cottage Art School Movement belonging to the Kerswells, inspired by William Morris, began in the 1890s and continued into the thirties:

Here's Coffinswell and Kingskerswell!
And here's for Abbotskerswell too!

'Tis where we merry craftsmen dwell,
And wondrous is the work we do!

This is a refrain in praise of the Aller Vale Potteries, which, as well as producing the usual quantity of roofing tiles, pipes, garden edges, chimney pots, bricks and flower vases, under the direction of the philanthropist John Phillips set up Cottage Art Schools where young people and farm labourers at slack times were encouraged to make pottery to their own designs. It arose here as the Kerswells already had a strong tradition of cottage industries dating from the eighteenth century, when woollen yarns were spun in Kingskerswell and woven into worsted at Abbotskerswell. String, rope and sack-making was undertaken in the villages and flax grown in the fields.

Other green lanes in the area

Those leading to Coffinswell over the A380, equally magical and strangely silent.

Links

There are buses between Newton Abbot and Torquay that pass close to Kingskerswell. The John Musgrave Trail. The Two Castles Trail in *Exploring Green Lanes in the South Hams*.

Question

What is the date on Daccabridge plaque?

Long Burrow Windmill, as photographed in 1980.

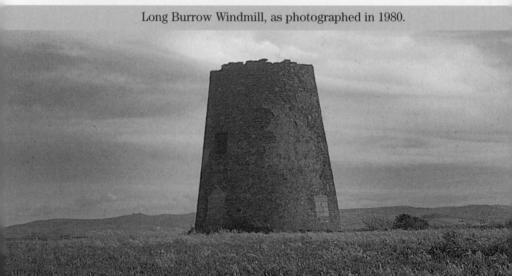

EAST OGWELL
to DENBURY

The fort which holds a secret, and has Celtic connections

OS Explorer 110

This walk takes you along footpaths and minor roads which are bordered by far busier ones. The proximity of Dartmoor cannot be ignored, nor the pattern of roads which once led from there towards markets and the sea in the south. The route includes a visit to the all-dominating Denbury Hill Fort. There is an extra route given which takes you over the A381 into Abbotskerswell, and eventually you can follow green lanes through to Kingskerswell, tracing connections to The Cottage Art School movement. (Look for a plaque on a house called Thatchers on Vicarage Road on the way to the Priory in Abbotskerswell, if you take this route).

Conditions: Some mud in lanes.

Distance: 3-4 miles.

Starting point: SX 853707. Beginning in Newton Abbot the safest way to get to East Ogwell is by leaving the old Turnpike Road, now the A381, which has been running between Totnes and Newton Abbot since 1832. Go through the park almost opposite the almshouses on this road, and through the grounds of the National Trust's Bradley Barton.

(1) The footpath is lined with some horse-chestnut trees at least 150 years old. Cross the bridge over the River Lemon, and turn left with the town mill leat running to the right by your side. There are quite a few willows here. Keep following the leat as you come out into an open space where there is a

small weir and an iron quay for controlling the flow. There is a granite bridge over the leat.

Keep following until you pass the entrance to Bradley Manor, a medieval manor built in the 1420s and now owned by the National Trust. Go into the woods on your left here, crossing over the River Lemon by a metal bridge. Keep to the right and follow the footpath signs up and over some steps, then a stile. You pass some signs indicating deep excavations – be careful. There is a lot of holly and oak here, and carpets of dog's mercury. This plant has perforated leaves to gain as much sunlight as possible from its position on the forest floor. You are walking through Emblett Hill, and you come out by the ford, where the mill once worked.

(2) Turn left up this winding minor road and you arrive at the top, passing Paddocks then Ridgewood. There is a thatched cottage on the corner called Torre. You are in Mill Lane, and come out by the Old Bakery. Turn left here if you wish to go up to Ogwell Green, which has good views over Dartmoor, dominated by Haytor. It is also a treat to find a village green of this size in Devon.

(3) Turn right and go straight down to the centre of the village with the usual signs of former trades preserved in the names of the cottages you pass – take Spadger's, for example. This is a dialect word meaning 'sparrow' – no doubt a lot of them were kept well-fed by the former granary and bakery. The Church of St Bartholomew dates from the fifteenth century. By the stile there is a cross with Celtic-shaped arms and an indentation on both sides for a statuette to have rested. The Celtic connection continues inside, where, built into the gables of the east and west ends of the north aisle, is a sixth-century burial stone enscribed *Caocli Fili Poplici* (meaning 'son of the people' or 'son of Peblig'), dating from Celtic times. Continue up past The Jolly Sailor pub, formerly The Church House Inn.

(4) Take the road to the left. The house on the right-hand corner here has a lintel inscribed RW 1718. His initials can be found on longhouses on Dartmoor too. Elm begins to intrude into the hedges here.

(5) At Stubbins Cross go round the right-hand side of the farm buildings and take the green lane along there.

(6) It twists and turns, following old fields once ploughed by Anglo-Saxon oxen; their name remains in Oxenham Wood, which you pass through having reached the end of the lane, turned left and then left again.

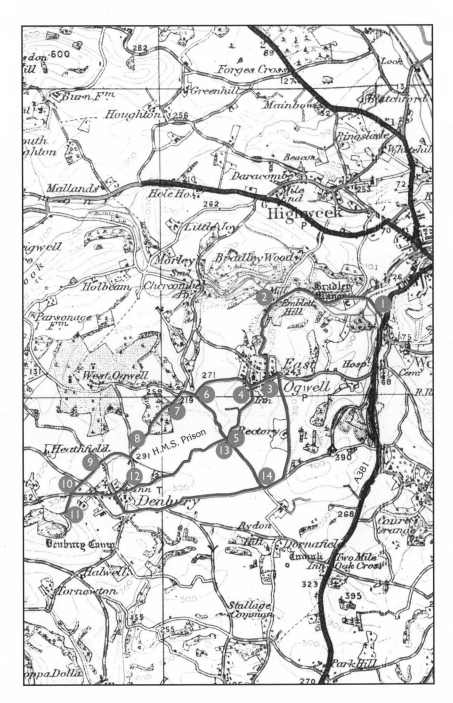

(7) This is West Ogwell Cross. There is a huge pollarded lime here, a sign of ancient woodland.

(8) At Start Cross turn right through the footpath, which begins with paving stones and becomes a green lane lined with ash and views of Denbury Iron Age Hillfort ahead.

(9) With Peartree Farm to your left, cross straight over the road.

(10) Here there is a crossroads. Heathfield is indicated to your right – ignore this and carry on round the base of the fort.

(11) At Denbury Down Cross go straight over the road and take the narrow path which leads up to the top of the fort (see *By the way*).

(12) On your return, turn right into the lane which leads into the centre of Denbury. The most dominating monument here is the water conduit dated 1771 at the crossroads close to the Church of St Mary the Virgin. This church is beautifully maintained, and has some subtle purple-coloured slates for its floor as well as some interesting wall plaques. On leaving, turn left into the minor road which will take you past the forbidding entrance to Denbury Manor House. This is believed to have once been a cell set up by the monks from Tavistock, possibly to keep control of the Celtic religion still active in the area during the early days of Christianity. Carry on past the long limestone wall to your left. On the right is Denbury Green, where some magnificent limes stand. Take the first turning turning to your left along a green lane back to Stubbins Cross.

(13) Between the first turning to your left and Rydon Cross look out for two fully grown elms in a hedgerow in the distance, recognisable by their wedding-cake-tier look.

(14) At Rydon Cross turn left and back to Stubbins Cross to (5) once again. You could now go straight into the heart of Newton Abbot, as the cattle once did by going through the churchyard and over the ford of the River Lemon – a reminder that there were once a lot more elms to see, as the name Lemon is a metathesis of the word 'elm'.

By the way

Denbury Hill Fort, named after the men of Devon, lies at the centre of this walk, and although it is ever-present it doesn't dominate. If I were a painter, I would say that it has been placed to draw your attention between the hills of Dartmoor to the north and the rolling countryside to the south-west. It was used as a meeting-place, shelter and castle for the Dumnonii, the last

Celtic inhabitants of this area, and is dated between 1000 and 300 BC. There is a rhyme collected by Risdon in the seventeenth century which reflects the story of this having been the place where the last King of the Dumnonii, Geraint, was defeated by the Saxons:

Whoever delves on Denbury Down
Is sure to find a golden crown.

This legend is kept alive by another verse which appeared in the local press in 1911:

If Denbury Down were levelled . . . ?
Denbury could plough with a golden share. [the blade of the plough]

As well as being a fortification and a small city, its links with other high points are reflected in the place names around: Halwell Cross, where the next seaward fort stands, and Loddiswell's Blackdown Rings can be seen from the top. After your first hundred yards in the lane, notice where a stream passes which once fed the conduit standing in the centre of the village.

Other green lanes in the area

Towards Woodland and Bickington.

Links

Buses pass along the A381 on their way to and from Newton Abbot and Totnes.
Staverton Walks (nos. 39 and 40), Kingskerswell Walk (no. 33).

Question

Besides the last King of the Dumnonii, there is another kingly connection concerning later invaders here. What is it?

English fyrdmen armed with axes and spears.

WOODLAND

On the edge of quarry country

OS Explorer 110

This is a circuit with quite a lot of minor-lane walking, but they are seldom busy. However, they once were extremely full with traffic crossing from shore to moor. Although The Rising Sun Inn seems strangely placed to us today, it was once at the heart of all journeys in this area.

Conditions: Steep in places, some standing water.

Distance: 3-4 miles.

Dogwood

Starting point: The Rising Sun Inn at SX 791697.

(1) Turn right out of the pub and climb up to Cross Park Cross on the right.

(2) There are good views on this corner over to Ashburton Clump. Take the green lane to your left by the far side of the triangle, and you are plunged into what feels like a very ancient lane, worthy of hedge-dating: there is a lot of oak, holly and dogwood here. As it descends round the ridge of a hill it loses a hedge on one side and runs alongside a very narrow field – known as a quillet plot. It becomes steep, with stony steps towards the bottom.

(3) Turn right into a beautiful, still, twisting lane, which climbs up to East Down, a fine farmhouse looking out over the moor. You soon come to West Down at the top. Walk by with a glance at the variety of farm equipment standing in the barns and yards.

(4) Take a sharp left into a very wide and eventually sunken green lane – unsigned, but from time to time used by 'schoolboy moto-cross' groups.

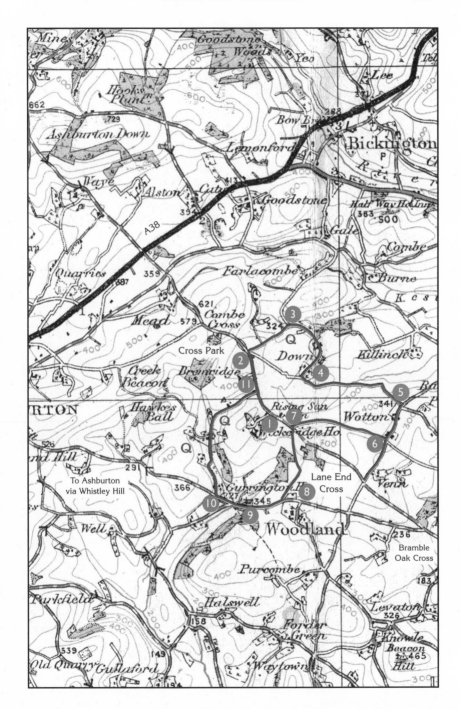

There are good views in all directions once you climb up towards the end of the lane, where a good stretch of cobblestones takes over. There is a very big stand of pines here – some Monterey flanking a field here which could have been a resting-place for cattle on their way to the markets or up to the shielings for summer. As such they would have been easily spotted by drovers, who often brought their cattle from a seaward direction to rest inside the safety of Denbury Hill Fort before going down to the cattle market at Ashburton. They were only using the fort for what it was primarily used when it was built in the Iron Age: as a corral for people and their cattle.

(**5**) At Wotton Cross turn right towards Higher Wotton. You climb up to Lower Wotton.

(**6**) On the corner where a round threshing barn stands back in the yard to your right, turn right into a wide green lane on the bend (unsigned). There are clumps of sweet-smelling marjoram clinging to the steep hedges here. Cobbles soon emerge, and then the lane narrows as you pass an oak gatepost cut square from the tree *in situ*. Look out for views over the moor from here onwards. As you pass under the pylon, look out for a fine Turkey oak on your right, and there are glimpses of pine trees in the distance.

(**7**) Turn right and you will reach The Rising Sun again, which seems oddly isolated to us today but which once stood midway on the routes directly between moor and shore, and between the markets of Ashburton and Newton Abbot. Many cattle were driven this way. You are high up now here, and broom begins to appear in the hedges.

(**8**) There is a footpath here down towards the church. Arthur Mee described coming across this church in 1938:

A remote grey cluster of a farm cottages and a church, it has hills and woods all around and lanes aglow with gold and purple in the spring-time.

(**10**) and (**11**) provide an alternative route back to The Rising Sun.

By the way

Woodland Parish tells the story of how land was prized not just for its agricultural value but also because of its mineral wealth. Records show that the Kitsons, who had been granted land from the time of Henry VIII's Dissolution of church lands – a grand nationwide reshuffling of assets – were the owners of Woodland and its numerous quarries. They produced a superior quality of green and purple slate. At Gurrington there was another slate quarry company, headed by Samuel Baskwill (not unlike Baskerville, a famous fictional character with connections in this area) as its Captain.

Other green lanes in the area

East Ogwell (no. 34), Ilsington (no. 36).

Links

There are buses to Denbury and Ashburton from Totnes towards these routes. The Dartmoor Way. The Ashburton Route. The East Ogwell and Denbury Route.

Question

Where can you see an ecclesiastical use of the region's slates?

Slaters.

ILSINGTON

Where highway users do not go their separate ways

OS Explorer 110

This is a walk full of communications history, and one that really requires two separate circuits to be made within the area. There are the stories of the Templer Granite railway running from Haytor to Teignmouth, of the Potteries, of the Enclosure roads of the early nineteenth century, and of the winter shieling roads for cattle alongside the packhorse trails horning to and from the moor. All these can be included in a circular

or a linear manner. It is a fascinating area, full of industrial and social history, and nearby Bovey Tracey can be an alternative starting and finishing point too. In this walk you will come across some special, locally made fingerposts. Mr Stuart Hands of nearby Bickington has made a lifetime study of these highway monuments, and this walk is dedicated to him.

Conditions: Muddy, rocky and very steep in places.

Distance: 5 miles for the complete circuit.

Starting point: SX 818772, Bovey Tracey Pottery roundabout. This route begins with a detour along a short section of what is known as The Templer Way.

(1) Take the road called Wallfield, leading off the roundabout, and follow along to the crossroads with the Ashburton Road where you will see a sign for The Templer Way.

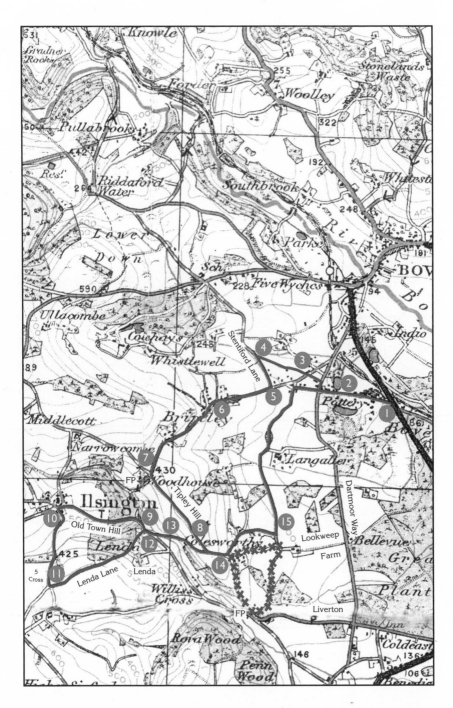

(2) Turn right for The Templer Way, which is signposted to the left a little way up. (3) Turn left along Moor Lane until you come to a bridleway crossing, which is where you enter this industrial way. You come across long granite slabs placed about three feet apart, some still showing the grooves of the iron truck wheels which brought the granite down from Haytor to Teignmouth between 1820 and 1850. In summer the lane is lined with rosebay willow-herb, hemp-agrimony and meadowsweet.

(4) At the end of the lane turn left into Stentiford Lane towards Ilsington, although the Templer Way stretches up towards your right. You will not have gone far before the smell of eucalyptus trees fills the air, from the plantation to your right.

(5) Turn right into Brimley Lane. (6) You are passing the Brimleys, where there was once a thriving community of masons, tinners and weavers, relying on their own bakery and resident craftsmen. Maybe this is because of its position on the old road from Ilsington to Bovey Tracey.

(7) At Woodhouse Cross, where there is an impressive moor stone boundary post set in the hedge, turn to the left and go up into Tipleyhill Lane. It is wide, and well used. To your right views of Haytor can be seen, and the tower of Ilsington church peeps up behind the woods.

(8) Take the road to the right at the top junction and you pass down a rocky road sliced through the wood. Some sections of the hedgebanks are stepped like mini-Giant's Causeways. At the bottom, where it joins the road, (9) turn right and look for the next green lane to your left. This is Lenda Lane, named after a pre-Saxon settlement – but do not take it. Carry straight on and up through Silver Wood and Old Town Hill, and you are in Ilsington. On your right you will pass by a Wilcocks of Buckfastleigh acorn-finialed fingerpost. Pass the Carpenters Arms, and pay a visit to the church.

(10) This is a beautiful church, and in view of what is to follow on your walk notice one of the bosses in the church, which shows three rabbits with joined-up ears. The notes on the church state that this was an alchemical symbol adopted by tin miners, which is to be found at Widecombe and Chagford too. The incidence of the rabbits and hares in decorative form has been traced back to the silk road in China. There have been silver lead mines in the area since 1475. It climbs up gently, passing oak and holly woods to your right.

On the corner opposite the pub, go down into Simm's Lane which runs along the side of a wood. Here on the right is a plaque dedicated to the memory of Sydney Reed in 1996, a member of the Motor Cycling Club. You then have to climb up a very steep slope with an exposed well-written rock face. At the top there is another plaque:

Erected in fond memory of Geoff Mafgette, a dedicated car member trialist, Morgan enthusiast and a gentleman.

Here is testament indeed to the co-existence of lane users.

(11) You come to the junction once known as 'Five Crossways' – a rarity as green lane junctions go. The lanes here all stick to high contours, and reflect communication patterns before the Enclosure Roads were built across Ilsington, Heathfield and its woodlands in 1809. They cut through common land in some cases, and caused hardship for some who lost their rights for grazing and furze-gathering for fuel. Take the lane to your left which runs down by a wood and contains a lot of holly in its hedges. Its steepness is broken up by granite slabs across the path.

(12) At its base turn right. (13) Take the lane to the left which you walked previously between (8) and (9).

(14) Turn left here, with views of Bovey before you. (At this point you may wish to make another diversion down to Liverton and on to Drumbridges. If you do so, notice that where you leave the green lane there is another acorn-finialled fingerpost.) (15) Turn left at the bottom at Colesworthy Cross, where it joins the Dartmoor Way and leads you back into Wallfield once again and the Pottery roundabout.

By the way

Notice the strange name on the map by (16), Lookweep Farm. Was this where the gallows once stood? One of Ilsington's heroes, Thomas Campion, was hung here in 1795. He had led a group of labourers into Bovey Tracey, where they had smashed the mill machinery in a protest against rising corn prices. In February 2008 it was said that there were only ten weeks' supply of corn left in the world. Will we have to Lookweep again?

Other green lanes in the area

The Bridford and Woodland Circuits.

Links

There are buses to and from Newton Abbot and Bovey Tracey. Brown sign cycle route/The Templer Way/Dartmoor Way.

Question

Which type of Right of Way is open to all vehicles?

IVYBRIDGE to BITTAFORD

China clay, shielings, stone rows and a great naturalist's home nearby

OS Explorer OL28 Dartmoor

This walk is triangular. Using the B3213 as your base-line along which the buses pass, you can make the triangle as wide or as narrow as you like. This route takes you along feeder lanes into the moor, to shielings (summer pastures) by ancient stone rows and crosses. It follows in part the old Clay Tramway.

Conditions: Stony in the green lanes and boggy on the moor.

Distance: 4-5 miles.

Starting point: SY 636561. The new Watermark Centre in Ivybridge is where the Library and Information Centre are housed if you want to stock up on information before you set off, or just have a coffee.

(1) Leaving Watermark behind, turn left and cross over the High Street by the bridge and into Harford Road by the River Erme. You pass the block on your right, which used to be a big coaching inn, The London. You reach Stowford paper factory on your left, which clings to the side of the valley in a way that presages the moor. You ascend with the Community College buildings to your right.

(2) At the junction with Cole Lane to your left, cross over first the road and then the railway bridge. There's a plaque set into the wall here to mark

the beginning of The Two Moors Way (TMW) on the 29th May 1976. You pass Stowford House to your left with its beautiful bow-fronted corner.

(3) On the bend take the public footpath to your right, marked "½ mile to the Moor". This is a wide, twisting stony lane with a gully to one side and granite stemming stones lying across it. These stones were put in to break the downward pelt of cattle and packhorses as they descended. Erme Valley Woods become visible to the left.

(4) There are large moorstone (granite) boulders along the stone-walled sides topped by pollarded beeches. The lane narrows, then widens again to at least twenty-five feet in places. There are bluebells under the hazel clumps, and some gorse, holly and sycamore where the lane horns out onto the Moor.

(5) Go through the gate and veer right, following an ascending line of cobbles and grass on an open way, some five to six feet wide with a distinct camber.

(6) Skylarks will join you now before you join the old tramway base and turn left to follow it upwards. The clay-pits of Lee Mill come into view. Remember that this track ran along up to the Redlake China Clay works, built in 1910 and closed in 1932.

(7) Here is a section lined with gorse bushes and some railway stone-walling by the TMW marker stone where stonechats feed.

(8) You sweep to the left round Weatherdon Hill and get your first sighting of what looks like a fellow walker far away on the left but is, of course, part of a stone row. This is Hobajons Cross. There are views over towards Harford on the left.

(9) Hangershell Rock, formed by huge lumps of granite remaining after the meltwaters and debris of the Ice Age receded, is off the track to your right. There is a scattered hut circle to your left, and closer still alongside the track a series of rectangular and circular cast-iron covers for the tramway. You pass over a stream full of the white star-shaped flowers of water-crow-foot. South Brent hill comes into view as the track widens.

(10) There is a tarn to your right. Veer round it to the right, and Spurrell's Cross comes into view.

(11) This is obviously a good place to stop and get your bearings (you may startle a group of snipe in the area too). From here, return to the track on your right and follow it to your left straight down towards the moor edge again. You pass between Ugborough Beacon and Butterdon Hill. You have to dodge about off the peaty, swampy track in some places.

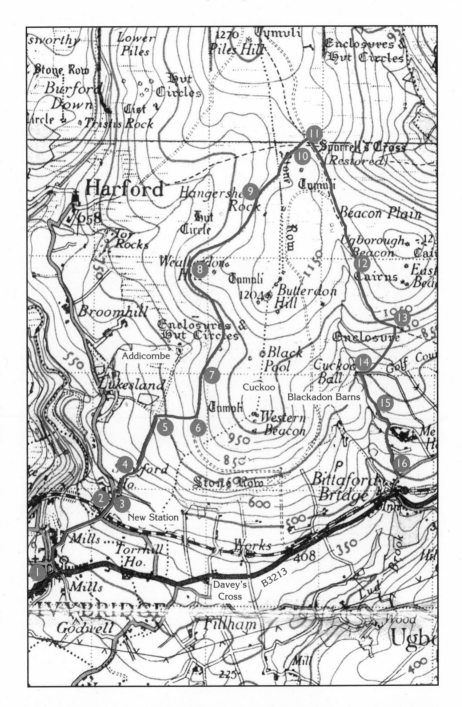

(**12**) The source of the Lud stream is to your right, and a small valley opens out below you. The spire of Ugborough church comes into view and to its left the outline of Forder Lane. (This is Route 21 from *Exploring Green Lanes in the South Hams*).

(**13**) Wrangaton Golf Course is just below you, so watch out as you descend and go straight down towards the left end of the walled copse opposite.

(**14**) Climb up and over the wall by the footpath sign into a path lined with granite boulders and a variety of stone-wall-loving plants, including stonecrop burnt purple by the sun.

(**15**) Go through a gate into a hawthorn-lined lane which comes out onto a minor lane at Blackadon Barns Cottages. You go through the Moorhaven Village complex, marked on your old map as Plymouth Asylum.

(**16**) After passing the main buildings and gardens, keep on the lane to the right which will bring you out through a small gate by a bigger cast-iron pillared entrance. A house called Holne Wood is to your right. At Hillside you follow a row of Cornish-built council houses and keep to your right down under the viaduct by the Old Sunday School Chapel. This will bring you out to the bus stop at Bittaford. If you wish to go further and through to Ugborough, turn left and continue along the road till you come to a green lane opposite on the right. This is Forder Lane, which is described in Route 21 in *Exploring Green Lanes in the South Hams*.

By the way

I have ended this route by saying that you could link up with another which goes inland. This is because these ways up onto the moor show how cattle were moved from one feeding area to another on a regular basis, to enjoy the summer shielings. Stowford Paper Mill was in operation before 1837, when its first paper-making machine was installed. Before that, all paper was made by hand, and as individual sheets from rags and cotton collected locally; do you remember the rag and bone man? By the time of the coming of the railway in the 1860s, the mill was employing 300 people and had become a proper mill town with its own Methodist chapel and cottages built to house the workers.

It now produces fine watermarked paper, as it has done since the 1850s. A watermark is an image created in paper during manufacture by redistributing the fibres which form the paper using a 'dandy roll'. This roll carries a three-dimensional version of the watermark design.

It is difficult to choose which moor feeder lanes to include in any exploration of green lanes. For the best exploration of these ways see Eric Hemery's *Walking Dartmoor's Ancient Trackways*.

Nearby Moorgate was the naturalist George Hurrell's home in the 1930s. He donated land at Lady's Wood to Devon Wildlife Trust, which became their first nature reserve.

Other green lanes in the area

When you reach Spurrell's Cross, you may decide to go straight ahead and leave the moor via Owley Gate and the lanes which lead down to Wrangaton or South Brent.

Links

The Erme-Plym Trail, The Two Moors Way, Lukesland Gardens, National Cycle Route 2. Paper Trail Route 7 in this book.

Question

What is the name of the river that feeds the paper mill?

Look out for stonecrop growing in the wall at (14).

ASHBURTON to BUCKFASTLEIGH

A tinner with a social conscience and some botanical rarities

OS Explorer OL28 Dartmoor

There is obviously much to be seen in the Dartmoor town of Ashburton, but this circuit out and round to its sister town Buckfastleigh will provide a good background to their industrial pasts.

Conditions: Steep in places, stony and muddy.

Distance: 4-5 miles.

Starting point: SX 755698. The church of St Andrew's in North Street. Notice to the right of the entrance the grave of one of the Napoleonic prisoners of war, François Guidon. As you are about to leave the town it is interesting to know that the prisoners held here were also allowed out. Milestones literally measuring one mile were placed on the hills around Ashburton.

Above: "This well, the waters of which are said to be good for weak eyes, was dedicated to Saint Gudula, the ancient patroness of the Bund. The Cross (probably 14th century) was removed prior to 1510. It was restored, re-erected and presented to the Parish of Ashburton 1933."

(1) Take the church path which runs round the back of the church, passing The Old Cattle Market, now Tuckers.

(2) Turn right into the Old Totnes Road. From here drop up on to North Street, now the main road from Totnes into the town, and notice the roof tile

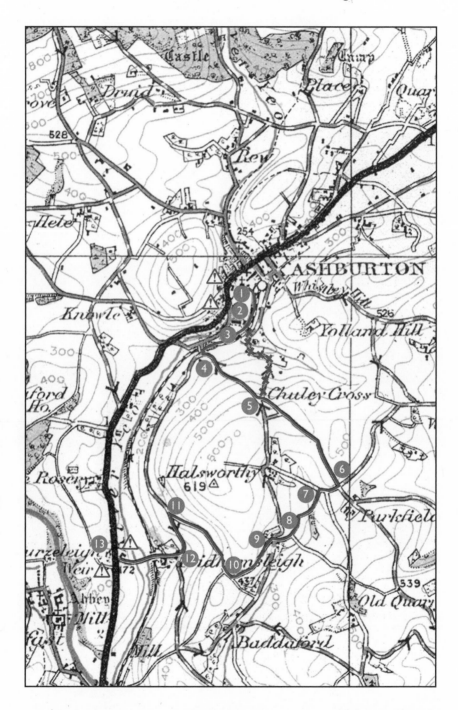

next to Laura Cottage on the opposite side of the road. It is of a horseman wearing some kind of eighteenth-century uniform and a three-cornered hat, and is there as a sign of hospitality for travellers passing through. However, as we are walking in the steps of quarrymen, wool merchants, weavers, tuckers and miners, we must take the Old Totnes Road again.

(3) Here it drops down to St Gudula's Well on the right, with its ancient cross and plaque. Carry on to the junction of the A38 sliproad. Parts of Ashburton were isolated by the making of the dual carriageway here in 1972, especially the area where the cattle market used to be at this end of the town.

(4) You must cross over here, and then take the footbridge over the A38 itself. (5) Then take the steep minor road to the left to Chuley Cross.

(6) Take the road to the right signed to Halsworthy, Bulland and Baddaford, and the sound of the roaring of the road begins to diminish, boxed away by square-cut low but dense hawthorn hedges. There are views over towards Ashburton, and perhaps the distant sound of a steam train in the Dart Valley below.

(7) Turn left at the byways crossroads. (8) Turn left, passing Bulland.

(9) This byway over the road opens out with views towards the A38 and Hembury Barn in the distance. Buckfast Abbey towers appear where it narrows, and the hedge contains a fair number of elderberries which ripen early on in the autumn here. Soon South Brent Hill comes into view, and the bridge over the A38 is visible as the traffic becomes audible. Up on this lane in the autumn there are giant sloes too; but in the spring months look out for the Pridhamsleigh Primrose.

Every year the first flowers to appear are single, arousing fears that it has disappeared, when suddenly the second flush, which comes a little later than the ordinary primrose, opens into full double flowers.

from *The Magic Tree: Devon Garden Plants History and Conservation* (Devon Books, 1989)

(10) Where the byway meets the bridleway, turn right. This is a beautiful grassy lane with some cobbles. There are views down to the A38 and Buckfast Abbey. There are stands of blackthorns and elders here.

(11) At the end turn left, which brings you down over the bridge with the Pridhamsleigh dovecot on your right, which is easily accessible over a stile. Cross the bridge over the A38.

(12) In the lane over the bridge, watch out for the prolific pink flowers

of soapwort growing close to one of Buckfastleigh's old woollen mills. These plants were used in the process of softening the cloth collected from so many cottagers in Ashburton, Buckfastleigh and Staverton and brought down to this important woollen-processing town. This was the work of the fuller, who cleansed and thickened the cloth.

(13) Turn left along the pavement to Buckfastleigh, or turn right to return to Ashburton.

By the way

Back in the town there is much to see, and down St Lawrence's Lane is where one of its fairly unsung heroes was born, lived as a child and first learnt to work tin: Richard Carlile (1790-1843). He is of interest to us in our quest for those who fought for the rights of the workers who once used the green lanes we are exploring. In 1813 he moved to London and became involved with Henry Hunt, the orator who tried to speak at the Peterloo Massacre in Manchester 1819. He got to know Tom Paine, the author of *The Rights of Man*. He launched a radical newspaper called *The Republican* – in 1843 it outstripped the sales of *The Times*. He was fined and imprisoned, but carried on printing what was thought of as seditious material. No doubt (like Thomas Wakeley in Route 14) he had observed the desperate circumstances of the miners and tinners amongst whom he grew up, and had done his best to help them. However, there are records going back into the fourteenth century which show that 'the poor men of Devon' – that is, the farmers – complained that the tinners were destroying good farm land as well as houses by polluting the watercourses and their fields with debris from their mining activities.

Other green lanes in the area

The Staverton Routes 39 and 40.

Links

There are buses which run from Newton Abbot to Totnes and pass through Ashburton.

Question

What other wild plant produces soap-like chemicals and was used in the production of textiles?

PRIMROSE

STAVERTON to PEN RECCA

Where slaters were not always welcome

OS Explorer OL28 Dartmoor

This route together with the next one (plus another, no. 22, in *Exploring Green Lanes in the South Hams*) attempt to make viable circular routes through this parish with its great number of green lanes.

Starting point: SX 774664. Beginning at Landscove Church, pause under the lychgate and see if you can make out this inscription:

District of the church of Landscove. Notice is hereby given that no persons are allowed to assemble or stand about within the precincts of this Church-Yard either during the service or at any other time. Parties offending in this way making any noise or making any nuisance or injuring the fence will be prosecuted and punished as the Law directs. John Robert Sowerby was the church warden plus John Philip.

No date is discernible, but the sign is not maintained and is fading fast. The church was designed by the cathedral designer John Pearson, and entirely paid for by Miss Champerknowne of Dartington in 1851 for the benefit of the slate quarry workers. The quarries were opened in 1838. There were caverns, slate-processing workings, and transport and steam engine houses for pumps – and very few places to stay overnight if you worked here.

(1) On leaving the church, turn left then left again at the road junction. You pass the old Vicarage and Hillhead Gardens and climb up towards the strangely suburban solid bow-windowed Thornecroft, with Hillside and Landscove House behind.

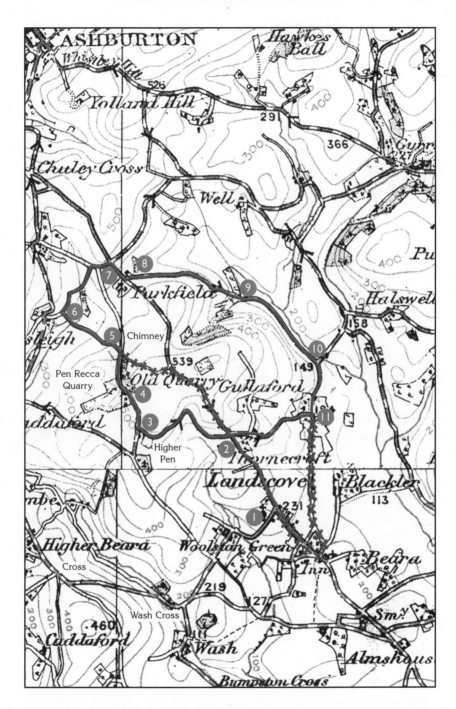

(2) Turn left into a lane by a lone telephone box. This is a beautiful ridge road leading towards Higher Penn, with sweeping views over to Staverton Hill to the right and Kingswear Beacon clump faraway to the left. There are small quarry features in the hillside to the right, and a water source to the left. Higher Penn is just one of what seem almost identically-built farmhouses of tall imposing dimension built in this region, which belonged to the Church of England for centuries.

(3) You are now on the way up to the Pen Recca slate quarry. Slivers of purple slate line the banks of this minor road.

(4) Here the chimney still stands which once gave draught to heat the boiler of the steam engine which worked these profitable quarries.

(5) Turn left here towards Bulland for the meeting of the byways.

(6) Take the byway to your right where the three byways meet. It is well cobbled, and well-used.

(7) Keep to the right, for you are making for Parkfield Cross. Turn right and pass the houses here, taking the byway to your left.

(8) Here is a beautifully maintained lane leading along a woodland edge to a muddy path at the bottom. The lane narrows on its way up, and becomes sunken and bracken-lined, full of butterflies and dragonflies. Turn right at the top.

(9) This byway runs along a ridge, with a low hedge to the left giving views towards the ridge of volcanic smooth-rounded hills towards Ashburton and further still over to Haldon. The lane has a blue slate surface, but is muddy in the middle. Conifers appear and there is a long tunnel-effect lane to negotiate, with evidence of pollarding.

(10) Carry straight on down into this minor lane. At the big road triangle, turn right here down to Gullaford.

(11) From here turn right to Thornecroft and down to Landscove Church once again, or carry straight on down to the Live and Let Live Inn (marked with crosses on the map).

By the way

These routes, which seem impossibly complicated to us today, were used to haul goods to and from the River Dart, down to the sea or up to the moor. They are routes related to agriculture, droving, fishing, poaching, hunting, mining and quarrying. Our reasons for (and directions of) travel have changed all this, and that is why these lanes have a maze-like quality, quite unique in Devon. If you think of the routes as lying between Staverton Bridge, Austin's Bridge and Whistley Hill in the far north near Ashburton, and use these as your guidelines, it will help you get your bearings.

Other green lanes in the area

It is best to refer to the present-day OS map for these.

Links

Buses run out from Totnes through Staverton to Broadhempston.

Question

Given the name of the slate quarry here, what nationality do you think some of the miners might have been?

Slaters' axes: the pointed wedges were used to cleave the slate.

Pen Recca slate quarry workers. *Courtesy of Totnes Image Bank.*

The local hunt by Pen Recca Chimney. *Courtesy of Totnes Image Bank.*

WOOLSTON GREEN to STAVERTON

Orchards and organics

OS Explorer OL28 Dartmoor

This further exploration of Staverton's green lanes takes you from Woolston Green to the edge of quarry country, then down to the River Dart and back up again.

Conditions: Very watery: even in summer you will need Wellingtons.

Distance: 4-5 miles.

Starting point: SX 777661. Woolston Green, Staverton.

Staverton Walk
Sketch by Steve C. Taylor.
c.1980.

(1) From the seat at Woolston Green, follow the road round to the right towards Pennywell Close until you come to the 'Unsuitable for Motors' sign. The lane is as wide as a cart track; notice the orchard to your right. The famous Tom Putt apples of this area originated around 1750 from a gentlemen of that name in Gittisham near Honiton. At the bend the lane becomes slatey, watery and eroded. At intervals, large stag's-head oaks appear in the hedges. Cider is still available from this area.

(2) At the end turn right and go straight on, passing Wash Cross. At the next T-junction after Gladingford Bridge, turn right and walk alongside Coombe Plantation.

(3) This lane is signposted to Higher Penn. It is well cobbled at the beginning, and runs alongside a stream which at some points runs into the lane and makes a damp path towards the end. Keep right and you will come to a beautiful square slate-hung house in the lane.

(4) Follow the lane round to the right. A very watery section follows in this byway, which is overgrown in the middle with mint and brooklime.

(5) Turn left towards Baddaford, and you are walking in orchard country still along this minor lane.

(6) Turn left again, doubling back upon yourself to go down the green lane here. It is an attractive but always damp lane – you will be glad of your wellingtons.

(7) At the end of the lane, turn sharp right along a minor road to High Beara. Turn right at the next road junction and follow the bridleway (8) to your right down to Ware and the busy road below.

(9) Turn right now along the road with great care. If you want to visit Austin's Bridge, then turn left and cross over back to Buckfastleigh.

(10) Take the byway up through the woods here to Five Lanes, a once-important junction.

(11) Turn right here and follow the ridge road down to Higher Beara, Higher Beara Cross, Wash Cross and back to (2) on this route.

By the way

You cannot help but notice the patches of orchard still bearing fruit in this parish. It has great fame as an area where cider was produced, and this is still available in local shops today.

It is said that it was near Austin's Bridge that Walter Raleigh was re-arrested and taken back to the Tower of London again. He had been released to go down to Dartmouth to help recover property stolen from his ship *Rowe Bucke*, which had come into port there from the East Indies. The spices, amber, musk, pearls, gold, jewels and silks had begun to disappear into local hands, and only he, with his local accent and understanding, could help recover the goods.

Other green lanes in the area

The Staverton and Woodland Routes.

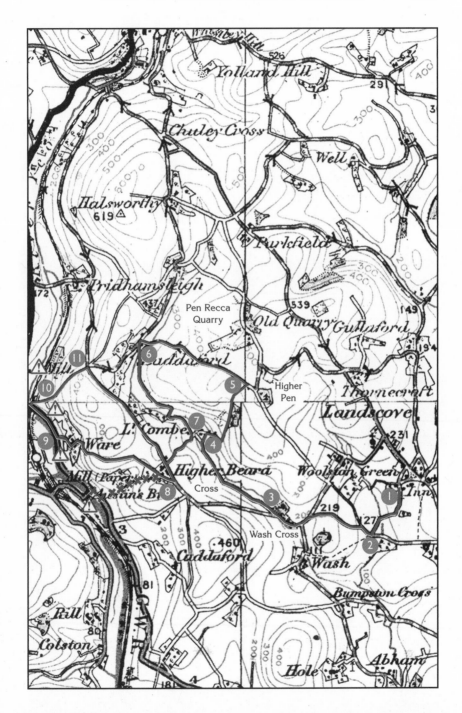

Links

There is a bus to Woolston Green from Totnes.
Route 22 of *Exploring Green Lanes in the South Hams*.

Question

Sugar Bush, Quench, Devon Crimson and Pig's Snout are all varieties of what?

MORELEIGH to TOPSHAM BRIDGE on the AVON

An Anglo-Saxon way
and a church of atonement

OS Explorer OL20 South Devon

This route begins with the story of a squire who killed a parson over a tithe dispute, and had to build a church as atonement. It is no wonder that such disputes arose, because a large tract of this land was granted to the Church by King Edgar in 962. The area involved was over 8,000 acres, and you will be walking one of the boundaries which fixed these Charter or Chapple lands,  and which is called on the map the Roman Road. The walk takes you from high ridgeway to valley bottom, with views of Dartmoor and Bigbury Bay.

Conditions: Steep and slippery in places.

Distance: 2-3 miles.

Starting point: The settlement of Moreleigh strings out along what used to be the turnpike road from Dartmouth to Modbury, built by one of Macadam's sons between 1759 and 1765. Walk past the pub to the best starting point for the walk, the Church of All Angels at SX 762526.

(1) Arthur Mee wrote in 1938:

Dramatic indeed were its beginnings, for it was built by a thir-teenth-century squire who had killed the parson of the neighbouring

village of Woodleigh during a quarrel over tithes, the Pope ordering
him to build a church to expiate his crime.

Within the church, notice the monuments to the Hallett family, especially
one on slate showing a carpenter at work. This family is of long standing in
the village, as carpenters and sometime funeral directors. Carry along the
turnpike with the views of the moor to the right and the sea to the left, passing a turn to Diptford on your right.

(2) You come to a fork: turn left here, and then sharp right into a green
lane which is wide and flat. Almost immediately on your right is a double
hedge-bank which runs along the whole length of the lane and is topped by
scrubby goblet-shaped oaks and holly. A double bank was used to reinforce
an important boundary such as the one marked by this lane. For such an
ancient lane it is remarkably unsunken, thus disproving the theory that the
deeper the lane the older it is.

(3) Towards the end of the lane, where its cobbled surface comes
through, there is a row of large beech trees to the right. Behind these trees,
just before the conifer copse, is a patch of moorland, recorded in Domesday
as 'waste land'. The name Moreleigh means a clearing on a moor, and this
was how the agricultural taming of these lands took place and made them
productive and valuable to those concerned. These areas were often far from
any nucleated settlement – no wonder disputes arose. To your left, through
gaps in the hedge, you can see the marks of a moto-cross circuit carved out
in the hillside. Suddenly we are at the end of the lane. Alone, even on the
brightest day, you will feel the age of this lane. In company, you will fall into
talking of other things and forget the lane. Yet it has taken foot traffic for
over a thousand years and remains unworn, a fine example of the magic of
green lanes.

(4) At its end, proceed a little further to the right until a gate appears on
the bend to your left. Through here is a double line of oaks which continue
the parish boundary between Woodleigh and Diptford. The boundary outlined in King Edgar's 962 Charter carries on down this lane and past High
Marks Barn to cross the Avon at Cock's Brook. Retrace your steps to the end
of the Anglo-Saxon lane and continue along this minor road, so high up now
that you will be escorted by skylarks past Preston Combe and on to Preston
Cross.

(5) This crossroads does not indicate the green lane to your immediate

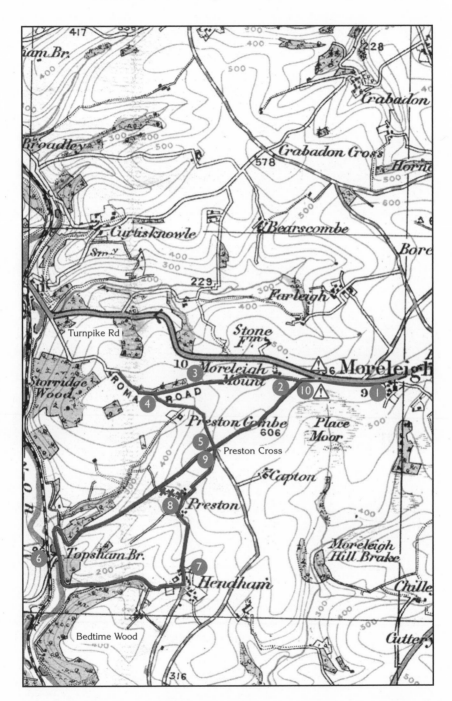

right which you are to take. It is a wide lane and completely unwooded, its hedgebanks being Devon earth banks. The skylarks are accompanied by the wind singing in the telephone wires. You start to descend to a green lanes T-junction. Keep to your right. It becomes narrower as it descends, and there is a wooded area to the right where underfoot outcrops of schists, shales and slates appear. There are deep multi-coloured grooves here, and the sound of the river Avon begins.

(6) You leave the lane by the beautiful curve of the river at Topsham Bridge. There used to be a eucalyptus farm here; this has now gone, but there are still one or two large specimens which, once warmed by the slightest beam of sunlight, give off that haunting Australian smell. Turn left and look under the road bridge, and you can catch a glimpse of the railway bridge built by the navvies of the GWR's Primrose Line which ran from 1893 to 1963. There are wagtails and dippers here, and peacocks strutting along the bridge parapets. This is a very tranquil spot. Continue to your left and notice over the river the buildings of the old railway station. You climb up with the intriguingly named Bedtime Wood to your right, now owned by the National Trust.

(7) At Hendham House turn left.

(8) You pass Preston, a stone-built house with a dovecot set in its walls, and here you can walk back along the long green lane you just came down by turning left if you wish. But it is best to keep on climbing to Preston Cross.

(9) Turn right towards Moreleigh Mount again. There are some fine views to be had along this lane, which brings you back to the beginning of the Anglo-Saxon lane again.

Turn right, and if you have time, when you come to the Diptford turning by the smallest post office in the South Hams, turn to your left and at the top on a hedge-bank in a garden you will see the only surviving example of a Totnes Urban District Council fingerpost still in place.

By the way

If an Anglo-Saxon charter exists in the area through which you are walking, then it is worth looking at for an exact description of features in the landscape, including hedges which have been there for over a thousand years. This is the case with the 962 Charter here. This information, along with the technique of dating hedges (see page 86), is conclusive proof of its age.

There are 1.6 million miles of hedgerow in the United Kingdom; a third of them are a hundred years old. Many are much older than that, especially in Devon where not many of the small medieval or earlier fields were swept away by the Enclosure Acts of the early 1800s.

Other green lanes in the area

There are many around the Gara Valley, and two in *Exploring Green Lanes in the South Hams*: Halwell's High Lanes (Route 4) and Loddiswell's Silver Lane (Route 12).

Links

There is a bus route from Kingsbridge to Totnes which calls twice a day into the village. The Avon Cycle Route. National Trust Woods, Aveton, Bedtime and Titcombe.

Question

You have seen the River Avon on this walk, but it runs very close to another river whose lower reaches you will find near Slapton. Which one?

DIPTFORD

Down the deep, slate-rich mines with 'Duchesses' and 'Peggies'

OS Explorer OL20 South Devon

This walk takes you high up out of the Dart Valley and along ridgeways where you only have to glance down to see that there are some very deep valleys nearby. One such you will find by delving down into the only green lane in this walk, but what it reveals is far from a tranquil haven.

Conditions: This green lane often streams with water, and is muddy and slippery.

Distance: 4 miles.

Starting point: SX 777585. The Church House Inn at Harberton is where you may wish to start from, before visiting the church, of course. This pub is now the only remaining one; there used to be eight in 1850. White's *Directory* lists five shops, a corn mill and a starch mill, and a shovel and reaping-hook manufacturer. Also, given the steep way to get into Totnes and to trudge out to the neighbouring farms, it is not surprising that there were six shoemakers as well.

(1) Climb up out of the village from the bus stop, passing Tristford Farm on the right. Note the interesting recesses in the wall to the left.

(2) Keep to the left at Belsford Cross. You then walk down through beech and hazel coppice, with the Harbourne River on the right. You pass over Leigh Bridge and climb up once again, passing the Old Smithy on the left.

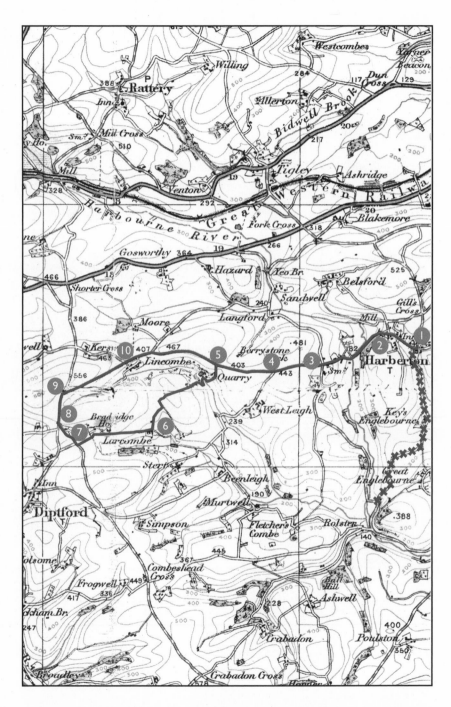

(**3**) Keep straight on over East Leigh Cross. As you climb there are marker trees, and skylarks soaring and singing above the high hills. Watch out for Berrystone Rock outcrop on the right. Is this the 'trap' stone referred to by White in his *Directory of Devon* 1850:

so hard as to resist the mason's chisel, and surrounded by dunstone and slate.

(**4**) At West Leigh Cross carry straight over. From here piles of slate become visible. There is a holly tree on the left, which means you are close to the Larcombe Quarry turn. There are views over the lower slopes of Dartmoor to your right.

(**5**) Turn left into this very muddy and steep lane. The derelict cottage to the right still stands empty. It was once home to a Mr Stone who worked, in stone, on the roads in the Diptford area. The surface of the lane has grooves in which once ran the wheels of the short tub-carts which hauled all the slate to the top. These quarries have been worked since medieval times. Look at the houses in the Totnes district and you will see tile-clad roofs of a light grey hue. (One of the quarries here was known as Greyhills.) At the bottom of the lane are two ruins connected with the mines, which are too dangerous to explore now. In 1983 the Green Lanes Project found old slate cleavers, boots, chisels and the base of some kind of steam engine. As you climb up, the lane is lined with some very big impressive 'shiners' (large slate hedging slabs) on either side; some are purple-tinged. The old paymaster's house stands at the left of the green lane.

(**6**) Follow the lane to the Larcombe group of farmhouse buildings and cottages. Another pile of slate, belonging to Stert Quarry, is to your left.

(**7**) Pass Bradridge House on the right. At Bradridge Cross turn right as the spire of Diptford church comes into view.

(**8**) Turn right again, which will lead you to Diptford Green.

(**9**) On the brow of the hill take the minor road to the right which is lined with closely spaced rows of holly and ash trees.

(**10**) You pass two turns for Lincombe on your right. From here it is the turn of oaks to line the route. On the left from here to (**5**) there is a narrow quillet plot running parallel to the lane, maybe a pound for stray animals or a cover belt for birds.

By the way

The photograph on page 222 shows fifty men employed at just one slate quarry. Those employed in the splitting could produce 30-100 tiles a day using a bettle, a wooden mallet and a steel chisel with an 8-inch handle. This must have been hard, difficult, and skilled work, as the piles of tiles neatly stacked in front of them show. The following table shows the names of the different slate sizes produced by the workers:

Standards	24" by 12" to 12" by 6"
Randoms	24" by 14"
Peggies	12" by 6"
Ladies	16" by 9"
Small Ladies	14" by 8"
Queens	36" by 18"
Princesses	30" by 15"
Duchesses	24" by 15"
Marchionesses	22" by 12"
Countesses	20" by 10"

From 'peggies' to 'queens', a lot of space must have been needed to produce them. The 1851 Census records very few quarry-workers by name, and yet there must have been many from other parishes who walked in daily. William Diggins was a quarryman at Stert, and Frederick Prout of Greyhills too. Management is more often mentioned, such as Henry Hatch, the foreman at Larcombe. Middleton and Sons were the quarry owners of Larcombe, which had its depot in Plymouth. The lanes you walk today must have been used on a regular basis by many slaters and quarry-workers.

Perhaps it now becomes more obvious why there were eight pubs in Harberton. It is said that a platoon of Napoleonic prisoners of war were taken from Ashburton and disposed of in these quarries, whose waste slate heaps are complemented by bottomless water-filled pits. It seems they do not rest in peace: it is a green lane which has always had a haunted feel about it. The last slate quarry here was Lincombe, which closed down in the 1920s. I met an ex-worker, now living in Ipplepen, who told me that they had smashed the slate into powder, and it was sent via the Avonwick railway to Plymouth; but he does not know why.

Other green lanes in the area

Wheeldon, Chapplelands, Moreleigh's Anglo-Saxon Charter Lane.

Links

The Kingsbridge-Exeter bus goes into the village of Harberton a few times a day. Ashburton to Buckfastleigh. In *Exploring Green Lanes in the South Hams*, Route 13, North Huish. Woodland Slate Quarries.

Question

What kind of tool was used to split the slate?

Slate quarry-workers at Larcombe. *Courtesy of Totnes Image Bank.*

EAST ALLINGTON

Good Queen Bess's Highway

OS Explorer OL20 South Devon

The focal point of this circuit is a rare lane indeed, as it is one which has its own map dating back to 1600; it is named 'Good Queen Bess's Highway'. This 400-year-old lane once provided access to the church from the great house at Fallapit: traffic went from here to the mill, and it was the way to the centre of the village. Clashes between these users may have led to a dispute arising, and a map having to be made to provide evidence and determine priorities. There is some quiet minor-lane walking on this circuit.

Stonebreakers by the roadside. *Courtesy of Totnes Image Bank.*

Conditions: Very muddy in places.

Distance: 3-4 miles, extendable to 6 miles.

Starting point: SX 767488. This walk can begin at any point in the village of East Allington. What is described here is one way.

(1) We start at Tollditch Farm, which is also marked on the 1600 map. The footpath begins on a farm track lined with horizontal stone walling, showing some fine sandy mortar in its construction. At the end of this wide stretch turn left into a very narrow green tunnel. There are railway sleepers stepped up at intervals here as you ascend, and there are still a few of the famous Kingsbridge slate shiners – large slabs of upended slate – lining the sides. At the top, the stone walling has become vertical. You come out into Greenhill Road, which takes you to a T-junction where The Fortescue Arms stands. To your right, just before the junction, notice the two troughs to the

left with a stream flowing into them – this old lane also ran towards the village's source of water.

(2) Turn right at the pub. The farmhouses you pass are faced with local slate, and there is a wide gully to the right. The church of St Andrew is forbiddingly large. It has fine cast-iron gates made by Lidstone of Kingsbridge, and the Rector, also a Fortescue (with the foreign-sounding middle name of Reymundo) tells us that he was here in 1848. He stayed until 1898. It is unusual to find an inscription above a church door, such as is found here: "I was glad when they said unto me, let us go into the house of the Lord." All the ways you walk, as ever, in Devon, were well used by pedestrians on a Sunday. From the top of the churchyard you look down on Fortescue House at Fallapit and can see up into the valley you will walk along later. On leaving the church, carry on up to the top of the hill.

(3) Take the road to the left towards Cole's Cross. Watkins, the original writer on ley lines, states that this place name indicates a point from which road surveying was checked by prehistoric man, and maybe fires were lit. You descend, then climb up again to Cross Farm on your right.

(4) Turn left at the next junction (or take the footpath as signposted) and there are views out towards Dartmoor here.

(5) Turn into the green lane here on the right. This lane was once opened up by the Green Lanes Project in the 1980s, and considered a bit of a waste of time and money as it was so short. But after twenty-five years it stays open as a valuable wildlife corridor. It has a great variety of wild flowers: an unusual white flowered lime-leafed balm, silverweed, bryony, hemp-agrimony, tall yellow agrimony and many more. My children once helped in the maintenance of this lane – let's hope the coming generations will do the same.

(6) Turn left at the end of the lane, where there are glimpses of the sea in the distance to your left. You pass a large clump of oaks and the drive to Higher Norton Farm.

(7) To your right is a sign (on the left of the road) for the bridleway, which opens out into rolling meadows. There are big fields here, with the odd stretch of straggling hedge and some conifers. During the Second World War these fields lost their hedgerows and were enlarged for the growing of such crops as potatoes and carrots on a big scale. There is a lot of bird-life here: swifts and swallows swooping over the wheatfields, and buzzards circling above the woodland into which you are headed.

(8) Go through a footpath gate and keep to the right. Cross two field gates.

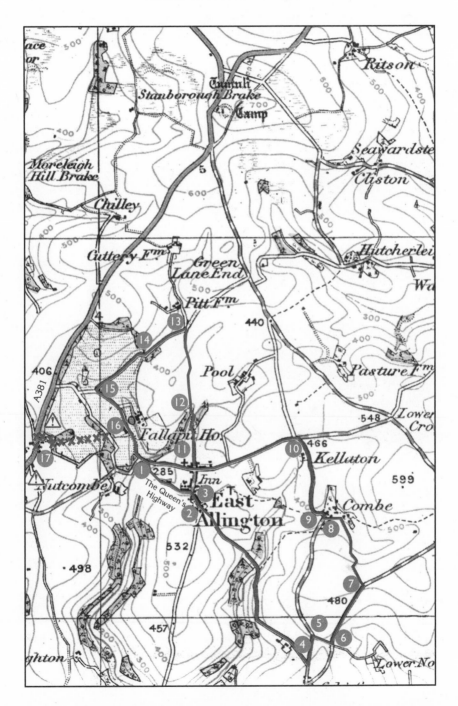

(9) Turn right into the road passing the concealed Coombe Farm on your right. At Hemsbrook, Welsh Mountain ponies may make an appearance. Climb up, passing the slate-clad, slate-built Kellaton Farm with its old raised winnowing bay threshold entrance.

(10) Turn left at Kellaton Cross, where you walk by a line of fine beeches; some dogwood appears in the wider hedges here. There is an interesting bench by the roadside as you go towards East Allington.

(11) Turn right into the public bridleway sign at Townsend, passing a farm on your left. This is the 'Whitestone yeat' shown on the old map at this point. Gates were often placed over roads to control the traffic (see *By the way*). You plunge down into a very straight, quite narrow lane, which becomes cobbled just before it crosses a stream and climbs up again.

(12) You come out into open fields. Keep to the left along the hedgerow and go through two gates, dodging the Dexter cattle as you go. After the muddy end to this lane there is a sign for Pitt Farm. From here you can extend your walk or (13) turn left as indicated and descend on the minor road back towards East Allington. Winnowing Close is to the right, and there is a sawmill to the left. Estate walls come into view, and the Fallapit's copper beeches stand out in the hedges and parkland.

(14) As you enter Fallapit Drive (the 'Vallapitt' of the old map), turn right and then right again and onto the A381. (15) Turn left.

(16) Take the footpath on the right, known as the old Warrener's path.

(17) This will bring you out onto the A381 too, but closer to the bus stop.

By the way

Good Queen Bess's Highway was maintained by the parish from 1555:

An Act was passed for amending of High-ways being now both very noisome and tedious to travel in and dangerous to all Passengers and Carriages. This provided that yearly every parish should elect two parishioners as Surveyors and Orderers for one year, who should take office on pain of a fine. The Surveyors nominated four (later six) days between Easter and Midsummer on which the Parishioners shall endeavour themselves to the amending of the said Ways. Voluntarily, of course.

The place names Tollditch, Whitestone and Yeat (meaning gate) on the old map and the Green Lane End and its nearby crossroads, are all associated with droving. The width and straightness of the lanes in the area confirm this historic usage. These routes must have been familiar to the cattle drovers of the South Hams as they moved their stock mainly towards Plymouth to supply the navy with fresh meat; they would have crossed the Totnes to Kingsbridge road and worked their way westwards.

Other green lanes in the area

Moreleigh Anglo-Saxon Lane and Gara Bridge. Others in *Exploring Green Lanes in the South Hams*, particularly nos. 6 and 7.

Links

The bus from Kingsbridge to Exeter goes into the village a few times during the day. The Dart Valley Trail.

Question

As you rest awhile near Kellaton Cross on a wayside seat, look beneath your feet to discover a link with another form of transport. What is it?

The Queen Bess's Highway as shown on the map in Elizabethan times. It is now a public footpath. *Courtesy of Mr J. V. Somers Cocks.*

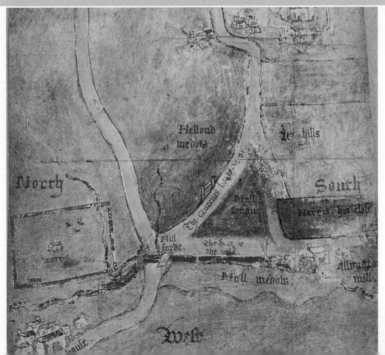

Behind SLAPTON: from HEMBOROUGH to STRETE

Hansel and 'Sketchall' – Jack Yeats in Devon

OS Explorer OL20 South Devon

This walk directs you towards the Gara Valley from the high lands of Capton, Woodbury and Hemborough itself. It follows a ridgeway down to the sea, well-trodden by farmers, fishermen, gypsies and smugglers throughout the centuries. All of these were very well sketched by Jack Yeats, the Irish painter who lived in the Gara Valley just before the outbreak of the First World War. I dedicate this walk to him. This walk can easily be made circular, but there is a bus from Strete which will take you to Dartmouth or on to Plymouth.

Photo courtesy of the National Gallery of Ireland.

Conditions: Steep in parts; muddy, overgrown and slippery too.

Distance: 4-5 miles.

Starting point: SX 832523 **(1)** Hemborough Post. This stands by the road towards the Sportsman's Arms pub on the A3122. Cross and take the road towards Bugford. It is believed that there was a small racecourse in the field to your left, but the pub takes its name from the pursuit of the many deer and hares which once lived in this area. Because of its proximity to the sea there are hillforts nearby, and hidden in the hedge back by the Capton turn is a World War II concrete lookout post. As you set out, notice the clump of windswept beeches in the distance which you will pass in time. There are many fine pedigree South Devons in the fields around.

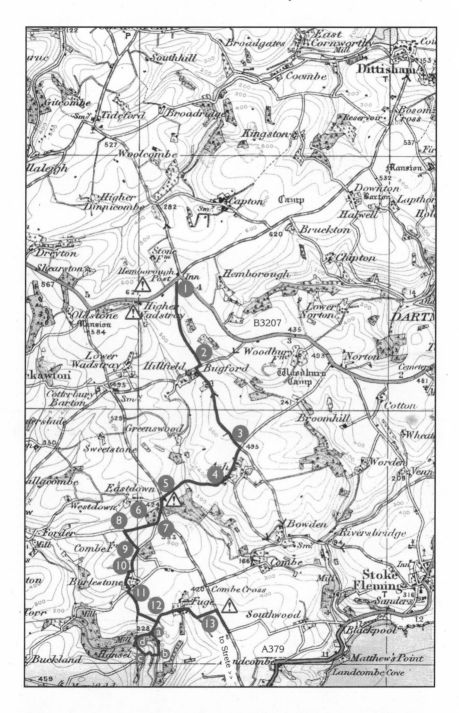

(2) At Bugford follow the road round to the right and then left, passing some fine cob-built barns as you proceed. Amongst Jack Yeats' water-colour and pen-and-ink sketches in the National Gallery of Dublin are those recording:

haylage, laying the fan shaped straw, Manning's sheaves well cut, well bent, well stood.

He had a great eye for detail, recording such everyday things as a makeshift gatepost, and pigs feeding. You climb up the lane through such fields.

At (3) Ash Cross there are views of the sea to the right. The line of beeches you saw at Hemborough appears in front of you now, and in the distance a new clump at Fuge appears. You drop down, passing a well set in the stone wall to the right, some of which is set vertically in local stone.

(4) At Two Ash Cross junction turn right and go through the farmyard gates into a lane marked 'Unsuitable for Motor Vehicles'. It drops down into a tunnel with plenty of exposed, slippery rock overhung with branches of ash and hazel. You go through woodland and towards the end of the lane, where clouds of rosebay willow-herb appear, is a gate marked 'Private Nature Reserve'. The rock becomes black underfoot.

(5) You emerge through a gate at Eastdown. Watch the road as you turn left. (6) Take a sharp right towards Forder. (7) There is a lot of sweet chestnut as you proceed. At the next T-junction, keep right. Most of the roads in the East and West Downs area have started to sprout grass and moss in the middle.

(8) The next green lane you take to your left gives you the next stage of the story, and from here you can look back over views towards Blackawton and Dartmoor.

(9) Turn right and keep right, passing a series of very old farm buildings at Burlestone. There is a trough and a tap set in the wall to your left, and a dovecot here.

(10) Veer right here (11) at the road triangle, and then veer up to the left, where sea breezes will greet you. There are yellowhammers calling for a little bit of bread and no cheese, as they fly up and down the lanes. You can now see down upon the chimneys of the houses in the Gara Valley to your right.

(12) Turn to your right where there is an 'Unsuitable for Motor Vehicles' sign. You drop down and follow the letters as indicated in the enlarged map. You pass by the first home in Hansel to your left by a fast-flowing stream (a). Turn left here down an always slippery road, and on your left is 'Snail's Castle', 'Cashlauna Shelmiddy', Jack Yeats' old home. Below on the right, in

the wood, are the ruins of his studio where he sketched with great mastery such everyday things as apples on shelves and his sleeping dog. This is where he wrote and illustrated a series of toy theatre plays for the children of Strete. (b) Go straight down into the lane with a magnificent tulip tree to your right. (c) Now veer to the right and take a narrow path where Himalayan Balsam and water pepper grow. This will lead you down to (d) where there is a bridge across the Gara. This is where the poet John Masefield and Jack Yeats used to race their toy boats. Turn right at the end of the lane by the Monterey pine, and you will come to Water Mill Cottage. From here you can cross the Gara again and climb up back to (a). Once back at (12) go straight across to Fuge. There is another set of fine farm buildings here: notice the elegant gateposts to Higher Fuge and another line of marker beeches.

(13) Take the footpath to the right, which will direct you onto the road into Strete. You pass the church and the old school on your right where Jack staged his toy theatre plays. You come out on to the A379 at Strete and the bus stops by The King's Arms.

By the way

From 1897-1910 the Irish painter Jack Yeats lived with his wife Cottie and their dog Hoollie (Hooligan) in the depths of the Gara Valley. Many came to visit him, including his poet brother W.B., bringing with him some friends from his Rosicrucian circle. John Masefield wrote *Jim Davies* here and, with Jack, became involved in protesting about the dredging at Hallsands. The latter's small canvas-clad ring-bound sketchpads went everywhere with him: to the racecourse, the sea, the fair, the school, the pub. He was a great wit and observer, seeking to catch what he called "the living ginger of life".

Other green lanes in the area

Those along the Upper Gara towards Blackawton.

Links

There are buses along the Dartmouth and the Coast Road for connections. *Exploring Green Lanes in the South Hams* Route 5.

Question

What is the name of the school where Yeats' children's plays were first performed?

Jack Yeats in the Gara Valley. *Courtesy of National Gallery of Ireland.*

BEESANDS

From the red mullet hewers of Hallsands to the slaters of Sunnydale

OS Explorer OL20 South Devon

This walk takes you back from the long shingle strip at Beesands up and into the green lanes which lead into Beeson village. You will be following the footsteps of generations of fisher-farmers and, more recently, of those who feared for their lives during the Second World War.

Conditions: Steep and slippery underfoot in places.

Distance: 4-5 miles.

Starting point: You will probably approach Beesands by coming along the Coast Path from Start Point or Torcross. Before you leave the village, make sure you visit the newly decorated and slated church of St Andrews. In 2008 they were using slates from Argentina, and not from Sunnydale quarry. It is beautifully tranquil inside, even on the most tempestuous of days. There is a plaque dedicated to the seven residents who lost their lives in enemy action on July 26th 1942. Another is to Florence Holdsworth, from the Holdsworth family of Widdicombe and Dartmouth. There is a bell here which was taken from a Barrow-in-Furness collier after it was wrecked in the Great Storm of 1891. The bell inscribed *Janus 1815* was used to summon parishioners until it became too heavy for the church joists. It stands next to the thriving Britannia Fisheries outlet.

(1) SX 819405. The Cricketers Inn on Beesands High Street. Just over a hundred years ago there was another pub here, a post office and a shop.

Facing the sea, turn right, and where the road ends veer right by a house called Seathatch (with a plaque saying "circa 1700") up onto the coast path where you will go through a tunnel of swept-back bad-hair-day blackthorn. There are remnants of other paths running close to the cliff, with some flat platforms still remaining. These were not put there for the view, but for the comfort of the 'hewers' who would watch and wait for the incoming shoals of fish. Once the 'hue' and 'cry' was set up, helpers would come from villages in the hinterland to help bring the fish ashore. One such watcher is recorded at nearby Hallsands, visible from most points on the beach at Beesands.

And she (Johanna the widow of Gervase: exemplar for some of the other tenants) shall sit upon the sea shore at le Hole (Hallsands) from the feast of the Purification until Hockday (2nd February until the second Tuesday after Easter) expecting the coming of the mullet and, with the men of Frittiscombe, she will catch the said fish and they shall have two thirds and the lord one third.

From the Account Roll of Salisbury lands, 1346. (John de Montacute, third Earl of Salisbury).

The dates here are significant, as the Lord wished to eat his fill of the tasty red mullet before Lent. Lucky Johanna, to spend the worst wintery months of the year just gazing out at the beautiful view!

You come over Tinsey Head and down onto Hallsands, where there are some new housing developments right on the beach.

(2) Just before the gate onto the beach turn right where the sign reads "N.T. Walks to Beesands". You walk along a willow- and elm-lined way which is quite wide in parts. Follow the grass track along a field edge and through a gate.

(3) There are some remnants of stone-walling here and some productive sloe trees, which are just bare spikey blackthorns in the winter. Follow the grass track along the field edge.

(4) At the T-junction, veer right up into a green lane. This lane is steep in parts, and has some good stone-walling along most of its length. This route up to Huckham Barn Cross has been used for centuries as a fairly easy way back to the farming communities inland. Maybe some of Johanna's friends from Frittiscombe would have come running along here to help with the red mullet haul.

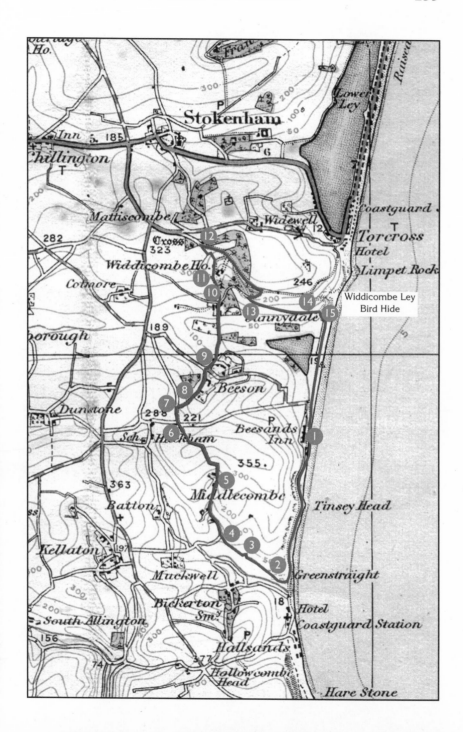

Widdicombe Ley
Bird Hide

(5) At Higher Middlecombe Farm you pass by a winnowing barn. Its open design allowed the wind sweeping up from the sea to funnel through, thus helping to separate the chaff from the wheat.

(6) At Huckham Barn Cross go straight over. You will see on the old map that there was a school near here. There is a packing station here now for an organic farm.

(7) Turn right here towards the settlement of Beeson. (8) You pass Beeson Farm with its large slate slabs, known as shiners, set into the walls. They probably came from the quarries at Molescombe, rather than being hauled all the way from Sunnydale.

(9) Veer right at the fork, and then left after the phone box. Turn right again and then bear immediately left between Lower Beeson Farm and Gull Cry. Veer left where the track forks, and follow the footpath. There are some lovely old sweet-chestnut trees along this track.

(10) At Widdicombe Farm take the footpath opposite and to the right through the gate and up the field edge alongside the wood. Do not take the lane to the right, although this is obviously quite old and follows a lane up from Sunnydale quarries to the house.

(11) Widdicombe House was built by the Holdsworth family from Dartmouth in the eighteenth century. It is built of local Meadfoot blue slate, and it is said to have hosted Captain Cook on his return from Tahiti. The garden was designed by Capability Brown, who got his name because of his assertion that he could see the 'capabilities' of a site for landscaping. When the house changed hands in the 1920s, records were shown detailing pineapple pits in the greenhouses; they also revealed an outstanding bill to the designer which perhaps was never settled. There are stands of sweet chestnut, oaks and limes in the gardens which are at least 200 years old. The chestnuts are particularly fine. The house was used during WWII by General Eisenhower as a Combined Services Headquarters. Although the gardens are beautiful they are rather overshadowed by the trees, so it is a relief to turn down towards the coast once you reach the drive.

(12) You pass a cottage on your right, and find yourself in a lane which reveals how the trees within the grounds to your right have recently been thinned out.

(13) You come out from the woods and follow the footpath signs over into the meadow where sometimes it is a green lane, and sometimes (where it loses its hedges), it isn't. Good views and sounds of Widdicombe Ley

accompany you as you are crossing the meadow where around 180 species of birds have been spotted.

(14) At the bottom of the meadow you go over a stile and into a green lane which takes you down to the shore. On the right just by the fingerpost crossroads here, there is the entrance to a World War II lookout point. Turn right for Beesands Cellars. You descend a slippery section of lane towards the beach, with the sweep of the bay towards Start Point lighthouse in front of you. We are lucky to be able to freely enjoy it and not to be dependent on watching for the catch to come in. Britannia Fisheries will be opening a new fish restaurant on the beach soon. Perhaps they should call it The Johanna.

(15) To your left is a group of cottages and an open green space, and the *base sandes* of Beesands. The quarry is now a nature reserve owned by the National Trust. At low tide there is a short cut to Torcross along the beach round Limpet Rocks. The colours and shapes of the slate here are varied and dramatic.

By the way

This space was where the slates were split into various sizes (see Diptford Route, page 218), hence the amount of broken slate around here. There is a photograph showing a long shed here, so the workers were not quite as exposed as you might think. There are many references to this quarry, which first appears on a map in 1747. The Devon historian Polwhele says that at this time it was producing the best blue slate in Devon: "It is large and a fine object of the sort."

If you go along towards the beach you will see the steep, seaward entrance over some steps carved out of the rocks. Henry Williamson, when on a walking holiday in south Devon, recorded in 1933 that there were at least four quarries here, and adventurous folk can prove this for themselves, but be careful. By 1885 the quarry was no longer worked. Some thirty years before this there are records showing that no more than twelve men were working here at any one time. What we probably have here is, as well as working as farmers and fishermen, some local men also working in the quarries. There were, after all, twenty-two quarries in the parish of Stokenham.

Other green lanes in this area

Those leading back from the coast, especially around Prawle.

Links

Green Lanes Walks: Beesands Strand and Land Leaflet, published by South Hams District Council. *Exploring Green Lanes in the South Hams:* Route 6. Slapton. The Coastal Footpath.

Question

What is the name of the way which runs by the beach at Beesands?

MODBURY

Where Cavaliers once fled in fear

OS Explorer OL20 South Devon

This route takes in the famous Runaway Lane down which the Royalists were pursued towards Plymouth by the Parliamentarians in 1643. Unlike them, we return to the town from which we begin. Once when I was with a group of children, we met a tortoise making a break for it down this lane. I wonder if he was ever recaptured!

Conditions: Muddy and steep in places.

Distance: 2-3 miles.

Starting point: There is a lot to see in Modbury, so spend some time exploring before you climb the hill towards the church. Go through the churchyard and keep to the left, which brings you out through a gate on to Church Lane. Turn right towards the main Plymouth road here, passing the Vicarage, and you will be walking along a raised cobbled pavement especially laid down for the Rev. Green and his family, who were here between 1860 and 1910 when the Vicarage was at the back of Runaway Lane.

(1) On your left is a sign which reads:

RUNAWAY LANE
Five Crosses 1 mile
Unsuitable for vehicles

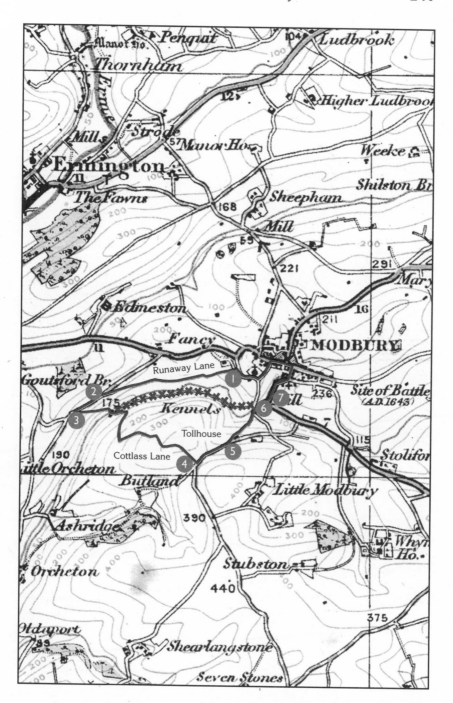

You enter a sunken lane where mosses and ferns grow from the over-hanging tree-root plates formed by large beech trees growing high above the hedge-banks. There is a bridge over the stream at the bottom, but watch out for patches of mud here. From here the lane flattens out along the field edge, and the pursuit of the Royalists must have begun at a canter as both sides were on horseback. Thirty Royalists were killed and eighty were captured. This led to Hopton setting up Plymouth as a Royalist stronghold. Ignore the footpath signs to the left here, and keep to the lane. To the left watch out for pollarded ashes in the fields. You climb up the lane, flanked by oaks. The Royalist runaways must have felt a bit apprehensive as they reached the top of the lane. It becomes ridgeway-like, running along the top contour line. It is very narrow, and bracken from the hillside grows into the lane through the thin oak-sapling hedge. At the top of the lane the Scots pines on the road to Orcheton come into view – always a welcome sign for drovers. Which way did the Royalists go when they reached the top? If they turned to the right they would be doubling back into Modbury, but the road to the left looks as if it would do this too. They probably went on via Goutsford and Sequer's Bridge in a north-westerly direction.

(2) Turn left into a minor road here. (3) Turn left again into Cottlass Lane. Ahead of you is the farm, which has nothing to do with warfare as the Cott element refers to a high settlement and not a sword. This was once a corn mill, which explains the different arches here through which the mill leat water was directed. Keep left up the steep track between the buildings. The walls here are rich in ivy-leaved toadflax and pixie cup lichen. The path begins to flatten out; there are views of Modbury, and fine glimpses over a field pattern which is so typical of the South Hams. The track has a grass surface towards the end where you come out on the road which leads towards the sea.

(4) Take a sharp drop to the left.

(5) An overgrown structure with a well-preserved arched doorway stands here. It is the remains of a tollhouse of the Kingsbridge Trust, dated at about 1827 to prevent evasion of tolls at Stoliford Gate on the Modbury-Kingsbridge road. The turnpike trust was abandoned around 1885 and this once inhabited tollhouse with it. Take the fork to the right here down towards the charmingly-named Swanbridge Mill.

(6) Here to your right is where the old gas works stood. Fired by coke, this lit up the from 1865 until 1920. On the bridge parapet to your left is an iron plaque which reads:

KINGSBRIDGE RURAL DISTRICT COUNCIL

Take notice that this bridge or culvert is insufficient to carry weights beyond the ordinary traffic of the district and owners, drivers or other persons in charge of locomotives are hereby warned that they will be held responsible for any damage caused by attempting the passage of the bridge or culvert without consent of the district surveyor.

By order William Beer, Clerk, Kingsbridge, July 1905.

Of course, the locomotives in question have nothing to do with the old Kingsbridge to South Brent railway line, but refer to the use of steam locomotives: traction engines for agricultural purposes. No doubt many a bridge was brought down, or lane widened, as those 'Farmer's Friends' made their seasonal forays into the South Hams. There is another green lane to the left here if you wish to enter Runaway Lane again from another direction.

(7) Take the footpath to your left, and pass alongside this lovely garden area to return to the Poundwell Street Car Park over an interesting slate stile and a narrow lane.

By the way

Modbury is a town I run towards rather than run away from. I first became interested in the Anglo-Saxon elements in Devonshire place names here, which led on to an interest in the Anglo-Saxon charters in the area. Many of these ran along old manorial boundaries which included green lanes. It is to Modbury History Society that I owe the fact that my first book *The Green Lanes of England* came to be published, as they were my sponsors. It was in the primary school here, with the invaluable encouragement of the, then headmaster, Gordon Waterhouse, that the first production of *The Lost Lane* play, which outlined the historical phases of a lane, first hit the cobbles. Thank you, Modbury!

Other green lanes in the area

Those going out towards Ringmore and Kingston.

Links

There is a regular bus service from Kingsbridge to Plymouth which passes through Modbury. The Erme-Plym Trail.

Question

What is the date on one of the slate stiles which you go over on your return towards the Poundwell Street car park in Modbury?

Part of the Rev. Green's way to the church from The Old Vicarage, seen to the right at the beginning of Runaway Lane.

TAMERTON FOLIOT

A land of mineral and agricultural wealth

OS Explorer 108

This is a walk firmly fixed on the Devon side of the Tamar, but owing much of its prosperous history to the fact that it is opposite lead-silver-rich Bere Ferrers. You descend to the site of the ferry and climb up to look out onto Cornwall's mineral-rich hills. The lanes are secret and secluded, and always there is a whiff of ozone on the breeze.

Conditions: Muddy, wet and steep.

Distance: 3-4 miles.

Starting point: (1) SX 469613. Go north from the church through the village, and at the junction of Horsham Lane with Whitson Lane take Horsham to the left. Along here on the right at Warleigh Lodge there is a footpath sign. Warleigh House below was home to the Foliots in medieval times, from which Tamerton gets its name.

(2) Take this signed footpath, which starts round the side of the building. But before you plunge down here, take a look at the view from the top to your left, over the Cornish landmass with the great Tamar Bridge and the little branch line's iron bridge below you too. The lane is packhorse-width, hazel-hedged and muddy underfoot. Half-way down this gives way to a very slippery rock face as you pass under the pylon.

(3) The green lane joins a minor lane on the left; you turn right into it and go down towards Blaxton. You go through a farmyard: Horsham Farm dates back to the thirteenth century, and its name means 'watery meadow for horses'. Veer left up a lane marked 'Unsuitable for Traffic'. There is quite a lot of holly in the hedgerows from here forward, as Blaxton Wood comes into view.

(4) At the next footpath sign turn sharp down to your left then left again

at a footpath sign which will take you out onto Blaxton Quay. The Tamar Valley Discovery sign of an apple will appear on some of these signposts – a bit confusing, for this side of the Tamar where agriculture and mining were of more importance than fruit-growing enterprises.

(5) As you reach the quay, notice a wall to your left with an overgrown bay tree at its end. This was the wall to the ruined cottage beside the ferry – where the ferry master and his family lived perhaps, and where there was a tide mill. To your left is the quay bar and some lime kiln ruins. There are more of these hidden on the left round the corner. From here, the tide permitting, you can cross over and go through the estuaryside woods towards Maristow. If not, then retrace your steps.

(6) At the end of the lane go to the left then straight over a flooded section of this minor road where (12) the Tamar Valley Discovery Trail starts. Ignore this, and go straight ahead where a gated green lane awaits you. There is barbed wire, but you can untie the binder twine and walk through. This is a magical lane which climbs up through a series of gates. Its beginning is flanked by large oak trees, and later by a Devonshire stone-faced bank. It is muddy towards the top where you go through Pound Farm to reach Pound Cross.

(7) You can take a minor road return from here. However, if you want to discover the estuary edge further, turn left.

(8) Take the first left turn towards Maristow.

(9) This minor lane takes you to Maristow, once an important loading place for Bere Ferrers silver on its way to London in the thirteenth century. Maristow House on the hill dates from the same period. The place-name elements of Mary, Christian and Stow Pagan show this to have always been a sacred place, and there is a chapel in the house dating back to the fourteenth century.

(10) Follow the sign for the Tamar Valley Discovery Trail (TVDT) to the left, down to the quay.

(11) At Creekside you can follow the Riverside path back to Blaxton or take the TVDT lane down to (12) and (6) and back to Tamerton Foliot again.

As you descend back into Tamerton, the church nestling amidst the hills, with no houses in view from this angle, calls out to be visited.

By the way

The name of Tamerton Foliot goes back to the naming of the Celtic river Tamar and also to the Foliot family first mentioned in King Stephen's reign (1135-54). One famous Foliot was involved in supporting the assassination of

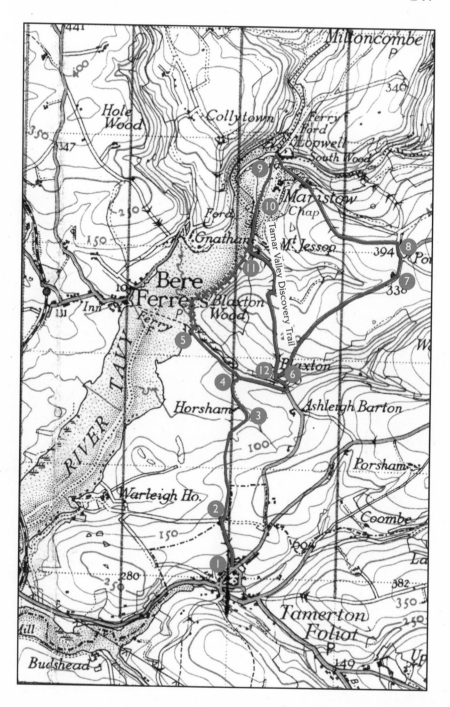

Thomas à Becket. The family of Copleston moved here from the Crediton area in the twelfth century (see Route 2 in *Exploring Green Lanes: North and North-West Devon*). Outside the church on the road towards Plymouth is a fine burnt-out oak tree, the Copleston Oak. In Queen Elizabeth I's day, John Copleston is said to have killed his godson here as they were leaving church. The boy was only complaining about the foul language his godfather was using – this was outright murder. However, by surrendering thirteen Cornish manors of his to the Crown, he escaped punishment. Things are a good deal more just at Tamerton today.

Other green lanes in the area

Those linking up with the Tamar Valley Trail to the north of Maristow.

Links

There is a regular bus service to Tamerton Foliot from Royal Parade, Plymouth.
The Tamar Valley Discovery Trail/The West Devon Way. There is a Nature Trail worth exploring down towards the river along Station Road.

Question

What is the name of the hill over in Cornwall with its mining chimney still intact on the top?

SYDENHAM DAMEREL and HORSEBRIDGE

Walking along the borderlands

OS Explorer 108

These parishes lie very close to the Devon Great Consuls mines shown on your map, but although this group was very important you will see that there were others in the area too which pre-date it. As you move towards the north, and the Duke of Bedford's residence at Endsleigh, you will be walking lanes which were once walked by his workers. There are connections here too with John Taylor, the engineer who built the  Tavistock Canal, as we are close to Wheal Maria where he was the manager as a young man of 19. You can begin this route at Sydenham or Horsebridge. The walk can be extended by following the Tamar Valley Discovery Trail.

Conditions: Often overgrown and damp underfoot.

Distance: 4-5 miles.

Starting point: SX 401748. **(1)** Horsebridge.

Writing about Greystone bridge further down over the Tamar, Hoskins says:

Among other things apart from telling us that granite is the great building stone of Cornwall, it should also dispel the myth that medieval roads were poor and nearly impassable. Why should you build a bridge like this if the roads on both sides were as bad as the books say? They were not, of course.

The same applies to this Tamar crossing at Horsebridge: dated 1437, restored in 1685, and showing signs of ecclesiastical influences in its architecture. It is said that at low tides, traces of copper-bearing stones can be seen beneath the shallow waters. There are kingfishers here which you can watch at ease, as this is not such a busy Tamar crossing as others. Before setting off, walk back into Cornwall and on the left at approximately 100 feet from the centre of the bridge you will find a granite stone inscribed with a 'C'. These were set up after Henry VIII's dissolution of the monasteries, which had been formally responsible for roads and bridges, to indicate that a county or other authority was now in charge of the crossings for at least 100 feet either side.

(**2**) Cross back into Devon and turn sharp right, taking the road to Lamerhooe Cross and Wheal Maria. (**3**) Go straight over here. Pass the lodge on the right.

(**4**) Turn left into a lane which is just a small cart's-width wide, and marked 'Unsuitable for Long Vehicles'. It has a flinty surface, and widens as it ascends, lined with oaks and hollies. A fine set of square-built cottages put up by the Duke for his workers both in and out of the mines can be seen across the valley in the distance. There are at least seven species of hardwood to count in these hedges. I felt that there were still miners here walking along as they once would have done on their way back to Sydenham or further afield.

(**5**) Here it widens out at a T-junction with a tempting-looking footpath to the left, but go straight on over a muddy patch to the end of this green lane.

(**6**) You come out at Hartwell. To your right is the way down to Chip Shop – a misleading notice for those looking for a fish supper, for it actually refers to the place where tokens obtained in lieu of wages when working for the Great Consuls Mines could be exchanged for goods and food provided by – guess who? There is a signpost in the area to Taylor's shop, which was the same place with the same arrangement. This payment system was known

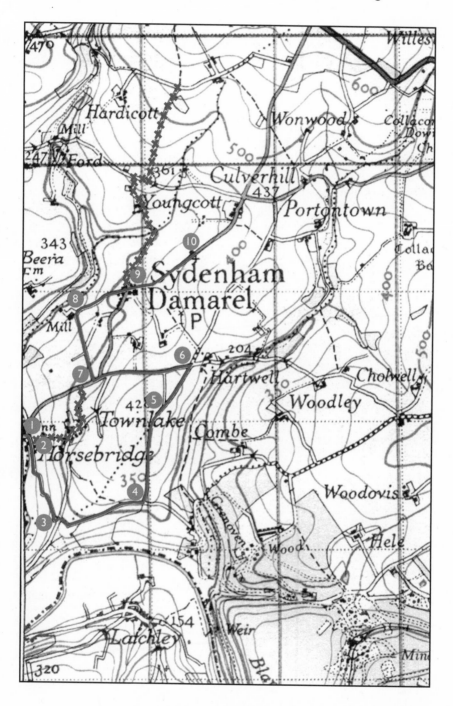

as truck, and it had existed in some form or another since the 1200s. The first use of it in a negative sense, i.e. 'to have no truck with', occurred in 1615.

Then came the Truck Acts, beginning in 1831 which gradually made sure that all workers were paid in coin and not in kind. However, seeing these isolated villages today, there would have been a very good reason for having a shop placed locally for your supplies in the nineteenth century. One of the most recent Truck Acts, that of 1960, gave provision for workers to be paid by cheque and not in cash. The truck system was also found in the lace industry at Branscombe too (see Route 22). Turn left, and as you progress you will find Hill Farm on your left at the other end of the bridleway not taken. Go straight on, admiring the magnificent oaks here, with glimpses between them out over Bodmin Moor in Cornwall. You pass a sign to Townlake on the left and then come to a delightful road triangle complete with a Sydenham Damerel millennium seat. This feels as if it developed as the dividing point for a two-way system: one to the right going directly to the village, and another to the mill. The latter is the one that we will take, so go a little further along the road.

(7) You come to a green lane on the right which has a very large sessile oak just by the entrance. Of all the green lanes traversed, the ones in this area are the most silent, and yet ironically they were once some of the noisiest in the county. There are Scots pines along the way here, a sign for drovers travelling long distances and needing a place to rest, or just needing route guidance. So why is there a line going down to the left just before the drive to Damerel House? Passing the drive, you drop down into a part of the lane where tarmac begins to appear again. There is some pedunculate grass here, presaging dampness to come. There is some stone-walling and big flints underfoot as you go downhill towards the end.

(8) You come out onto a minor road with the mill to your left. Beera Farm to the left is in that fine square granite style belonging to the area. The lane to the village becomes seriously green at its centre as you climb towards its end.

(9) You come out at Chiselwood, a reference to the two carpenters who were here in the 1870s. Go straight over by Churchtown Farm and the church of St Mary's. Outside stands a low shaped column of granite which I mistook for a cheapstone – that is, a stone set in a market-place for striking bargains on. However, when you enter this single-aisled church you will see that it is in fact a survivor of the fire which occurred in 1956 when the church was struck by lightning. The pinnacles of the tower are covered with yellow

lichen, *Xanthoria parietina*, and round the base the granite is covered in a furry coating of stag's-head lichen. When Mee was here in 1938, he commented upon the row of Irish yews leading into the churchyard. They are still there, having been restored in 1977. As we are so close to Cornwall, note the number of Tozers buried close by.

(10) Go down the yew avenue and turn right into the lane which passes Woodside and a footpath on your right (one which will take you back to Horsebridge). In front of you on the right is the Methodist Chapel, dated 1926. However, its isolated position and dull exterior point to its true origins. Over in the car park, which looks out towards Bodmin Moor, and from where you can just see the lichen-covered pinnacles of the church, is a plaque set in the wall which reads 'Bible Christian Chapel 1832'. This is one of many of the Cornish branch of Methodism set up to appeal particularly to working men just after the close of the Napoleonic wars. From here you can also see where other mines were once worked. You can continue and join up with the Tamar Valley Discovery Trail before returning to either Sydenham Damerel or Horsebridge.

If you do return to Sydenham to catch the Friday bus back to Tavistock (see *Links*), then stand opposite the church. As you wait on the tyring platform set in the tarmac there, which must have been in front of the blacksmith's forge, imagine the heat and the sweat involved in placing the iron rim round the felloes of a new cart-wheel!

By the way

There were eleven farmers in Sydenham Damerel in 1870, but no mention of quarrymen or miners. Yet throughout this district many men must have been employed in this industry. Their absence from any occupational records is probably due to the fact that many were employed on a seasonal basis. Just as there were fisher-farmers on the coast, so too there were mining farmers in the many areas throughout south and south-east Devon where this industry was big business for a while. But this, in its turn, caused quite a lot of trouble. Those true miners coming across the border from Cornwall to work in Devon Great Consuls found that the pay was far less than in their native county. This was due, in part, to the fact that farm labourers in Devon would accept lower wages for mining work. A strike took place in 1866, and policemen and troops were brought into Tavistock. The miners were asking for the right to set their own price on any lode which was to be worked. At the time they were paid £3 12s for a five-day week. (The agricultural worker's rate at this time was about £2 10s).

Other green lanes in the area

There is a very short circuit containing some green lanes around Horsebridge and Lamerhooe Cross.

Links

There is a community bus from Tavistock every Friday.

Question

Although called Horsebridge, how many packhorse recesses are there set in the parapets?

BERE FERRERS to BERE ALSTON

Fortunes reversed beyond a physician's healing

OS Explorer 108

This walk takes you from the fertile pear-drop of land, once silver and cherry-laden, between the Tamar and the Tavy. It climbs up onto that high ridge where Cornish granite meets Devonian slates, revealing mineral wealth and miners' paths rising and falling like fortune itself. There is some minor-road walking, and a good choice of footpaths and green lanes throughout this de-industrialised

land. You can walk between the two Beres, the word meaning 'peninsula', using the train to Plymouth or the bus back into Tavistock.

Conditions: Steep, muddy, overgrown and above all, silent.

Distance: 4-5 miles.

Starting point: If you have never taken the train from Plymouth to Gunnislake, then do so now, before it closes. This route begins from Bere Ferrers station, where the train stops after a long stretch of woodland from St Budeaux which looks out over Brunel's 1869 bridge and the estuary.

(1) SS 453635. Mind how you get off the train here. Arthur Mee records that ten men were killed when getting off the train here on their way to Salisbury Plain to serve in the First World War. This is a station which has kept its steam and diesel trains on-site, and where the station house, although

not open, is full of signs that it once was. The line of buddleias opposite the platform truly live up to their name of 'butterfly bush' when the sun shines. Follow the signs – some cast-iron (as illustrated on page 254) and with diamond-shaped finials – right down into the village on the edge of the water. This is where the oldest mining settlement in the country based on mineral wealth was once to be found.

The church is in a stunning position overlooking the Tavy and opposite Blaxton Quay, close to Plymouth. Although often locked, the church has this reminder of how a fatal falling from fortune can be – and this time, not from a railway platform. You will find it at the back of the East window by the river, and it is in memory of Walter Pyke in 1752:

By a fall I caught my death
Which no man knows his time nor breath.
I might have died as soon as then
Had I been with physitians men.

He fell from a ladder while cleaning some of the oldest stained glass in Devon, next to that of Exeter Cathedral. Return in the direction of the station, and take the road straight ahead towards Clamoak and Hole's Hole. As you go over the railway line, take a look at the greenness of the track here: like any green lane, grass is growing in the middle of the line. Greystones is to your left. You climb up this minor lane, which has been hewn out of slate here and has pennywort leaves and Jack-by-the-Hedge leaves as big as saucers, so dank and damp are the banks. Clam Oak Farm is to your left.

(2) You go down and then up again, and towards the top on the right opposite a granite gatepost with a tear-and-feather post (marks indicating where explosives were placed to split stone) take the lane (unsigned) to your right. To your left the wood sinks away where a huge quarry close to Weir Quay below was once worked. The lane begins wide, with striations of slate covering its surface. There are cobbles underfoot, and some white-faced slate forms the surface towards the top. Breaks in the hedge reveal views of Cornwall close by. There is a great variety of wild flowers in the hedges and surfaces along here: poppies, purple mallow and pineapple weed. As you reach the top the lane's surface breaks up where Lower Birch Farm brings its daily dose of mud out into the lane.

(3) Turn left here, and go straight down to the beginning of a wood where there is a footpath sign on the left; this points to the right, where the

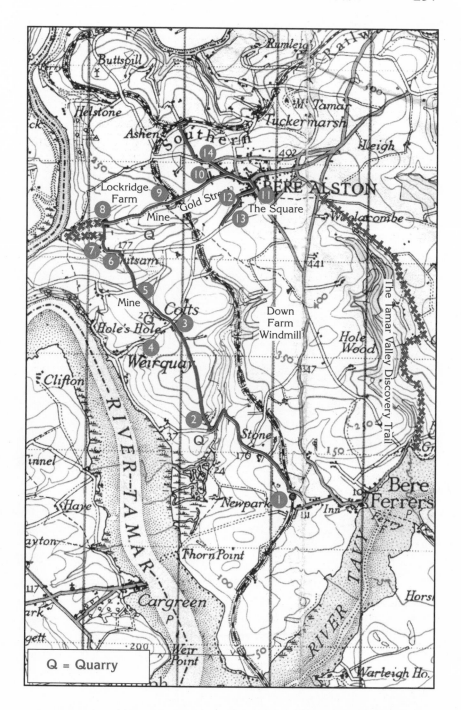

lane behind the Cotts begins.

(4) The lane snakes up with a little open quarry of yellow sandstone and hogging (a type of road surface using pebbles and sand) on the right. Under the trees there are patches of stone walling. Suddenly, on the right there is the chimney – dead, ivy-clad and solitary – standing in a slight hollow with its silent memories.

(5) You come out of the wood, and to your left is a stunning view over the river to Pentillie House, or Castle as it is known: a beautiful square honey-coloured building. This was the centre of the cherry orchard area over the water. You come up by the end of the row of Cotts with a 'VR' post box to your right. Turn left and go along to the next junction, with rows of what appear to be espaliered lime trees to your left. Veer right at the next junction, then straight down into an unsigned green lane to your left. This carriage-width lane can be damp underfoot. There are views of Kit Hill in front of you, at its end there is an 'Unfit for Motors' sign. (6) Turn left, and you go down into a lane with grass in the middle and an enclosed orchard to the left.

(7) You turn right through the top part of Whitsam Farm. You are close to an area where black cherries, pears, plums, strawberries and apples grew and, before the railway came in 1890, were shipped out up the river to Plymouth from Weir Quay. The lane you turn into past the barns is wide and has some slate striations underfoot; but it is the wide hedgerows which impress most. At the end of this brief section is a notice explaining that they are being managed for conservation purposes over the next ten years.

(8) Go straight across the meadow and over a stile by a holly and hazel coppice wood. Keep to the left, then over the stream and up to the right where tall blackthorn and once bulace trees line the way, and up to Lockridge Farm. This farm dates back to 1453; given this fact, hedge-dating in the area is worth trying (see page 86 for hedge-dating theory).Walk past the farm into a wide lane, and notice the patches of the pretty yellow flowered St John's Wort along the way. You go through a gate with granite 'tear and feather' patterns on its pillars.

(9) There are views of Kit Hill to the left. You come up into Bere Alston through a group of council houses with granite facing blocks.

(10) You come out of Lockeridge Bridge Lane opposite the Fire Station and Drake's Park. Turn right towards the centre and pause by the little square opposite the Parish Hall. There are benches topped with chess boards here, and it is a charming place to rest as the swifts wheel and scream oppo-

site you under the Parish Hall eves. Go further into the town and notice how much more mining-like it feels as compared with Bere Ferrers below.

(11) By the Edgcumbe Hotel turn right towards Underways along Cornwall Street. This was formerly known as Pepper Street, and was in 1851 occupied by over 500 miners from West Cornwall.

(12) The unusual-looking collection of houses to your left was built by mining manager Percival Johnson, and provided good accommodation for some workers. It had its own Town Hall and workshops. From here you can choose to go down back to Bere Ferrers by many routes. The Tamar Valley Discovery Trail is marked out here.

(13) If you are making for Bere Alston Station, then retrace your steps to the Fire Station and carry on down Station Road. Notice the Jet Garage still has a sign advertising Sleep's Automobile Engineers.

By the way

This area is full of green lanes and footpaths which outline perfectly the story of its past, from silver lead mining and slate quarrying to market gardening, within a hilly area which must have been intensely farmed to feed an expanding population. Each way has many stories to tell. In the Tamar Valley Discovery Trail guide, Selena aged thirteen and her brother Joseph Gregory aged ten are enumerated as having been employed in the mines for who knows how many hours a day. Let's hope it wasn't always raining when they emerged to walk back up home to Bere Alston. Just as the name of Tavistock Canal's John Taylor lives on in the Taylor Woodrow Company, so does the name of Johnson in the mining company Johnson Matthey.

Other green lanes in the area

Many, especially towards Tuckermarsh, and those traceable through "Silver and Salvation' by Avril Henry (see Bibliography).

Links

There are buses from Tavistock and trains from Plymouth to the Bere Peninsula. Tamar Valley Discovery Trail (see Bibliography). Tamerton Foliot (no. 47).

Question

Where can you find your compass bearings in Bere Ferrers?

Along the TAVISTOCK CANAL· towards MORWELLHAM

'Blood upon the copper, Oh how I fade away.
Working in the darkness day by day'

– from Devon-born Seth Lakeman's song about this area

OS Explorer 108

For me, any circuit around Morwellham is a return to an area which first taught me the truth about green lanes. Whatever else they are now used for, they are first and foremost routes to work. John Taylor's Canal, begun in 1803 and not finished until 1817, is the main focus of this route, taking the towpath through lands which once reverberated to the sounds of heavy industry. Technically the canal is not a green lane because it is not bounded by hedgerows either side, but now,

Sketch by H.T. Streeton.

because of its recreational value, its new-found silence gives it a place in any list of green lanes worth exploring. This area is rich in both natural history – the Tamar Valley is an Area of Outstanding Natural Beauty – and industrial history – it is a UNESCO world heritage site, making it difficult to take a short route in any direction, as what you discover will lead you on. This is what exploring green lanes is all about.

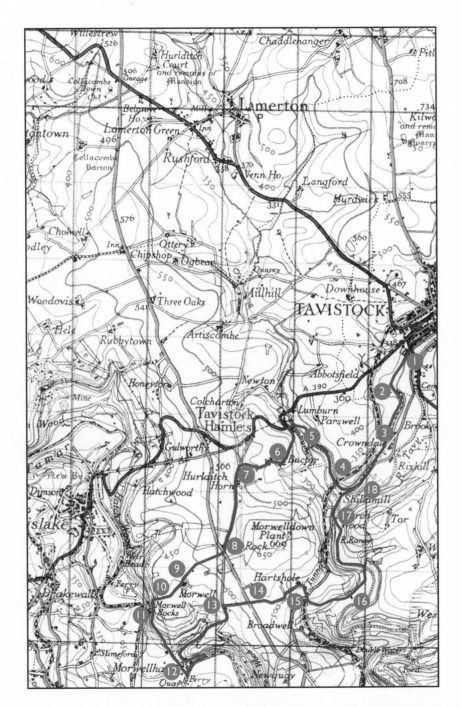

Distance: 6-7 miles.

Conditions: Nearly all on the level, with some minor-road walking and some muddy ups and downs in the green lanes.

Starting point: SX 478743. This is where The Quay Centre stands along the canal in Tavistock. Having had a good look round this stalwart moor town, make your way westwards to the left of the Centre along Taylor's Canal to West Bridge.

(1) You pass under the A390 with the school to your left, some allotments to your right and the canal in between. It is well maintained here, and there are always mallards and White Campbell ducks to be fed here.

(2) This area is known as Monkswood. There is a bridge here leading to the new housing estate to your left. Carry straight on along the towpath, where you pass under a tall, tree-lined way, the canal now flowing darkly beside you. Crowndale Woods, now managed by the Woodland Trust, are ancient. There is horsetail to be found here, and sticklebacks in the canal.

(3) You emerge from the trees into meadows by Crowndale, Francis Drake's birthplace, where there are both masonry and iron bridges across the canal. There is a barn entrance to your left on a level with the canal from which you can imagine produce and goods being loaded and unloaded in the nineteenth century. The path continues with a cobbled surface and is lined with hazel. But the tree most dominant in this area is the hawthorn – not straggly hedgerow specimens, but ones which grow straight, tall and sturdy. In spring they drip with sweet-smelling white blossom. I say sweet; however, one of the reasons why may blossom is considered to be unlucky if brought into a house is that it is reputed to presage a death in the dwelling. Sniff again, and you can smell red meat on a slab if the wind is in the wrong direction. You are now walking along the contour of one of the containing hill ridges above the Tavy. When Taylor first started to build his canal he obtained the rights to any mineral wealth he might find along the way. There are two shafts hidden to your right as you come into a fine beech avenue. Some of these look older than the canal by at least fifty years, and there are some good examples of bracket fungus wedged in their elephantine pollarded branches. Between numbers (3) and (4) of this route there is a guide post to your left where you will join the canal again at number (19) on this route.

(4) The viaduct of the Bere Alston to Tavistock railway over the river Lumburn came to the valley in 1859, and spans the canal as you pass under.

Along the edge of the canal now the rough jagged edges of rock-face intrude into the water, evidence of just how the navvies tore through the rocks to build the canal.

(5) Through the trees here you can see where the canal doubles back upon itself, and where it served the copper lodes at Crebor discovered in its construction. The lode produced up to 3,000 tons of copper every year, and, as John Taylor had obtained a licence to construct the canal and prospect at the same time, things went well. He was obliged to give the Duke of Bedford a tenth of the proceeds from the mineral lodes. Mills were also powered by water from the canal. This is the junction for the swing bridge too which was restored in 1998. From here you can follow the canal further along for a short stretch before it becomes prohibited. In the 1930s the canal was dredged and an extension made to a reservoir, from which a pipe conducted the water down the cliff to Morwellham to provide electric current by means of a hydroelectric plant which is still in operation today.

From here take the lane to your right which gives you views up to the first of the very square granite-built houses you will see on this route. This one is called Higher Parswell. Just before the end of the lane there is a path to the left which will take you up onto Crebor back lane. This is greening up nicely, and after a gentle climb with a wooded quarry to your right you come to Buctor Farm on the corner.

(6) There is a fine collection of granite-built barns here, and notice the carved granite window-frame as you approach. Could this be something borrowed from Tavistock Abbey after Henry VIII 'dissolved' all religious houses? There is some evidence here on the right of the lanes which ran from prosperous Crebor down to join first the canal and then the railway (see Route 18 for further evidence).

(7) You come out at Five Acres Cross, and there is nothing for it but to turn left down towards Rock. This is a straight road and takes traffic heading for Morwellham including buses, so be careful.

(8) At Rock crossroads, before you take the footpath to your right notice on the opposite side of the road a granite post with the words Morwellham Quay just about visible.

On the fingerpost here you will find directions to Chip Shop which, as mentioned in Route 48, has sent many a hungry tourist off on a wild goose chase towards Gulworthy – the chips referred to are tokens to be traded in at shops owned by the canal and mining companies. You are passing along a tarmac drive towards Morwell Barton lined with beech hedges. You get glimpses of this fine house on the left. It was the country residence of the Abbots of Tavistock, and a chapel was built here in 1391. The rest of the house dates from the fifteenth century.

(9) From here you go through three gates along the side of rich meadows with woodlands in front and Morwell Wood to your right.

(10) As you go through a gate and before you go straight ahead down into the woodland, notice the green lane tunnel which runs to your left. This is part of the inclined plane railway built for transporting minerals down to the docks below and which you will find emerging (now recently excavated) when you come to the quay below.

(11) Follow the path in the woodlands to the left, and take time (and care) by a post marked Morwell Rocks to look out over the view below you. There is the River Tavy, and views across to the chimneys of Gunnislake. This wide path through conifer woods takes you down to the quay passing the way to Morwell Farm on your left. Obviously this is a good half-way point on your route.

(12) There are two ways you can leave the quay. If you follow the directions to the George and Charlotte Mine there is a footpath sign which will take you up through the woods and bring you out above the reservoir or along the lane by Lower Sheepridge Farm. Or you can just walk up the hill past the Methodist chapel on the left to the crossroads at Sheepridge.

(13) Turn right here and look back over the Tamar Valley and over to Gunnislake on the hill.

(14) Take care and cross straight over at the next crossroads following the sign to Hartshole Farm. Here you will meet another square granite house, and where the lane swings to the right before it meets the minor road ahead there was once an important junction. The railway entered a tunnel, and roads ran down to the river and up to Tavistock.

(15) Go straight over and through the metal gate on the left. This is still a well-used lane, but is very overshadowed first by uncoppiced hazel and ash and then by sinking down between fields where it is shored up by some good stretches of stone walling. There is holly to be found in the hedgerows above – a sign of ancient woodland. This lane would make a good candidate for some hedge-dating.

(16) You emerge into a minor road with a woodstore in front of you and a lane leading to the weir to your right. However, turn left and continue through on this tarmacked road. You will soon come to a clearing where the

roaring Tavy comes close up to the road. The Rifle Range marked on the present-day OS map is indeed still in operation, but this is a public byway and the participants in this sport will do you no harm as they let you pass through.

(17) You merge with a minor road to your left, and just before you get to yet another square granite house at Shillamill, notice a green lane disappearing to your left. This marks the route of the Crebor copper once again.

(18) Pass the mill, and where the orchard to your left stops and woodland begins, you will find a granite stone marked 'MW'. Climb up the bank here, which will bring you back up on to the canal. Turn right to return to Tavistock.

Other green lanes in the area

Many which are being documented and restored by the Morwellham Quay World Heritage Site project.

Links

Buses run to Morwellham from Tavistock.

Question

Whose statue do you pass at the beginning of this walk?

By the way

I conclude this exploration of the green lanes of South and South-East Devon with a poem which was written for me by a group of schoolchildren over twenty years ago. As you stand by the touristic and educational busyness down at Morwellham Quay, you can see the ways by which the workers once arrived and departed. Wherever you live, the same thing could have happened too, once you step off a minor lane and enter a green one. Happy exploring.

THE MAGICAL LANE: COMPOSITE POEM BY ST PETER'S SCHOOL, TAVISTOCK (c.1985)

Approach the winding, whispering lane
Wet leaves blown against my trembling arm
Mud squelches under my cautious feet
Dark trees stoop threateningly with the wind

A murky gloom hangs in the air
Chilling grey fingers touch my face
A leaf, a hand, a bat, a ghost
A magical mist wraps itself around all.

A band of ancient hunters stalking their prey
The fading echo of a distant packhorse.

Mist descends warning of danger
The clashing of quarterstaves pierce the night
Deep in the forest the sound of tunnelling miners
One approaches carrying a flickering lamp
Could it be a miner wending his way home?

I see an overgrown wall, was it a tollhouse or a smithy's forge?
Do the ghosts of Henry and George haunt this track?
As my imagination fades away
My feet feel the hollowness of the creaking bridge
The trickle of water brings me back to reality
But I'll never forget the magic of the lane.

Canal tow path and Shillamill viaduct.

POSTSCRIPT

There are many lanes that you will know of, which are not included in these volumes. However, the main areas where green lanes are to be found in Devon have been covered in my three books. Those which lie in between these groupings can be brought into the picture, even though they will never appear as well organised as our present-day highway system. Too many travellers have made short cuts, detours, erasures and extensions to an ever-evolving pattern of social and economic needs for the picture ever to be complete.

Highway history as a subject is less revered than that of railway history, even though it covers a greater period of time and mileage. However, it is more difficult – and more intriguing – to explore.

Let us hope that these green lanes will remain havens for wildlife, and continue to tell their stories to you well into the future:

As long as the length of the green lane are the stories it will tell.

BIBLIOGRAPHY

Ashton, Rosemary: *The Life of Samuel Taylor Coleridge*. Blackwell, 1996.

Beacham, Peter (ed.): *Devon Building, An introduction to local traditions*. Devon Books, 1990.

Belsey, Valerie: *Devon Roads – Past and Present*. Past and Present Publications, 1993.

Belsey, Valerie: *The Green Lanes of England*. Green Books, 1998.

Belsey, Valerie: *Discovering Green Lanes*. Green Books, 2001.

Belsey, Valerie: *Exploring Green Lanes in the South Hams*. Green Books, 2003.

Belsey, Valerie: *Exploring Green Lanes and the stories they tell: North and North-West Devon*. Green Books, 2008.

Booker, Frank: *Industrial Archaeology of the Tamar Valley*. David and Charles, 1985.

Born, Anne: *A History of Kingsbridge and Salcombe Estuaries*. Orchard Publications, 2002.

Brooke, Alan and Brandon, David: *Bound for Botany Bay*. The National Archive Press, 2005.

Clark, E.A.G.: *The Ports of the Exe Estuary 1660-1860*. University of Exeter, 1960.

Clist, Brian and Chris Dracott: *The Book of Hemyock*. Halsgrove, 2001.

Devon County Council Booklet: Geology, 2006.

Eckhart, Sheila: *Browsing in the Blackdowns*. White Tree Books, 2003.

Farquharson-Coe, A: *Devon's Waterways*. James Pike Ltd, St Ives, Cornwall.

Fox, Harold: *The Evolution of the Fishing Village: Landscape and Society along the South Devon Coast 1086-1550*. Leopard's Head Press, Oxford 2001.

Hands, Stuart: *Road Signs*. Shire Publications, 2002.

Harman, Richard (ed.): *Countryside Character*. Blandford Press, London.

Hawkins, Michael: *Devon Roads*. Devon Books, 1988.

Hemery, Eric: *Walking Dartmoor's Ancient Trackways*. Hale, 1975.

Henry, Avril: 'Silver and Salvation: A Confessor's Itinerary 1400-1500 Throughout the Parish of Bere Ferrers' in Vol. 133 of The Devon Association Transactions.

Hoskins, W. G.: *Fieldwork in Local History*.

Hoskins, W. G.: *Devon and its People*. Wheatons, Exeter, 1959.

Hoskins, W. G.: *One Man's England*. BBC Publications, 1978.

Hostettler John: *Thomas Wakeley, An Improbable Radical*. Barry Rose Law Publishers, 1993.

Hutchinson, Orlando: *Travels in Victorian Devon, Illustrated Journals and Sketchbooks (1846-1870)*. Devon Books, 2000.

Jarvis, Robin: *Landscape and Locomotion*. The Coleridge Bulletin, New Series, Spring 1999.

Lane, John and Walshaw, Harland: *Devon's Churches, a Celebration*. Green Books, 2007.

Macfarlane, John: *The Wild Places*. Granta Books, 2000.

Jones, Robert H.: *All about Otterton*. Keverel Press.

Mee, Arthur: *Devon*. Hodder and Stoughton, 1938.

Minchinton, Walter: *Windmills of Devon*. University of Exeter, 1977.

Norris, Gerald: *West Country Rogues and Outlaws*. Devon Books, 1986.

Pevsner, Nicholas: *The Buildings of England, South Devon*. Penguin, 1952.

Pilkington, Francis: *Ashburton: The Dartmoor Town*. Grey Matter and Devon Books, 1978.

Rackham, Oliver: *A History of the Countryside*. Dent and Sons, 1986.

Rattenbury, Jack: *Memories of a Smuggler*. 1837.

Scott-Giles C.W.: *The Road Goes On*. The Epworth Press, 1946.

Sheldon, Gilbert: *From Trackway to Turnpike. An illustration from east Devon*. Oxford University Press, 1928.

Simmons, Jack: *A Devon Anthology*. Macmillan, 1971.

Sisman, Adam: *The Friendship, Wordsworth and Coleridge*. HarperCollins, 2006.

Slater, G.: *Coldharbour Mill*. Uffculme, Devon.

Street, A.G.: *England Today in Pictures*. Odhams, 1947.

Uffculme, The Book of. Published by the Uffculme Local History Group, 1988.

Waller, John: *The Real Oliver Twist*. Icon Books, 2003.

Wills, Richard: *The Book of Ilsington*. Halsgrove, 2000.

TIMELINE

To help you identify the various periods through which the lanes you are walking have survived (adapted from Oliver Rackham's *Woodlands*).

4,600 million	Origin of the Earth
500 million	Land plants
340 million	Big plants
140 million	Broadleaved trees
70 million	Present genera of trees
2 million	Beginning of Pleistocene glacial cycles (glaciations and interglacials)
200,000	Present human species
3800–2000 BC	Neolithic in Britain; beginning of cultivation and woodmanship
2000–750 BC	Bronze Age in Britain
750 BC–40 AD	Iron Age in Britain
40–400 AD	The Romans in Britain
400–1066 AD	Anglo-Saxon England
1066–1536 AD	Middle Ages in England
1348–1349	The Black Death (one-third of the population perished)
1536–1539	Dissolution of Monasteries by Henry VIII (redistribution of property and land)
1642–1645	The Civil War

Timeline

1751	First turnpike road in Devon (at Stonehouse, Plymouth)
1775-1783	The American War of Independence
1789	The French Revolution
1801	First General Enclosure Act (common land no longer available)
1815	Corn Law passed, forbidding foreign corn to be imported cheaply. English corn prices dropped significantly. Repealed in 1836.
1815	The Battle of Waterloo
1819	Reform of Penal Code. You were less likely to be transported for minor offences.
1824	Average wage for labourers 9s 4d a week (50p approx.)
1834	Tolpuddle Martyrs (a group of farm labourers uniting for better wages. They were deported.)
1834	New Poor Law Act (Workhouses established)
1844	First railway comes to Devon (Bristol to Exeter)
1870	Average wage for labourers 12s a week
1900	Average wage for labourers 15s a week
1914–1918	First World War
1920	Tarmacking of roads begins
1939–1945	Second World War
1977	First section of motorway opens in Devon

~~ERS TO QUESTIONS~~

~~~e end of each numbered route~~

Route 1: CADBURY

~~hat~~ is the name of the house by which the well stands?
~~Inneford.~~

Route 2: WHIPTON

~~tion~~ How many children survived the Bampfylde who built the Almshouses?
~~wer~~ Four.

Route 3: BRIDFORD

Question The luminous escaping gas which was sometimes seen close to mines was called *ignis fatuus*. What does this mean?
Answer Foolish fire.

Route 4: DUNKESWELL

Question The three colours which predominate in the church are to be found in the American flag. What are they?
Answer Red, white and blue.

Route 5: FENITON

Question On the station you will find its former name. What was it?
Answer Sidmouth Junction.

Route 6: BUTTERLEIGH

Question Which monarch was kind enough to ensure that poor boxes were put in every parish church?
Answer Queen Elizabeth I.

Route 7: CULLOMPTON

Question 1) We are in cob-building country. Which modern public building pays homage to this?
Answer The bus shelter at Bradninch.
Question 2) What type of ship is carved on the exterior walls of Cullompton church?
Answer An Elizabethan cog.

Route 8: TIVERTON CANAL

Question What do you call the path which runs beside a canal?
Answer A towpath.

Route 9: KENTISBEARE

Question One of the Blackborough churchyard pillars carries
a special mark. What is it and what authority put it there?
Answer OS Trig mark (see photo on right)

Route 10: UFFCULME to SPICELAND

Question What kind of poplar tree can you see at Five Fords
and elsewhere in this area?
Answer The black poplar.

Route 11: ASHILL

Question Which nationality is well represented in the Allhallows Lane graffiti?
Answer Kiwis from New Zealand.

Route 12: CULMSTOCK to CULM DAVY

Question What is a turbary?
Answer An area of peat bog used for cutting blocks for domestic fires.

Route 13: HEMYOCK

Question There is a boundary stone at the beginning of this route which provides
a clue to its milky past. What is inscribed here?
Answer Wilts United Dairies Boundary 12.

Route 14: MEMBURY

Question There is quite a lot of dogwood growing in the hedges in this area. Do
you know what its slender branches were used for in medieval times?
Answer The making of arrows.

Route 15: STOCKLAND

Question Which country would you have been transported to if you had damaged
the bridge in Stockland?
Answer Australia.

Route 16: HAWKCHURCH

Question Where was the clock at Middle Holditch made?
Answer Dublin.

Route 17: KILMINGTON

Question How old is the block of stone outside Kilmington village hall?
Answer 1,000,000,000 years.

Route 18: COLYTON

Question What is the traditional industry here (which is still in operation) called?
Answer Tanning (at Colyton).

Route 19: AXMOUTH

Question What year was the concrete bridge at Seaton built?
Answer 1877.

Route 20: ROUSDON

Question You are walking along one of the oldest roads in the county? When was it established as a turnpike?
Answer 1758 (see page 147).

Route 21: BEER

Question In which famous London building is Beer stone to be seen?
Answer St Paul's Cathedral.

Route 22: BRANSCOMBE

Question At (5), watch out for some realistic-looking animals which are always a potential hazard for walkers. What are they?
Answer On top of the stone pillars just at the beginning of the drive are statues of greyhounds looking as if they might leap into action as you approach.

Route 23: NEWTON POPPLEFORD SOUTH

Question A diamond of a lane. Along one of these lanes you will find a diamond in the rock face. Which one?
Answer Passaford Lane, about halfway up there is a diamond carved in the red sandstone on the right when ascending.

Route 24: SIDMOUTH to OTTERTON

Question What is the name of the trees which line either side of Bicton College drive?
Answer Monkey puzzle trees.

Route 25: EAST BUDLEIGH

Question In the church you will find the name, an Elizabethan-sounding one of Raleigh's stepmother, spelt backwards. The primary school is named after her too. What was her name?
Answer Joan Drake or Naoj Ekard.

Route 26: NEWTON POPPLEFORD NORTH

Question How can you tell an elm leaf from a hazel or a beech leaf?

Answer Here are sketches of the basic shapes, but you can also tell by texture, beech is shiny, hazel quite thin, and elm quite downy. Sketches from left to right are beech, elm and hazel.

Route 27: OTTERY ST. MARY

Question What kind of animal was driven across the Ford at **(10)**?

Answer Geese; this is Gosford.

Route 28: TEIGNMOUTH

Question You pass through plenty of red seaside hills on this walk, but a small fragment, carefully labelled, comes from other red lands. Which one?

Answer Outside the church of St George in Holcombe is a basin, mounted on a granite pillar which comes from the Red Sea Hills Geheist Gold mine in the Sudan.

Route 29: SHALDON to RINGMORE

Question How many feet (or metres if you prefer) is The Beacon above sea level?

Answer 169 metres or 549 feet.

Route 30: IDEFORD to BISHOPSTEIGNTON

Question What is the name of the high headland visible on the other side of the estuary?

Answer The Ness.

Route 31: DAWLISH

Question There is a farm above Dawlish which dates back to the signing of the Magna Carta. How do you know?

Answer Pitt Farm has a date plaque of 1215.

Route 32: STARCROSS

Question There are some industrial archaeological remains here not connected to the former quay, where are they?

Answer By the station, Brunel's Atmospheric Railway Pumping house.

Route 33: KINGSKERSWELL

Question What is the date on Daccabridge plaque?

Answer This bridge has a plaque which reads: "This bridge was repaired by ye county in 1693."

Route 34: OGWELL to DENBURY

Question Besides the last King of the Dumnonii, there is another kingly connection concerning later invaders here. What is it?.

Answer There is a plaque in the church which says that Aldred, the priest from this little community, crowned William the Conqueror in Westminster Abbey in 1068. This caused a near riot to explode around the Cathedral, but Denbury's priest held fast.

Route 35: WOODLAND

Question Where can you see an ecclesiastical use of the region's slates?

Answer On the roof of the parish church.

Route 36: ILSINGTON

Question Which type of Right of Way is open to all vehicles?

Answer A byway.

Route 37: IVYBRIDGE

Question What is the name of the river that feeds the paper mill?

Answer The River Erme.

Route 38: ASHBURTON to BUCKFASTLEIGH

Question What other wild plant produces soap-like chemicals and was used in the production of textiles?

Answer Bracken.

Route 39: STAVERTON to PEN RECCA

Question Given the name of the slate quarry here, what nationality do you think some of the miners might have been?

Answer Penn Recca is a Welsh name, so some slaters could have come over via north Devon to work here.

Route 40: WOOLSTON GREEN

Question Sugar Bush, Quench, Devon Crimson and Pig's Snout are all varieties of what?

Answer Apples, which are used in today's production of cider from this area.

Route 41: MORELEIGH

Question You have seen the River Avon on this walk, but it runs very close to another river whose lower reaches you will find near Slapton. Which one?

Answer The River Gara.

Route 42: DIPTFORD

Question What kind of tool was used to split the slate?
Answer Cleavers of varying sizes (see p.207).

Route 43: EAST ALLINGTON

Question As you rest awhile near Kellaton Cross on a wayside seat, look beneath your feet to discover a link with another form of transport. What is it?
Answer The supports are shaped around the initials GWR (Great Western Railway).

Route 44: BEHIND SLAPTON

Question What is the name of the school where Yeats' children's plays were first performed?
Answer The National School.

Route 45: BEESANDS

Question What is the name of the way which runs by the beach at Beesands?
Answer Greenstraight.

Route 46: MODBURY

Question What is the date on one of the slate stiles which you go over on your return towards the Poundwell Street car park in Modbury?
Answer 1884.

Route 47: TAMERTON FOLIOT

Question What is the name of the hill over in Cornwall with its mining chimney still intact on the top?
Answer Kit Hill.

Route 48: SYDENHAM DAMEREL

Question Although called Horsebridge, how many packhorse recesses are there set in the parapets?
Answer Four.

Route 49: BERE ALSTON

Question Where can you find your compass bearings in Bere Ferrers?
Answer On the central column of the fingerpost illustrated just below the finial (see p.254).

Route 50: THE TAVISTOCK CANAL

Question Whose statue do you pass at the beginning of this walk?
Answer Sir Francis Drake.

INDEX

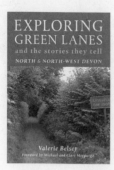
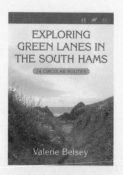